take a hint from the heavens...

1986 is packed with promise. Make the most of it with the predictions, insights, clues and suggestions America's most popular astrologer, Sydney Omarr, has prepared for you!

Learn about the "geometry" of relationships—who you get along with, and why ... pore over celebrity sun signs and personality profiles ... discover how and why the movements of the zodiac affect men and women so differently ... and much, much more. Whatever your desire, whatever your dilemma, let Sydney Omarr's time-tested wisdom guide you through 1986, and watch your dreams become exciting realities!

For Expanding Your Personal Knowledge of
Astrology, SIGNET Brings to You

SYDNEY OMARR'S ASTROLOGICAL GUIDES FOR YOU IN 1986

- [ ] **ARIES** .... (136764—$2.75)*
- [ ] **TAURUS** .... (136772—$2.75)*
- [ ] **GEMINI** .... (136780—$2.75)*
- [ ] **CANCER** .... (136799—$2.75)*
- [ ] **LEO** .... (136802—$2.75)*
- [ ] **VIRGO** .... (136810—$2.75)*
- [ ] **LIBRA** .... (136829—$2.75)*
- [ ] **SCORPIO** .... (136837—$2.75)*
- [ ] **SAGITTARIUS** .... (136845—$2.75)*
- [ ] **CAPRICORN** .... (136853—$2.75)*
- [ ] **AQUARIUS** .... (136861—$2.75)*
- [ ] **PISCES** .... (136888—$2.75)*

*Price is $3.25 in Canada

Buy them at your local bookstore or use this convenient coupon for ordering.

NEW AMERICAN LIBRARY
P.O. Box 999, Bergenfield, New Jersey 07621

Please send me the books I have checked above. I am enclosing $_____
(please add $1.00 to this order to cover postage and handling). Send check or money order—no cash or C.O.D.'s. Prices and numbers are subject to change without notice.

Name_____

Address_____

City _____ State _____ Zip Code _____

Allow 4-6 weeks for delivery.
This offer is subject to withdrawal without notice.

SYDNEY OMARR'S
DAY-BY-DAY ASTROLOGICAL GUIDE FOR

Taurus
(APRIL 20–MAY 20)

1986

A SIGNET BOOK

NEW AMERICAN LIBRARY

NAL BOOKS ARE AVAILABLE AT QUANTITY DISCOUNTS
WHEN USED TO PROMOTE PRODUCTS OR SERVICES.
FOR INFORMATION PLEASE WRITE TO PREMIUM MARKETING DIVISION,
NEW AMERICAN LIBRARY, 1633 BROADWAY,
NEW YORK, NEW YORK 10019.

Copyright © 1985 by Sydney Omarr

All rights reserved

Sydney Omarr is syndicated worldwide by Los Angeles Times Syndicate.

SIGNET TRADEMARK REG. U.S. PAT. OFF. AND FOREIGN COUNTRIES
REGISTERED TRADEMARK—MARCA REGISTRADA
HECHO EN CHICAGO, U.S.A.

SIGNET, SIGNET CLASSIC, MENTOR, PLUME, MERIDIAN and NAL BOOKS
are published by New American Library,
1633 Broadway, New York, New York 10019

First Printing, July 1985

1 2 3 4 5 6 7 8 9

PRINTED IN THE UNITED STATES OF AMERICA

CONTENTS

1 **Defining Terms**   7
- *Astrology*   7
- *The Zodiac*   8
- *Sun Sign*   9
- *Element*   9
- *Quality*   11
- *Element and Quality Together*   12
- *Planet*   13
- *House*   15
- *Rising Sign*   16
- *Horoscope*   17
- *Aspect*   18
- *Transiting Planet*   19

2 **Your House of the Sun**   21
Your "Piece of the Pie"

3 **The Geometry of Relationships**   32
What Signs You Get Along with—and Why

4 **Twelve Places at the Table**   35
Personality Profiles of the Signs

5 **Moods of the Moon**   44
Day-by-Day Changes

6 **Venus and Mars**   55
Love and Sex ... Peace and War ...
   Cooperating and Competing

7	Venus Sign Position Chart 1910–1975	70
8	Mars Sign Position Chart 1910–1975	76
9	The Planets As "Stars" Astrological Cast of Characters	80
10	Astrotrivia—Rating Yourself in the Best Game in Town	95
	I Sun Signs of the Rich and Famous	95
	II More Celebrity Sun Sign Lore	97
	III Fascinating Facts About the Signs	99
	IV Where Do You Belong?	100
	V Which Animal Best Suits You?	102
11	Sun Sign Changes 1920–1975	105
12	TAURUS: The Big Picture	113
13	TAURUS: Objectives and Obstacles A Game Plan for Being the Most Successful TAURUS Under the Sun	116
14	Pairing Off with TAURUS Your Compatability with Other Signs of the Zodiac	120
15	The TAURUS Sex Role Dilemma	124
16	The TAURUS Female Child ... Young Woman ... Mate ... Mother	126
17	The TAURUS Male Child ... Young Man ... Mate ... Father	129
18	TAURUS Help Wanted Selecting a Career/Your On-the-Job Style	132
19	How "Pure" a TAURUS Are You? Your Moon Sign ... Your Rising Sign	134
20	Find Your Rising Sign	139
21	TAURUS Astro-Outlook for 1986	142
22	Fifteen Months of Day-by-Day Predictions	143

1

Defining Terms

What Are Those Astrologers Talking About?

Everyone knows it is more fun to visit another country if you know a bit of the language, and it's a lot easier to find your way around, too. The same idea applies to astrology, which is still foreign territory to many people. Astrology has its very own language, but it really isn't difficult to get a handle on it as long as you understand a few important terms. What follows is a kind of "Astrological Phrase Book," a brief compendium of the most basic words and concepts in the astrological language. Once you've learned them, you'll find you know a lot more about the why of your sun sign as well as information that will help you understand other astrological factors that make you what you are. Best of all, your new language can help you enjoy and explore one of the most exciting, underdeveloped territories under the sun—modern astrology!

Astrology Is an Ancient and Practical "Science"

The first definition of astrology in the standard dictionary is "astronomy," and at one time in history the two studies were synonymous. The word astrology derives from Greek and literally means "the science (or study) of the stars." However, even in earliest times astrology has had much less to do with the "fixed" stars, which appear to remain in one place, than the planets, which move. (The word "planet" means wanderer.) Early man noticed that, as these heavenly bodies moved, their movements coincided with certain earthly events—mainly the changing of the seasons. Gradually, the movement of the planets was observed to coincide with other important worldly events, such as wars, and the science of "divination" (prediction) by the planets was born. Astronomy and astrology lived happily together until the Christian church banned the latter in about 1550, condemning it as mere superstition. Astrology bounced back in the 1700s, when it came into use as an indicator of human personality, as well as a way to foretell future events. However, this so-called modern astrology is based on the same premise the ancients set down thousands of years ago: "As above, so below." Simply put, what it means is that the positions of the planets, which represent the cosmic order, are related in a significant and observable way to both human behavior and events in human life.

The Zodiac Is a "Circle of Signs"
The zodiac ("circle of animals") is an invisible band in the sky which corresponds to the apparent yearly path of the sun, moon, and the major planets around the earth. It is the "apparent" path in the sense that it is what we *observe* from here on earth. Obviously we know that the earth and other planets revolve around the sun, but the study of astrology (and astronomy) takes earth as the reference point.

The 360-degree circle of the zodiac around the earth is divided into twelve thirty-degree segments—the twelve astrological signs. Throughout the year, as the sun appears to move, it passes through each of these segments in about thirty days. Zero degrees Aries, the vernal equinox or beginning of spring, is the beginning of the zodiac and the start of the seasonal year. It is at that point, on or about March 22, that the sun crosses or intersects with the *ecliptic*—another imaginary band that is (in the mind's eye) the extension of the earth's equator. Another major intersection of the sun's path and the ecliptic takes place at the fall equinox about September 22, the beginning of the seventh sign of the zodiac, Libra. (Equinox means equal days and nights, which is what we experience briefly in the early spring and early fall.) The zodiac "finishes" with the end of the twelfth sign Pisces, about March 21, then begins again with Aries.

Though the segments of the zodiac (the astrological signs) are *named* for the constellations of stars in the sky, they do not correspond with them. The constellations served as convenient visual markers for the ancient astrologer/priests, but the zodiac—and astrology—has always been based on the seasonal year, which never changes. The position of the constellations have changed with reference to our point of view here on earth, however, due to the slipping of the earth's axis. The constellations return a couple of degrees every year and have been doing so for centuries. That's why when the modern *astronomer* says "Aries," he is referring to a group of stars that is in a different position in the sky than the segment of the zodiac the *astrologer* calls "Aries."

Your Sun Sign is Determined by the Month and Day You Were Born

The twelve segments of the zodiac are the twelve astrological signs, from Aries through Pisces, and it takes the sun exactly one year to pass through all twelve signs. A person born when the sun is passing through a particular segment of the zodiac is said to be born under that sign, and it is his/her sun sign. For example, a person born October 14 is said to be born under the sign of Libra. Your sun sign is the most important component of your astrological personality, it is the "real you." However, there are nine other planets besides the sun, and at the moment of a person's birth, those planets are passing through certain segments of the zodiac, or signs, as well. You will learn about some of these lesser influences on your personality in this book later on.

An Element Is Part of a Sign

Obviously your sun sign is a lot more than simply a piece of the sky, or it wouldn't have any meaning. The meaning it has is based on two ancient astrological concepts, the *four elements* and the *three modes*. When these two factors are combined they form the basis of all astrological descriptions of human personality. You can't *see* an element or a quality; they are only to be understood in terms of analogy, but they are fundamental to everything else in astrology, so it is important to understand them.

The four elements, defined by ancient philosophers as the basic components of everything and everybody, are *fire, earth, air,* and *water.* It is doubtful that even in earliest times this breakdown was to be taken as a physical reality: The elements are really four different ways we experience both things and people. For instance, if a thing or a person was experienced as hot rather than cold, sharp rather than dull, active rather than passive, it was said to partake of the *fire* element. And it's easy to see the connection.

Later on, during the Renaissance, the four elements were called "humors," starting a whole new way of typing people. *Fire was the humor choler*, and people who were said to have too much of it were those angry, impatient types who are subject to modern-day diseases like high blood pressure and heart attacks. *The earth element was called black bile* and could cause extreme melancholia (depression) in a person who had too much of it. *Air was the sanguine or rosy humor* and meant a lighter personality. *The water element was the humor phlegm*, and people with too much of it had rather "soggy" personalities and tended to be fat, as well. If the relationship between the elements (or humors) and the signs of the zodiac is beginning to ring a bell, it should. Here's the way the twelve signs break down into elements:

Fire signs: Aries, Leo, Sagittarius
Earth signs: Taurus, Virgo, Capricorn
Air signs: Gemini, Libra, Aquarius
Water signs: Cancer, Scorpio, Pisces

The four elements as four primal types of being exist today in the way many psychologists categorize people's thought processes. Once again, the relationship to the ways in which the twelve astrological signs really do perceive and react to the world is uncannily correct:

The fire signs are instant reactors who put it all together very quickly; things rarely have to be spelled out for a fire sign. These types of people also see the future possibilities inherent in the present and want to bring them about *now*. Obviously, fire signs tend to be impatient, but they have strong wills. Fire is the principle of *action*.

The earth signs are more pragmatic and slower to react. If they can't literally see something or touch it, they have difficulty visualizing it. They operate out of *sense perceptions* and are the realists of the zodiac—the builders who provide stability and continuity. Earth is the principle of *sustenance*.

The air signs see everything as connected to everything else. They are sequential thinkers for whom there must be a beginning, a middle, and an end to everything. For the most part these people operate on *logic* and act only when they can see the sense of their actions. The air signs are endlessly curious and represent the principle of *connecting and reasoning*.

The water signs tend to feel their way through life. What is most real to them is what their emotions tell them; they do what their emotions tell them to do as well. They are imaginative thinkers, the poets and artists of the zodiac. The water principle is that of *caring, nurturing, and protecting*.

A Quality Is Part of a Sign

There are only four elements, but there are twelve signs. In astrological arithmetic, the *three qualities* which divide the *four elements* make up the difference. It isn't easy to grasp the concept of the elements, but the qualities (or "modes" as they are sometimes called) help a lot, because they make the elements a lot more tangible. Called *cardinal*, *fixed*, and *mutable*, the three modes can best be understood as *kinds of motion*.

Cardinal motion is start-up movement. It is the principle of bringing into being. Cardinal goes forward, so, the cardinal signs are *initiators*.

The four cardinal signs are those that start the four seasons:
Aries (*spring*)
Cancer (*summer*)

Libra (*fall*)
Capricorn (*Winter*)

Fixed motion means staying in place. Fixed things have come into being, and now simply are. The fixed signs represent stability, and are difficult to move. The four fixed signs represent the middle of each season:
Tarus (*spring*)
Leo (*summer*)
Scorpio (*fall*)
Aquarius (*winter*)

Mutable motion means flexible motion. Things that are mutable are changing, able to turn into something else. The mutable signs represent the *ability to adjust, and to accept change.* The four mutable signs are those that end the seasons:
Gemini (*spring*)
Virgo (*summer*)
Sagittarius (*fall*)
Pisces (*winter*)

Elements and Qualities Together Add Up to Signs
When you put elements and qualities together you begin to get a picture of what they add up to—the twelve astrological signs. Here is how each quality modifies each element.

Fire element/Cardinal quality = Aries
This get-up-and-go sign has all the flash and dash of fire plus an added dose of a pioneering spirit by virtue of its cardinal quality.

Fire element/Fixed quality = Leo
Leo burns with the ardor and enthusiasms of fire, but gives off very steady heat due to its fixed quality.

Fire element/Mutable quality = Sagittarius
Sagittarius represents the kind of fire that spreads, igniting everything and everybody in its path—which is rather erratic because of Sagittarius's mutable quality.

Earth element /Cardinal quality = Capricorn
Capricorn is the most active builder of the earth signs because of its cardinal quality. Capricorn's brand

of reality demands that something be brought into being.

Earth element/Fixed quality = **Taurus**
This strong sign stands and waits, holding things and people together. Taurus is the warmest and most nurturing of the earth signs, and is always "there."

Earth element/Mutable quality = **Virgo**
Virgo's practical sense knows that all things must change. This mutable sign represents the principle of stability with flux; that is, permanence in the face of change.

Air element/Cardinal quality = **Libra**
Libra's air nature moves forward, actively connecting people and things into partnerships via its cardinal quality of initiation.

Air element/Fixed quality = **Aquarius**
Aquarius is the most immovable of the air signs, representing the permanance of ideas and their practical application.

Air element/Mutable quality = **Gemini**
This very movable sign represents changing thoughts and opinions, the breaking up of static ideas so that new ones can come about.

Water element/Cardinal quality = **Cancer**
Cancer is the most initiating of the water signs because of the cardinal quality. Though shy, Cancer generally moves quietly but effectively to the forefront.

Water element/Fixed quality = **Scorpio**
Scorpio's powerful self-control comes from the emotional water element that is contained and compressed because of this sign's fixed quality.

Water element/Mutable quality = **Pisces**
Pisces extreme emotionalism—as well as this sign's creativity—comes from feelings that constantly change and move into new areas, creating new outlets.

Planets Are the Most Important Factor in Astrology
"Planet" is probably an even more important word in the astrological language than "sign." How can that be?

Because it is the placement of the planets in various signs which indicates personality and it is the movement of the planets through the zodiac that indicates events. In other words, without the planets the signs would have no application to people and what happens to them.

As early man noticed that the planets moved in fairly regular patterns, he began to associate certain characteristics with each of the planets, and each planet gradually took on a "personality." In a number of different cultures, certain planets were hooked up with certain gods, because it was the gods who really controlled life on earth. The moon was virtually always a female god—like Diana or Artemis. Jupiter, always a "good guy" planet, was known as Vishnu, the preserver, to the Hindus. Before he got his Roman name of Jupiter, the Greeks knew him as Zeus, a lusty fellow who had a heart of gold. (You'll get a complete rundown on each of the planets in Chapter p, "The Planets As Stars.")

From these planetary "personalities" came the idea that each planet caused a certain kind of behavior or event by virtue of its own nature. For instance, Mars, always the war god, is still regarded by modern astrologers as an indicator of strife and conflict. When predicting events, the astrologer looks at what sign and what house Mars will be passing through at a certain point in time to see what kind of influence it is most likely to bring into a person's life.

When looking at personality, the astrologer determines which sign a person's Mars is in at the time of the person's birth to see how that individual is most likely to assert him-/herself. The sun, the most important planet makes us what we are in totality according to which sign the sun is placed in at our birth; i.e., our sun sign's Venus is the planet of relationships, and its placement in a specific sign shows how a person is likely to relate to others.

In short, planets indicate *action*, and the signs in which the planets are placed indicate *the kind of action*.

Since ancient times, astrologers have recognized seven planets. The sun (which is really a star), the moon (which is really a satellite of our own planet, earth) Mercury, Venus, Mars, Jupiter, and Saturn.

With the development of the telescope, three more planets were discovered (although there is some evidence that early astrologer/priests divined their existence). Uranus was first spotted in 1781, Neptune in 1846, and Pluto as late as 1930. Some astrologers/astronomers anticipate that there are two more to be found, so that there would be twelve planets instead of the current ten.

A House Is an Area of Life—and a Planet's "Home"

Just as there is a great circle in the sky called the zodiac, and it is divided into twelve equal units of *space*, there is another circle which is based on units of *time*. As we all know, the earth makes one complete rotation on its own axis every twenty-four hours. Imagine yourself standing in one place during a twenty-four-hour period and making a mark on the sky every two hours while that sky appears to pass by you as the earth turns. At the end of twenty-four hours, you will have marked off twelve different units of sky. A "house" is simply one of those pieces of sky that has passed by during your day-long vigil. Toward the end of your day of skywatching, twelve houses will have gone by, and "house one" will be coming up again.

When an astrologer draws up a natal horoscope—which is simply a map of the sky when you were born—he/she does it by drawing a picture of the sky as it appeared from the exact place of birth, at the exact time of your birth. What happens is that the twelve houses are lined up in a very specific way—a very different way than if you had been born *in another place at the same time* or *at the same time in another place*.

What is most important about the particular lineup of the houses is that each house represents a different area of human life, and how those areas are positioned *for you* has a tremendous effect on your astrological makeup. For instance, the second house is the house of income and personal possessions and has a lot to do with attitude toward money and how easy or how difficult it will be to come by in your lifetime. The seventh house is the house of partnership and offers clues about who you are likely to marry. If you know the time of your birth within one hour or so, you can add a very important dimension to your astrological self-knowledge by reading the chapter "Your House of the Sun—Your 'Piece of the Pie,' " because the house of the horoscope into which the sun falls in your horoscope usually indicates what area of life will absorb you during your lifetime.

Your Rising Sign Is the One that Starts the First House

Your rising sign is sometimes called the ascendant, because it is the sign of the zodiac that was "ascending" on the eastern horizon at the time of your birth, no matter what time your birth occured. It is the "sunrise sign," corresponding to the nine o'clock position on the face of an ordinary clock. The astrologer's "clock" starts at this position and is read counter-clockwise around the circle of the face. If you were born around sundown, your rising sign will be the one 180 degrees *opposite* the sign you were born under. For instance, if you are an Aries born at sundown, your rising sign will be Libra. If you are an Aries born at sunrise, your rising sign is probably Aries as well.

Why is your rising sign so important? Because it starts the first house of personality, or your very individual way of presenting yourself to the world. No matter what your sun sign is, your rising sign will cover it to a greater or lesser degree (which is why it is so difficult to guess someone's Sun Sign when you first meet them). The rising sign has to do with appearances and can actually influence your physical looks.

If you don't know the time of day you were born, you can't determine your rising sign (although some astrologers can by doing what is called a "rectification," based on the events in your life so far). However, even those who do not know their rising sign can have their horoscopes read; what the astrologer does is put your sun sign on the first house, and do an analysis of what is called a solar horoscope. If you *do* know your birthtime within an hour or so, you can use the rising sign chart in this book to determine yours.

Planets in Signs in Houses Make Up a Horoscope
The whole basis of astrology is that anyone born in a particular moment in time partakes of the qualities of that moment in time. Actually, the same applies for things; for instance, a business that has its beginnings at a precise astrological moment also has a horoscope which can be read, and tells a lot about its potential for success or failure.

An astrologer looks at the particular moment in drawing up a horoscope—or "picture of the hour." A horoscope is basically a map of the sky, showing exactly where the planets were in relation to the signs and the houses, to each other, and from the particular reference point of your birthplace. It is also called a "natal chart" or "natal map."

Everyone's horoscope has ten planets and twelve houses. Those ten planets can be in a variety of signs, and in a variety of houses. Each planet means something different according to its own nature, how that nature operates in a particular sign, and what area of life the planet is most likely to affect by virtue of which house of the horoscope it falls into. Sound complicated? It is, and only a highly trained astrologer can interpret the many factors and put them together for you in a meaningful way. The most exciting part of astrology is the fact that *no two individuals are ever exactly alike*—not even twins, who are born a few minutes apart.

Although you can find out a lot about your astrological personality right in this book, many people like to take the next step and have a personalized horoscope drawn up for them and interpreted by a professional astrologer. There are a number of ways to find a good person to do this for you; in astrology, as in every other profession, there are variations in the level of competence. Two places you can start your search are:

National Astrological
Society
62 West 39th St.
New York, NY 10018

American Federation of
Astrologers
Tempe, AZ 85282

An Aspect Is the Distance Between Planets

Among the more sophisticated factors an astrologer looks for in your horoscope are the *aspects*. Within the 360-degree circle of the horoscope (and the zodiac), planets form certain aspects to each other by virtue of the distance between them. Some distances are considered harmonious, and some are inharmonious, in terms of how those two (or more) planets work together. It's all a matter of mathematics. The soft or harmonious aspects are the sextile (60 degrees apart) and the trine (120 degrees apart). The hard or inharmonious aspects are formed when planets are in square to each other (90 degrees apart) or in opposition, 180 degrees or exactly half a circle apart. These are only the major aspects, and there are lots and lots of minor ones between, but you can get a good picture of interplanetary relationships with only these few.

For example, if your sun sign is Aries, and at the time of your birth the planet Saturn was in the sign of Libra, or 180 degrees away from Aries, you are likely to have a more serious (Saturnine) disposition than the typical "happy" Aries. Depending on your point of view, this can be a positive note in your horoscope, because you will have greater powers of concentration than many an Aries—or a negative note, because you will be less happy-go-lucky. In another example, a person with a Capricorn sun sign may have a horoscope in which Jupiter, the planet of expansiveness, is 120 degrees away from the sun—either in the sign of Virgo or Taurus— and therefore in "trine" aspect to his/her sun. The result: a much more outgoing, giving Capricorn than the run-of-the-mill type. On the other hand, such an easy aspect could expand Capricorn's acquisitive nature too much, and make for a megalomanic (someone who craves worldly goods and power).

The ancients separated aspects into "favorable" and "unfavorable," but psychologically-thinking modern astrologers know that it is not that simple; it all depends on the total horoscope, plus the individual's reactions to the particular vibrations of the planets in that horoscope.

A Transiting Planet Affects Your Life Now

When someone goes to an astrologer for the first time, he/she usually has *two* readings—separate, but interrelated. The first will be an interpretation of your natal chart or birth horoscope. This tells you about your given personality—the traits, problems, abilities, and advantages you are most likely to have by virtue of the placement of the planets in the sky at the time of your birth. The second reading will have to do with what you can expect in your life at the present time and the near future. Your birth horoscope always remains the same, but the planets in the sky keep changing their relationships to your birth horoscope throughout your lifetime. The astrologer will acquaint you with the current "transit"—or movements—of the planets and how you, the individual, can expect them to affect you. For instance, if an astrologer notes that Uranus, the "earthquake planet," is approaching your fourth house (the house of emotional security, the place where we really live), the astrologer might alert you to the fact that big changes are in the offing: even a total shaking of the foundations, or a pulling up of roots. This is a major transit, and many people change their residence, partners, or jobs when it occurs. Similarly, but on a less critical note, the astrologer may notice that the planet Venus is going to make a transit over the place in the zodiac occupied by Mars in your birthchart. This could indicate a firey romantic interlude or the rekindling of an old flame.

There are two important things to keep in mind about astrological predictions. The first is that your natal horoscope—your "birth imprint"—really determines how you will react to life's events. To put it even more strongly, your innate personality will really *create* the events of your life, because "character is destiny." There is no doubt that the planets create conditions, but we must take responsibility for how we cooperate with those conditions. The second thing is that *there are very few hard and fast rules*. There are guidelines, to be sure, and most of them have ancient roots; a lot of astrological prediction is based on the case history technique. However, since no two sets of conditions—

the one in the sky and the one in an individual birthchart—are ever *exactly* the same, it is virtually impossible for any astrologer to tell you specifically what is going to happen.

2

Your House of the Sun

Your "Piece of the Pie"

The prime symbol in the very symbolic language of astrology is the perfect circle; it represents the sky around us, the cosmic atmosphere into which we are all born. All astro-math is based on division of the 360-degree figure, which since ancient times has been regarded as having mystical qualities. When thinking about the houses of the horoscope, however, it helps to use a very down-to-earth analogy. Look at that circle as a great "pie in the sky," which is divided into twelve cosmic slices—each slice representing one house and a different facet of human experience.

Just as there are ten planets in everyone's horoscope, there are twelve houses. However, not all those houses may be occupied by a planet; it all depends on where the planets were in the sky at the moment of your birth. The placement of any planet in a specific house is a *very* important factor in your individual horoscope, but the most important is the placement of the sun. No matter what your sun sign, your House of the Sun has a lot to tell you about the life you've been "given" to live on this earth. As your sun sign is the prime indicator of *character and personality*, your house of the sun points to the *area of human affairs* that you are most likely to find yourself concentrating on in your lifetime.

In the sense that it helps define the boundaries of your life, your house of the sun is your "piece of the pie"—that slice of life within which you will live. Does your house of the sun totally box you in? In a way it does, but it is more productive to think of the dimensions of your house of the sun as *guidelines* about where you can most profitably focus your energies.

Here's the way it works:

- The *sun* is the most important planet in your horoscope. It is the planets that do the "acting," and the sun plays the leading role.
- Your sun sign determines *how* your sun (the real you) acts, i.e., the characteristics of the character you play.
- Your house of the sun is the "stage" on which you will play out your role.

For instance, if your sun sign is Scorpio (the great investigator) and your house of the sun is the twelfth (hidden things), you find yourself drawn to some kind of career in which you must "dig" to do your investigating. Ergo, you might make a good psychoanalyst, archeologist, or genetic researcher. Or, your greatest pleasure in life might be reading mystery novels or spy thrillers—or writing or editing them.

In order to figure out which piece of the pie you've been served, you have to know your birth-time within an hour or so. If you were born during Daylight Savings Time or War Time, you have to subtract one hour from your birth time to determine the "real sun time."

Each house is described here from three different angles:

- The matters or principles connected with it
- The people/places/things related to it
- The problems and the possibilities of having your sun in that house.

Birth time, 4 to 6 a.m.: **Sun in First House**

- *First house matters:* Exploration . . . use of the physical body . . . being on the scene . . . breaking new ground . . . independent action . . . emergencies . . . conquest . . . controversy . . . strategy . . . competition . . . being in the vanguard.

- *First house people/places/things:* Entrepreneurs ... acrobats ... cutting instruments ... rock music ... metals ... satire ... hardware ... the head and face ... opticians ... adrenalin ... new products ... commodities ... salesmen ... fighters ... firemen.
- *Problems and possibilities:* With your sun in the first house, your sun sign personality is quite strong. Regardless of what your sun sign is, you should be able to make clear-cut decisions and have a good sense of your own identity. If you are to gain control over your life, you are going to have to banish fear from it and develop both the moral and the physical courage that is available to you. Though your will should be strong, you will have to keep yourself from a tendency to tyrannize others. When you feel most defeated is the time your first house sun will come to your rescue. The one thing that could keep you from living out the very vivid life this house placement gives you is inflexibility and intolerance. Be willing to listen.

Birth time, 2 to 4 a.m.: **Sun in Second House**

- *Second house matters:* Calmness ... conservation ... ability to make grow ... eroticism ... collecting ... comforting ... administrating ... luxury ... stabilizing ... building up ... perpetuating ... patience ... using ... making stronger ... indulging.
- *Second house people/places/things:* Possessions ... money ... the voice ... landscape gardeners ... brokers and bankers ... love/passion ... personal adornment ... life-sustaining skills ... buying and selling ... security needs ... nurses ... food and shelter ... good music ... creature comforts.
- *Problems and possibilities:* You should be able to establish yourself firmly and securely in whatever you choose to do; self-adjustment should come easily to you. Your economic life could be relatively worry-free but you must resist valuing money and

possessions for their own sake and becoming overly materialistic. You must develop the will that is given you and turn it into willpower, or you could lose self-respect. You are a good manager, but if you allow yourself to become too settled, you will fear to take the necessary risks to make your life less limited. Though things come to you fairly easily, do not let yourself over-indulge in any of them, including rich food.

Birth time midnight to 2 a.m.: **Sun in Third House**

- *Third house matters:* Connecting ... associating ... verbalizing ... dexterity ... inquisitiveness ... distribution ... novelty ... thinking and reasoning ... cause and effect ... exchanging ... bringing the news ... being responsive ... "here today, gone tomorrow."
- *Third house people/places/things:* Short journeys ... realatives (especially siblings) ... speech/languages ... high school teachers ... role-playing/entertaining ... computers ... graphic arts ... handwork ... transportation ... the nervous system ... handwriting .. repair men ... gossip ... comedy ... ventriloquists.
- *Problems and possibilities:* You should be an excellent communicator who reports things clearly and accurately. In your desire for information, however, you could become rather superficial and a bit of a talebearer. If you don't focus your mental energies carefully, you may waste the gift of curiosity your third house sun gives you. You must also learn to live with uncertainty, and to keep your opinions flexible. If life scares you, you are likely to become very defensive and locked in to your ideas. Develop your capacity for listening as well as your talent for talking.

Birth time 10 p.m. to 12 a.m.: **Sun in Fourth House**

- *Fourth house matters:* Adaptability ... change ... instinctiveness ... fluctuation ... protecting ...

imagination ... softness ... the subconscious ... survival ... enveloping ... integrating ... fertility ... mothering.
- *Fourth house people/places/things:* Dreams ... the past ... roots ... home and family ... physical sensation ... museums ... caterers ... water and other liquid ... introverts ... obstetrics ... boats ... domestics ... imagination.
- *Problems and possibilities:* Via your fourth house sun, you are given the possibility of understanding yourself and your motivations quite thoroughly. If you handle your life in a mature way, you will establish a warm and comfortable home for you and your family. However, you must strive for real self-knowledge if you are not to become simply self-absorbed and self-centered. Your imagination is considerable, and you could be highly creative; the down side is that you could develop irrational fears that verge on paranoia. Work to see the world clearly at all times and try to conquer your tendency to play the introvert. No mater what your sun sign, the placement of that sun in the fourth house will make you instinctively avoid the limelight. Get out there and shine!

Birth time 8 to 10 p.m.: **Sun in Fifth House**

- *Fifth house matters:* Being at the heart of things ... pleasures ... power ... ambition ... generosity/giving ... "gilding the lily" ... showmanship ... stability ... management ... territorial rights ... self-expression ... autocracy ... organization.
- *Fifth house people/places/things:* Philanthropy ... corporations ... impresarios ... holidays and vacations ... romantic love ... children ... gamblers ... gold ... circuses ... nursery teachers ... fashion and fashion designers ... public life.
- *Problems and possibilities:* Even if you have a "shy" sun sign, your fifth house placement of the sun will force you into some form of self-expression that is possibly very creative. You also have a capability

for approaching life with a joyful, expectant manner; however, your pursuit of pleasure and play could become extreme. Consciously avoid any pleasure that threatens to get out of control. Your affairs of the heart could be many, but it is important to keep alert for anything that smacks of an abusive partner; it's possible you could enjoy the drama of an unhappy situation. Develop your capacity for warmly accepting others.

Birth time 6 to 8 p.m.: **Sun in Sixth House**

- *Sixth house matters:* Competence/skill ... specialization ... refining ... categorizing ... analyzing ... obedience ... realism ... responsibility ... purifying ... invention ... making things work ... ministering ... discriminating.
- *Sixth house people/places/things:* Service ... critics ... crafts ... libraries ... closets ... public health ... the harvest ... small animals ... dependents ... dental hygienists ... research ... diagnosing ... numbers work ... chemists.
- *Problems and possibilities:* With your sun in the sixth house you have the potential of becoming a true master at something; however, if you allow yourself to get bogged down in life's details, you could possibly end up being a wage slave. No matter what your sun sign, your instincts tell you to be of service to others. While you are capable of great self-sacrifice, you must avoid the temptation to be overly humble and to assume the servant role. You are mentally very keen, and can break things and jobs down into smaller parts in order to accomplish them. Do not let the state of your own health become an obsession. With the sun is the sixth house, your basic constitution should be quite strong. Don't worry!

Birth time 4 to 6 p.m.: **Sun in Seventh House**

- *Seventh house matters:* Sharing ... comparing ... give-and-take ... peacemaking ... negotiation ...

making things beautiful ... creating balance ... fairness ... sociability ... gratification ... advocacy ... diplomacy ... aestheticism.
- *Seventh house people/places/things:* Divorce lawyers ... love poetry ... marriage brokers ... the kidneys and lower back ... illustration ... resort managers ... public relations ... fine arts ... receptionists ... boutiques ... jugglers ... tailors ... pianos.
- Possibilities and problems: You have a great need to identify with others, and can create a wonderful rapport with them easily. However, your need for a life partner could make you overly dependent. If you have an independent sun sign, this could create a serious life conflict. With this placement, you are able to adjust to new people and new situations easily, but you must avoid a tendency not to stick with a position when you really believe in it. You have the potential of forming very warm, balanced and intimate relationships; however, if you do not handle this gift in a mature manner, you could develop a fear of intimacy, and shy away from it or become an outrageous and insincere flirt.

Birth time 2 to 4 p.m.: **Sun in Eighth House**

- *Eighth house matters:* Release of blockages ... probing ... anonymity ... procreation ... rejuvenation ... willpower ... endurance ... controlling ... investigation ... aloneness ... demolishing and rebuilding ... crisis ... elimination.
- *Eighth house people/places/things:* Puzzles ... generals ... political parties ... labor lawyers ... the healing arts ... death and dying ... taxes ... spies ... superathletes ... crime detection ... statesmen ... sex symbols ... geologists ... explorers ... mating instinct ... sanitation engineers.
- *Problems and possibilities:* A light sun sign (like Gemini or Libra), the placement of the sun in this house will add depth to your character. You will feel compelled to investigate things that are hidden or

even dangerous. While it is good to probe, you must beware of a tendency to concentrate on what is morbid. All things being equal, you will be highly sexed; however, with insufficient self-knowledge, your healthy sexual instincts could turn into obsession with the subject—or a total advoidance of it. Learn to live with your dynamic physical body and you will live with others quite happily. Also, encourage your religious or mystical feelings, which are quite real. You have the potential of totally transforming your life at one point or another.

Birth time noon to 2 p.m.: **Sun in Ninth House**

- *Ninth house matters:* Anticipating ... aspiring ... moving around ... expanding things ... speculating ... idealism ... advising ... unpredictability ... search for truth ... search for opportunity ... taking aim ... magnanimity ... excess.
- *Ninth house people/places/things* Casinos ... ambassadors ... passport offices ... luck ... international transportation ... trading/high finance ... dancers ... aristocrats ... large animals ... higher studies ... lawmaking ... profiteers ... veterinarians.
- *Problems and possibilities:* Even if you have a routine-loving sun sign (like Virgo), this placement of the sun will give you the desire and the ability to constantly renew your life, and to adapt to new patterns of behavior. You will feel strongly about one religious or ethical system or another, or at least have a very strong personal philosophy. However, you could become rather dogmatic and rigid in your opinions. Your adaptability is admirable, but a desire for the new and novel could be the "downside" of your openness to new experience. Exercise control. With certain sun signs, there may be a tendency toward inner battles between opportunity-seeking and a firm set of principles. You are a spender—of both your money and your physical resources.

Birth time 10 a.m. to 12 a.m.: **Sun in Tenth House**

- *Tenth house matters:* Realism ... structure ... ambition ... rigidity ... integrating ... limitation ... disciplining ... reputation ... social position ... creating the useful ... contraction ... coolness ... convention.
- *Tenth house people/places/things:* Figures ... fame ... common sense ... property ... correctional systems and facilities ... ceramics ... money lenders ... efficiency experts ... the bones ... the elderly ... sculptors ... watches and clocks.
- *Problems and possibilities:* You have the capacity of becoming a respected member of whatever group you move in, because your public image is very important to you. If you play your cards right, you can arrive at a sense that you are fulfilling your destiny. However, if you become obsessed with power and appearances, you could end up living a shallow, meaningless life behind your strong facade. It is most important with this placement of the sun to find the right outlet for you to express yourself and get positive feedback from others. You won't be happy starving in a garret, because both money and recognition are too important to you. This position of the sun often brings fame.

Birth time 8 to 10 a.m.: **Sun in Eleventh House**

- *Eleventh house matters:* Helping ... experimentation ... humanitarianism ... association ... liberalism .. freedom ... suddenness ... awakenings ... combining ... freethinking ... rationality ... caring ... breaking through ... observing coolly ... predicting.
- *Eleventh house people/places/things:* Paradoxes ... stunt men ... electricity ... zealots ... divorce ... fireworks ... the social sciences ... reform ... geniuses ... aviation ... weathermen ... brotherly love ... magnetism ... groups ... friends ... causes.
- *Problems and possibilities:* If you are a very personal

sun sign (like Cancer), you will gain a lot of objectivity with the placement of the sun in this house. You should have very high aims and goals, and some of them will undoubtedly involve helping the less fortunate in some way or another. Though this is admirable, if you don't set yourself on a definite path in life and stick to a definite plan, you could simply drift along, with only vague ideas about where you can shine. It is important to be quite realistic with the sun in this house. Your own crowd is important to you, but you must avoid becoming such a part of the group that you lose a sense of your own individuality—which is potentially very great. Some people with the sun in the 11th house are downright wacky, but often very achieving people.

Birth Time 6 to 8 a.m.: **Sun in Twelfth House**

- *Twelfth house matters:* Dissolving ... ambiguity ... disguising ... retreating ... sensualism ... enchantment ... paying dues ... healing spiritually ... insubstantiality ... confinement ... persuading ... comprehending the incomprehensible ... merging ... pretending.
- *Twelfth house people/places/things:* Makeup ... escapism ... alcohol and drugs ... drama and dramatic actors ... films ... advertising ... pastoral work ... fishing ... astrophysics ... con men ... magicians ... hospitals ... alibis ... myths ... prisons.
- *Problems and possibilities:* Yours is not an easy house of the sun to have—especially if you are a very self-expressive sun sign type like Leo. You may feel that life is confining you in some way or another; what you are really sensing is your gift of the ability to transcend self to a much higher spiritual level. You should be an expert at coping with intangibles and sensing the nuances of any situation. In a sense, you have a kind of ESP which can be developed for life success. However, the real down side of the twelfth house sun is that it

can lead to a very confused, unfocussed attitude toward life. It is essential that you give yourself a definite structure to work within if you are to free yourself from the worries and cares of life. By all means avoid any form of escapism that is dangerous.

3

The Geometry of Relationships

What Signs You Get Along with—and Why

The first thing most people want to know about their sun sign is what other signs they are compatible with. It's a natural question, and a good one to ask an astrologer, because one aspect of astrology, called "synastry" (literally, "stars together") concentrates on the subject of relationships. When practising synastry, the astrologer compares the two birth charts of the two people involved to find what connections there are between them. It is a complicated process, but it provides excellent clues about how two people will relate to each other. What chart comparison does is *describe the nature of the relationship*. Actually, to an astrologer there are no "bad" or "good" relationships; there are just a lot of different kinds and each has a special character. Of course it is true that some relationships end up on the rocks, sometimes devastating one or both parties involved. But, even in such cases, the astrologer looks at it as a "karmic" relationship—one in which people *had* to come together in order to learn some life lessons.

While comparing two complete horoscopes is the ideal way to look at a relationship, there is a very simple method of looking at two sun signs, and coming up with an overall prediction of how two people will relate to each other. This method goes back to the great circle of the zodiac and to the division of the twelve signs into four elements: fire, earth, air, and water.

Here's the lineup of signs in each element:

Fire: Aries, Leo, Sagittarius

Earth: Taurus, Virgo, Capricorn
Air: Gemini, Libra, Aquarius
Water: Cancer, Scorpio, Pisces

The general rules of thumb for element-mixing are as follows:

Great	Good	Semi-tough or Difficult
Fire and air	Fire and fire	Fire and water
Water and earth	Earth and earth	Earth and air
	Air and air	Fire and earth
	Water and water	Air and water

Here's the way it looks mathmatically:
 If you divide the 360-degree circle of the zodiac by the twelve signs, you find that each sign is 30 degrees away from the next.
- Signs that are 30 degrees apart—or next to each other—are semi-tough.
- Signs that are 60 degrees (two signs) or 180 degrees (six signs) away from each other are the best combinations. (The latter, 180 degrees away from each other, makes these signs polar opposites, and in astrology polar opposites attract.)
- Signs that are 120 degrees apart—four signs away from each other—are in the same element, and their relationship is good, but far from perfect.
- Signs that are 90 degrees or three signs away from each other have the most difficult relationships of all. They are said to be in "square aspect" to each other.

When you look at the four elements in terms of what they signify in the physical world, you get a good idea why some elements get along more easily.

Fire turns water into steam (hot air).
Water puts fire out.
Fire scorches earth.

Earth smothers fire.
Air fans fire and makes it brighter.
Fire warms up cool air.
Water softens up hard earth.
Earth makes water keep its shape.
Water and air do nothing (unless you add heat).
Air blows earth around.

What about combinations of the same element, such as fire with fire? In effect, they tend to neutralize or cancel each other out. Or, they can simply be too much of one element for comfort.

- Two fire signs together could experience "burn out" fairly quickly.
- Two air signs might analyze each other to the death of the relationship.
- Two earth signs could depress each other a lot.
- Two water signs could make for an overly "heavy" relationship.

4

Twelve Places at the Table

A Mini Astrodrama in Which the Twelve Signs Play Themselves

No matter how accurate or colorful any description of a zodiac sign may be, it is still a description—not the real thing. A sign is simply an abstract concept until it takes form in a living, breathing human being. There are obviously as many different types of people as there are individual horoscopes, and no two are exactly alike. However, the twelve signs of the zodiac are still the best guidelines we have for sorting out human behavior into broad but meaningful categories. There are even fiction writers who use the zodiac signs as prototypes for characters they create because it makes them more realistic, i.e., more like people you are likely to meet.

What follows is fiction, but it gets closer to the truth about each zodiacal sign than a general description ever can. The twelve characters in this docudrama are obviously caricatures, because their behavior is highly exaggerated. But it is exaggeration for emphasis, and for the purpose of bringing to life the twelve signs of the zodiac, which don't really exist except as real people. Like real people, these twelve characters have foibles; but they have fine points too. As you read this drama, you may find yourself drawn to some signs and put off by others. Make mental notes of which signs you find yourself most sympathetic with and check out your findings in the parts of this book about astrological compatibility. It could prove very interesting—

and very revealing. As each sign of the zodiac has a sex or gender, they are portrayed here as male or female accordingly. But the basic behavior pattern is applicable to both sexes.

The twelve signs of the zodiac are invited to dinner at that great dining room in the sky. When they arrive, they find that their host (who shall remain signless) has slipped up, and there are only eleven places set at the table. Since it is a fancy affair, each sign is trying to be on his/her best behavior. However, the situation is a bit unsettling, so in the course of trying to resolve it, they all relapse into their natural zodiacal characteristics.

Aries An energetic young man, he comes bounding into the room, almost tripping on an untied shoelace. He is dressed rather casually for the occasion, and looks as if he got dressed rather quickly. When he realizes what the situation is, there's no doubt in his mind how to handle it.

"Only eleven places? Don't worry; Pisces will probably never show anyway. But, I got here before anybody else (the doorman will prove it) so I should definitely get a seat. In fact, I should sit down *first*. No, I don't need to wash my hands or anything. I'm *starved*, so I hope you aren't having anything like the gooey mess with the French name you had before. A hamburger will do just fine. And don't serve it cold like you did the last time. Hey, there's a great-looking dish over there, ha ha! Seat me next to her, will you Cancer? Well, she looks like a nice warm type, so I think I'll go let her warm me up. By the way, I'm organizing a sky-diving club. Want to join? Seriously, if you can't afford the membership fee, I'll put it up for you, because I'd love to have you join. Oh, you're doing okay now? Glad to hear you're off the rack. Got any pretzels?"

Taurus An attractive young woman with faint dimples in her roundish cheeks and a slightly unruly but pretty mass of curly hair comes sauntering into the room. She is dressed in a soft and pretty outfit that looks expensive, and has her handbag clutched tightly under her arm. She looks around the room with moderate curiosity. As the host walks up to her, she gives him a warm smile; when she speaks, her voice is low and melodious—but firm.

"Only eleven places? You mean, only eleven *chairs*. All you have to do is set another place and give me a pillow to sit on. I don't mind, as long as I'm comfortable. And I smell something wonderful, so I know the food is going to be delicious. To be honest with you, that's really why I came. I don't like to go out much, you know. What I really like is curling up in my warm and comfy bed—with someone warm and comfy, of course. (Are you busy later on?) But, now that I'm *here*, there's no way I'm not going to eat. What's for dessert? Who's that nervous-looking lady over there? Virgo? I'll go try to make her feel comfortable."

Gemini It's hard to tell just how old this fellow is as he springs in the door; he could be any age, though he looks about eighteen. He is dressed in the very latest style, though nothing he has on is really extreme. His eyes dart all over the room, and he is carrying a notebook under his arm. When the host tells him about the eleven places, he is so busy listening to another conversation, he almost misses it. When he reacts, it is in a typically casual way.

"Don't worry about me; I don't need a place. I'll just float around the room, because what I really came here for is the conversation. I'm writing a book, you know—it's called *1001 Opening Conversational Gambits* and tonight I'm researching. I see you've got some really fascinating types here. How did you make up the guest list? Are they all married? Why did they come alone? What's the menu? Who's the chef? Can I see the wine list? Who's that blowsy-looking type over there? Taurus? I'll bet *she's* got a story. Where's the telephone? I've got to make a call."

Cancer A sexy, voluptuous woman of indeterminate age pauses at the door; she seems shy, but conscious of the impression she is making. Her clothes are a bit unusual, and some things are from the thrift shop. However, her antique jewelry is genuine, and the whole effect is glamorous. When she discovers there are only eleven places, she is visibly upset, and there is a touch of a whine in her voice as she speaks.

"I wish I'd known; I could have stayed home with the children. They have colds, you know. If you want, I'll simply leave; but I really don't want to go home by myself; I'll get scared and have bad dreams. Upset? Yes, I am upset, and when I get upset I can't eat. Unless it's really soothing and nourishing. Did you know that a touch of heavy cream in mashed potatoes is simply heavenly? Chicken soup? I make it by the gallon. Say, you look as if you could stand a little fattening up. Well, all right. I *guess* I'll stay—unless I change my mind, of course."

Leo This is a fine figure of a man—fairly tall, rather muscular, and with a thick crop of curly hair that is somewhere between blond and red. He is elegantly dressed and his gold cufflinks probably put a real drain on Fort Knox. His grand entrance is smooth and practised, and his handshake is hearty and warm. When his host tells him the news, he takes it very personally.

"Well, let me tell you, this is embarrassing! I mean, all these people here to see me, and I may have to stand? I've given bigger parties than this, and they've always gone off without a hitch. Let me handle things for you the next time. For now, just get that chair over there and squeeze someone in—Virgo won't mind. No, *here*; not *there!* While we're all waiting I guess I can entertain everyone with my tantrum act. What? No, I'm only kidding—though I am mad. I'll do my Hamlet number instead. Like my cufflinks? They match my Gold Card. I've ordered another pair with sapphires, too."

Virgo A rather prim woman stands quietly at the door looking as if she would like to blend into the woodwork. She is dressed very neatly, but conservatively, with flat-heeled sensible shoes. In her handbag she carries a surgical mask to wear in case any of the other guests has a cold. Her reaction to the news that there are only eleven places is swift and shrill.

"Well, it certainly isn't *my* fault. I answered the invitation the minute I got it. I *always* do! Why didn't you check on things more carefully? If you had, this wouldn't have happened, and you wouldn't have all these people standing around thinking terrible things about you. I don't mind for myself, you understand, I don't eat much anyway; you never know what you're going to get. I'll stay in the kitchen and help the cook clean up. You can't be too careful about these things, you know. You wouldn't believe the sanitary conditions I've found in *some* kitchens. Not mentioning any names, of course. Oh, *why* did you mess things up this way; you are simply impossible...."

Intermission: Our host walks away as Virgo continues to complain. As he checks on the guests, he discovers that Libra has just arrived. Sagittarius and Pisces are nowhere to be found, but Scorpio, Capricorn, and Aquarius are waiting to greet him. Because he looks like he's a bit uncomfortable, the host talks to Libra first.

Libra A very attractive male, wearing all the right things, walks tentatively into the room, looking as if he is searching for someone. He is visibly uncomfortable alone. His gaze scans the room, quietly appraising everything and everybody in it. He seems to approve, but in his nervousness, he approaches the table, and starts rearranging one of the settings, then rearranging it again. All this is done very tactfully and gracefully. In fact, he looks as if he couldn't make an awkward gesture if he tried. His host approaches him and breaks the news. Libra's reaction is smooth and unruffled.

"Oh, how *clever* of you to arrange this little puzzle for us. It will make things so much more fun. Of course, we've got to make things absolutely fair; we wouldn't want to hurt anyone's feelings. I could leave if it would help, but ... Oh, how nice of you to tell me I'll definitely have a place; it makes me feel a lot less awkward. I rarely go places alone, you know. Who would I like to sit next to? Well, the Capricorn lady looks like a sturdy and sensible type. But on the other hand, Scorpio is a *knockout*. Is she attached? Hmmm, Taurus looks like she'd like to chat, but oh, that Cancer! Decisions, decisions; I'll make up my mind later on. Where did you get that *great* painting?

Scorpio A slim and sexy woman dressed totally in black comes slinking into the room. Her style and movement are absolutely magnetic, and every eye turns to look at her. But she gives no visible response that she is aware of it. She doesn't seem to be feeling anything at all, but when her host approaches and tells her what is going on, she is seething with quiet rage.

"Do you really think you are going to get away with this? I suspected something when I got that weird invitation. Who in the world would ever come as they are and let everybody else know what they're really like? No matter how many times you tell me it was an innocent mistake to set only eleven places, I'll never believe it. Nothing in this world is innocent. And when it comes to drawing straws, just remember you owe me one from the last time. You know, the *last* time! Who's that wimpy looking guy over there? Gemini? Maybe I'll amuse myself with him for a while. I need a new conquest; I'm getting out of practice."

Sagittarius While Scorpio has been talking with the host, a tall rather rangy male has come loping into the room carrying a suitcase. He is a bit disheveled because his flight was late. He throws the suitcase in a corner and starts putting himself back together—a bit absentmindedly because he is looking around the room with a big smile and a lot of anticipation. He moves toward the host and gives a slap on his back that is almost *too* hearty.

"Only eleven places? Why worry? We'll work it out somehow. Life's too short to get uptight anyway. Had the greatest trip, and I'm turning right around tomorrow and going to the Orient so I can practice my Chinese. Say, are you serving Chinese food? I love Chinese food—and a good beer to go with it. At least I hope you're serving better wine than you did last time. You're looking a little pale . . . been partying too much lately? Ha ha, only kidding. Who's that guy over there with the flashy cufflinks? And the mouse with the sensible shoes? Think I'll see if I can loosen her up a bit. Did you hear I'm going to win the lottery again? What do you mean, how do I know? I just *know*. And I've got a great idea for an international fast food chain I'm going to bankroll with my winnings. I'm gonna call it 'The Great Gobler' and serve only turkey sandwiches. Hey, I'm thirsty. Where's the bar?"

Aquarius An intellectual-looking gentleman—sort of an absentminded professor type—has been standing in the doorway quietly puffing his pipe and scrutinizing the crowd. His jacket and pants don't match, but he isn't aware of it. An even stranger—but typical—sartorial note is his electric blue tie with orange stripes. He's got his earphones with him; if things get too dull, he'll listen to some hard rock or electronic music and be in seventh heaven. When he finds out about the missing place, he gives a thoughtful answer and makes an impractical suggestion.

"Oh, well, rather than make anyone feel left out, we could cancel the whole dinner and bring the food to the local shelter for the homeless. Ah, you don't care for that idea. Too bad; I'm becoming more and more concerned about poverty in our own backyard. Of course, I'm no bleeding heart like Pisces, but fair's fair. Want to hear about a new invention I'm working on? It's an electronic stamp sorter that will revolutionize the whole philatelic world. Huh? Oh, that's stamp collecting. Glad you asked me to come alone, since I'm free as a bird now. My last attachment got so *sticky!* I've sworn off. At least off those emotional types who want you to get so involved. No, I never get lonely—I've got too many friends for that. By the way, I can just sit on the floor in the lotus position, and get some meditating in at the same time."

Capricorn A rather handsome, perfectly put together woman has been quietly observing the crowd and the room, mentally putting a price tag on everything. What she has on is very expensive, but understated and in excellent taste. In her handbag she carries a petition with her name on it. She wants to run for local office, and is hoping to pick up some supporters tonight. If they are "her kind of people," that is. Her reaction to the host's situation is sober but logical.

"Well, it's obvious someone will have to go, but I

trust your judgment to decide who is most important—if you know what I mean. Your appointments are in excellent taste; I see you like Tiffany as much as I do. Who's that rather tacky looking type over there? Cancer? Where *does* she get her clothes? I have little sympathy for people who can't get their act together and run their lives successfully. She's probably a poet. Ah, well, different strokes for different folks; fantasy has no place in *my* life, you know. By the way, I have some excellent ideas about how to shape things up in the community; will you sign my petition? At dinner, are we going to discuss great books? I just bought a whole series . . . all leather-bound, of course. They look smashing in my living room."

Pisces Meanwhile, a rather wispy but very pretty woman has been wandering in and out of the doorway, looking as if she isn't quite sure she is in the right place. She is dressed in a misty fabric of very pale colors; there doesn't seem to be a clear-cut edge anywhere. In fact, if you don't rub your eyes, you might think you are seeing an apparition. The host knows it's Pisces and catches her just as she's about to drift out the door again. He doesn't bother telling her about the missing place, because he knows she wouldn't understand why that was important.

"Late? Am I late? I lost my watch two weeks ago. Or was it three? Oh well, what's time anyway in the larger scheme of things? Hungry? Not really, though I can't remember the last time I ate. *Love*—it's *love* that's food for the soul, and that's what I care about nourishing. I wonder if any of these people have had any *real* soul food lately. No, don't worry, I won't try to convert anyone tonight. I'm too, too drained because of my current work. What kind? Well, it really isn't a job-job, I mean where you make money, and all. I've started a shelter for homeless animals in my apartment; I cry so much when I see a stray that I can't stand it. Who? Ho, he left some time ago. Something about there being 'other fish in the sea.' What in the world do you suppose he meant by that? By the way, I'm a little short of cash. Do you think you could lend me . . . ?"

At this point, things are at a stalemate, but the situation will quickly resolve itself in one of twelve ways. Take your pick: This time *you* can choose the ending you like—and the one you think makes best astrological sense.

A. Aries gets in a fight with Leo and has to go to the emergency room.
B. Taurus gets really tired and hungry and decides to go home, cook a hamburger, and go to bed early.
C. Gemini runs out of note paper and gets laryngitis at the same time.
D. Cancer gets a call from the babysitter and is so worried she goes home to take care of her children.
E. Leo gets so irritated that no one is paying attention to the bruises Aries gave him that he leaves in a huff.
F. Virgo gets a stomach ache and decides to leave. Besides, it's time for her mineral bath.
G. Libra isn't able to make up his mind and gets a headache in the process.
H. Scorpio decides it's definitely a plot to humiliate her, and bows out less than graciously.
I. Sagittarius gets a little drunk and leaves early to get the plane.
J. Capricorn leaves as soon as she gets her petition filled up because there isn't anyone there *really* worth knowing.
K. Aquarius decides to go teach people at the shelter to use his stamp-sorting machine so they can get jobs.
L. Pisces remembers she has a date with her spiritual advisor and that she forgot to feed the animals.

5

Moods of the Moon

How to Successfully Navigate Its Day-by-Day Changes

Never underestimate the power of the moon. It is the closest planet to earth, and the only one whose effect on human life can actually be measured. Even the most skeptical antiastrology person has to admit that the moon rules the tides. If you stand on the beach for even a half hour or so, you can literally *see* how the moon works its magic as the water flows higher or lower, according to the time of day. There are places in the world where the tide rises as much as forty feet from its lowest to its highest point—that's *power*. If you think about the fact that humans are about 98 percent water in our chemical makeup, it's much easier to accept the fact that the moon has the same powerful effect on us as it does on the tides.

Like the "female" she symbolically is, the moon also changes her mind—or her sign—more quickly than any other planet. If you look at the day-by-day predictions in this book, which gives the position of the moon for every day, you will see that this changeable planet moves into a different sign about every two days.

As it moves from sign to sign, the moon brings a different kind of energy to the earth's atmosphere. Those who are particularly sensitive—like Cancers—feel it most strongly. But even the most stolid types are often moved by the effect of the particular sign the moon occupies on any given day, though they may not want to admit it.

Are we then slaves to the moods of the moon? Not if we understand its energies and cooperate with them. If you work *with* the moon and not against her, you can actually make life a lot easier for yourself. For instance, there are certain activities that go more smoothly when the moon is in a particular sign, just as other activities are more difficult to accomplish. Scheduling things accordingly could prevent a lot of frustration. You don't have to become a complete "lunatic" (ancient meaning, "one ruled by the moon") to benefit from its positive vibes, but simply go with the flow. Keep in mind, however, that the moon's effect will be *modified* by your sun sign, so be sure to check out your individual daily prediction. For instance, for *any* sun sign, the days when the moon is in that sign should bring a surge of energy. Whether you handle that energy positively or negatively is up to you.

Here's a rundown of the moods of the moon and the human activities that go with them.

When the Moon Is in Aries There is a very *physical* tone to this day. People may be throwing their weight around in more ways than one. Impatience, independent action, and quick tempers can sprout up all over the place. The good news is that most people will be feeling rather decisive, so some things can be completed. The bad news is that decisions may be totally unilateral; what *you* want may be exactly what someone else *doesn't* want. Similarly, people may be invading each other's territories; "keep off the grass" signs won't mean much today. Rule-breaking is the order of the day, and so are the consequences that go along with it. However, if there's a big mountain to scale, today's the day to begin the climb. If there's a formidable task that requires a lot of get-up-and-go to accomplish, today's the day to plunge in with both feet. If there's something you've been hesitating to tell someone, today you'll get the nerve to say it, but it may be difficult to be tactful. Try, anyway. On the up side, people will be feeling in the mood for some fun and frolic—practical jokes are very "moon in Aries." Even the boss may get in the spirit of things. It's a good day to:

Make a sale	Sharpen knives
Do heavy housework	Stop worrying
Do some baking	Make a clean break
Start a diet	Start an exercise class
Buy a lottery ticket	Do something on your own
Get a haircut	Try a new recipe
Have your eyes checked	Throw a last-minute party

When the Moon Is in Taurus Today, the amber light goes on, and people start to proceed with more caution. Rather than being adventurous, most people will feel like sticking with routine tasks. It is not a good day to try something new. In this more conservative mood, people will tend to hold on to what they have; don't try to borrow money from a friend today. Concentrate on making your own money grow, instead. Speaking of increase, this is an excellent day to "make your garden grow" in every sense of the phrase. Along with a quieter mood of the day, you may feel like pampering yourself a bit; allow yourself at least one luxury. Chocoholics, beware, however; this is a day for food binges and all forms of dietary excess. Creature comforts are a lot on everyone's mind; in fact, it may be difficult to crawl out of that comfortable bed in the morning. And more than a few people will be crawling back into it fairly early—with their favorite person. Sexual cravings are high on the list of "moon moods" today. Enjoy!

It's a good day to:

Put something off until tomorrow	Put up preserves
Buy clothes or jewelry	Have a massage
Get your teeth filled	Start singing lessons
Start a savings account	Sell high on the market
Stick to your guns	Buy a plant
Buy candy	Buy real estate
Stay home and watch television	Hug somebody

When the Moon Is in Gemini There's a touch more energy in the air today, and people will begin moving around a lot more. For some, there will be a lot of nervous energy and the scattery feeling that goes along with it; don't force yourself to concentrate if you can avoid it. It's a day to make connections—call, write, or bump into both new and old friends. Wits are generally sharp today, and people could be cracking jokes all around you. On the other hand, they may also be spilling some secrets. Gossip is easy to start today, and it could spread like wildfire. Mind your mouth! Anything requiring manual dexterity can easily get done today; even those who are usually clumsy may find they have nimble fingers. The tendency today is to do things quickly, if a bit superficially. If there are a couple of things that require a once-over-lightly treatment, get them out of the way now. If you haven't been invited to a party, give your own—or at least plan to get together with some buddies for a little socializing; the time is definitely right.

It's a good day to:

Get your hair cut	Use your hands
Join a club	Pay bills
Have a tooth pulled	Eat out
Sign up for a new course	Take a walk/drive
Send a letter	Call your brother/sister
Try something new	Tell a fib
Learn a language	Do two things at once

When the Moon Is in Cancer In Cancer, the moon is in her very own sign—and you'll know it. All those "moon" characteristics—like changeableness, sensitivity, and the desire for security—will be heightened. Cancers, of course, will feel it most strongly; and the other water signs, Scorpio and Pisces, may be even moodier than usual. The general tendency today is to do things that make you feel comfortable and feel good. For some, that means eating a lot of food; for others, it could be hitting the bottle a bit. People tend to feel a bit sorry for themselves during the transit of the moon through Cancer. When two people who live together are both feeling that way, the result can be a rather touchy day—and evening. As much as you want the comfort of others, you are better off on your own and working off those anxious feelings by yourself. Not for safety, but for comfort's sake, the best place to go today is no farther than your own backyard. You'll probably be feeling very stay-at-home anyway. However, it's an excellent day for memories. Reminisce with somebody you love, or get out that old photo album by yourself. You might find yourself shedding a tear or two, but it's all in a good cause.

It's a good day to:

Bake something delicious	Hug your children
Buy something old	Take care of somebody
Put up preserves	Go without makeup
Buy property	Call your mother
Start a habit	Buy something for the house
Plant something	Entertain at home
Pamper yourself	Give your hair a treatment

When the Moon Is in Leo Today, everyone feels like "coming out of the woodwork." Just as Cancer moon makes you want to hide, Leo moon makes you want to get out there and be seen. Nothing but the best will do on this day, so it could be a rather expensive one. Most people will be more generous than usual—both with their money and their affections; many a new romance has started under a Leo moon. Leo is also one of the more playful signs, so a lot of you will be in the mood for fun and games. Eating out is very Leo moon—and so is picking up the check. Today, you may have to fight for it. However, the boss may be a lot stricter than usual, and even those with nobody to "boss" will try to push somebody around. If you've got children, today you will appreciate them very much—no matter what they do. Most people find themselves reaching for the newest thing in the closet under this transit of the moon. If they don't have anything new to wear, they'll probably go out and buy it—on credit. No matter what time of the year it is, you'll be looking for a little sunshine or at least a warm place. On the beaches or by the fireplaces are where most people would like to be today—wishing life were one long vacation.

It's a good day to:

Borrow money	Buy jewelry
Get a new hairstyle	Invest in the market
Start building something	Do something creative

Follow a hunch	Prepare a gourmet meal
Steal the spotlight	Dress up
Be brave	Kiss somebody new
Be waited on	

When the Moon Is in Virgo   Now it's back to work, and back to reality. There's a sharp distinction between the Virgo moon mood and what precedes it, so you may shock yourself. Perhaps by deciding it's really time to get organized and then actually *doing* it. On the home front it's a great day to rearrange all those sloppy closets and cupboards. On the job, you couldn't pick a better time to wrestle with that nasty detail work you've been avoiding. However, all is not good news under Virgo moon. For one thing, by contrast to Leo moon's generosity, people will be positively stingy today—both with their money and their love. Even the best of situations could deteriorate today when one or the other of the involved parties decides to point out the other's flaws. Your best course under the Virgo moon is to check that impulse to criticize. People can become highly self-critical during this transit, too. One extreme example of the going-over some people can give themselves during a Virgo moon is to develop mysterious maladies or to discover aches and pains they never felt before. Not to worry; they'll be all better by the time the moon moves into the next sign. Virgo moon is also inspection time, so the boss may be particularly sensitive to messy desks today and sloppiness in general. Keep things buttoned up and tidy for best results.

It's a good time to:

Start a diet	Start a new job
Get a physical	Sew or mend something
Bake bread	Read a good book
Quit smoking	Get a complete makeover
Buy a pet	Call your maiden aunt
Try to do without something	Feel like a martyr
Buy health food	Do a puzzle

When the Moon Is in Libra   Now it's time to kiss and make up. Any relationships that suffered from the ragged nerves of Virgo moon time can be nicely patched up today. Pleasantries should be easy for one and all. In fact, even people who are normally rather gruff should smile a bit more today. Libra moon is one of the most social of moon periods; meeting and greeting should be prevalent activities. Most people will want to put their best foot forward, too, so the impulse to dress up and look your best may come upon you. You may feel rather self-indulgent as well; hard work is not as compatible with the Libra moon period as rest and relaxation are. It's definitely a time of togetherness, so even habitual loners may be looking for company. Most people will feel they need people—possibly one special person. Romance blossoms under the Libra moon in its purest form. It's not so much sex people want now as romantic love and companionship. No one's actually made a count, but it's a fair bet that more flowers get sent under the Libra moon than at any other time. Physical beauty is also highly important, so Libra moon is a great one under which to get yourself a whole new look or to redo anything that needs it. Something that's off-balance will bother you more at this time.

It's a good day to:

Be tactful	Forgive and forget
Redecorate	Add color to your life
Give a party	Luxuriate
Fall in love	Sign up for a dance class
Join a singing group	Buy a stereo
Buy something beautiful	Buy a down comforter
Try a new makeup	Learn about wine

When the Moon Is in Scorpio Things could easily get heavy today, and the tendency will be to go to extremes. Haters will hate more; lovers will love more passionately and physically. The sex drive is stimulated in many people during this transit of the moon. With all those intense emotions flying around, it's not surprising that people easily get hot under the collar—and/or imagine that somebody is out to get them. However, there is an up side to the Scorpio moon, and that is the extra jot of will power it gives the most weak-willed people. If you've got to dig in your heels and clench your teeth to get something done, today's the day you will be able to do it. People *endure* a lot under the Scorpio moon. The only problem is that they may develop some resentment toward those they believe should be enduring with them. However, the tendency is to keep silent. In spite of the intense emotionalism of the Scorpio moon, there isn't a lot of outright complaining. People will let the pressure build up inside of them and then burst out into violent rages. If your temper isn't good under the best of circumstances, control it during the Scorpio moon, by all means. It's also a time when people tend to feel a bit claustrophobic; a good walk in the fresh air can work wonders at this time.

It's a good day to:

See a psychiatrist	Have good sex
Buy a house	Face up to a crisis
Open a secret bank account	Read a good mystery
Make a firm decision	Take body-building
Do your taxes	Get a prescription filled
Throw away what you don't need	Buy life insurance
	Change your life
Do some strenuous exercise	

When the Moon Is in Sagittarius Things definitely lighten up when the moon moves into Sagittarius—and people loosen up, too. In fact, one danger under this moon is getting too relaxed—with your diet, your money, or your generous spirits. Moderation is not the mood of the day, so you may have to force it on yourself. It is not a good time to try to stop smoking—or to stop doing anything self-indulgent. There's definitely a "live and let live" attitude in the air when the moon is in Sagittarius, so bad relations should be easily improved. A spirit of good will is pervasive, as well as a lighthearted attitude. One thing that means is that even normally conservative people will be willing to take chances; those for whom a more liberal outlook is a natural state of affairs could really go too far out on a limb. If you gamble, bet *only* what you can afford to lose today. The place everyone will want to be today is outdoors. In fact, more than one person will simply disappear from the scene to do something either adventurous or relaxing. It's an excellent day to think big, but you may find the follow-through a bit difficult. The big picture is what's easiest to see right now; leave the fine brush strokes for another time. Enjoy the spirit of fun and generosity that should be in the air.

It's a good day to:

Make a long-distance call	Go to church
Plan a trip	Enjoy a hobby
Buy a dog (or a horse)	Learn a new language
Contribute to a wildlife-foundation	Do something charitable
	Borrow money
Try a new approach	Run away from it all
Sell anything to anybody	Get a bigger place
Try your luck/feel lucky	

When the Moon Is in Capricorn In sharp contrast to the "easy come, easy go" feeling of the Sagittarius moon, the moon in Capricorn brings on a much more serious mood. You could call it the "workaholic's moon," and even those whose work style is less intense will find themselves wanting to get a lot done. It's important to *accomplish something* when the moon is in Capricorn, if you are to feel comfortable. Most people want to tread only on solid ground at this time, so there could be a bit of distrust in the air. No one wants to waste time—and least of all on things or people from whom they are not likely to derive some kind of benefit. Another curious facet of the Capricorn moon mood is a tendency to feel older and more serious; some lighter types dislike the feeling so much they will go out of their way to look young. It's the kind of day that matronly secretary in the office is likely to appear in something rather frilly. People can really handle things under the Capricorn moon too; endurance is *very* Capricorn. That means those who exercise will work out harder and longer; those who normally do not push themselves will do at least a little self-prodding. A good image is paramount to many people when the moon is in this sign, and the tendency is for people to be quite status conscious. Self-control is the order of the day, in every respect.

It's a good day to:

Start a new job	Make a list
Buy antiques	Keep your money

Buy anything for investment	Go to the dentist
Wear anything with a good label on it	Start a diet
	Work late
Bet on a favorite	Ask for repayment of a debt
Go to the chiropractor	
Buy insurance	Clean house

When the Moon Is in Aquarius When the moon moves into the sign of Aquarius from the sign of Capricorn, it's as if somebody took the cork out of the bottle. Suddenly, the rather repressed mood bursts into a desire for change—a *need* for change. This is one of those days when people tend to make rash moves like quit a dull job, call it quits with a clinging person, throw out everything in their closet and start all over again. Reaching this point is easy to do under the Aquarian moon. However, it's usually very positive. What's important at this time is to try something new, not just get rid of something old. Some people decide to experiment with a new recipe, a new lover, or a new hair style. It's the kind of day when a woman with long hair will decide to get a crew cut. On the relationship side, the mood now is one of brotherly love and friendship rather than highly charged sexual encounters. Wanting to be with friends and feeling like part of a group is what's important now. No one is a stranger under the Aquarian moon, and talking to people on the street is very common. The thing to be careful of under this moon is doing something irreparable—like finally telling the boss what you really think of him. He/she could easily decide that it's time for a change of personnel.

It's a good day to:

Do something kinky	Buy/wear something crazy
Try a new food	Color your hair
Do something friendly	Contribute to a charity
Start flying lessons	Move to a new place
Do something impulsive	Buy a television/stereo
Join a club	Make a new friend
Make a speculative investment	Be fair

When the Moon Is in Pisces This is a time when people wear their hearts on their sleeves and feel *very* vulnerable. There's a lot of ultrasensitivity under the Pisces moon, and a lot of crying on shoulders—if you can find one that isn't already occupied. Mixed in with the emotionalism is a real feeling of empathy with others; now's the time people feel that everyone is in the same boat. However, it may be a bit difficult to keep things afloat today, because there isn't a lot of firm direction from anyone or anything. It's confusion time, and even the clearest of messages can get a little garbled. Indecisiveness will spread like the plague, so don't expect to get any clear-cut answers today. Creative people get more creative under the Pisces moon, and anyone could feel just a bit poetic. Romantic relationships are heavenly under the Pisces moon as long as they don't get out of control. Keeping certain other things under control—like drinking and other forms of escapism—is a wise precaution, too. The most satisfying and least dangerous escape is to hold hands with someone you love while you watch a real tearjerker movie. Lots of people call in sick under the Pisces moon, and there's a good reason: Most people don't like to cry in public.

It's a good day to:

Put on weight
Fall in love
Develop ESP
Find God
Buy flowers or perfume
Swear off something
Get hooked on something

Write a poem
Take in a stray dog or cat
Visit the sick
See a therapist
Stay home and read
Pamper yourself
Buy a camera

6

Venus and Mars

Love and Sex
Peace and War
Cooperating and Competing

Next to your sun sign, your moon sign, and your rising sign, the positions of Venus and Mars in your horoscope are probably the most important indicators of your personal psychology. This is because Venus shows your affectional nature and Mars shows your sexual nature. To put it another way, *Venus shows your wants and needs in romantic love while Mars shows your sexual style and your manner of expressing it.*

In a broader sense, Venus and Mars are the principles of peace and war. Venus wants to cooperate and relate to others, to share life experiences. Mars is totally concerned with self and getting what you want. Everybody's got a Venus and Mars in their horoscope because every human being has to both live with others and assert him-/herself. It's all a matter of degree. If you want to, you can think of Venus as the "higher" side of human relationships; Mars the "lower." However, you've got to keep in mind that—like all other opposites in the universe—both *cooperating* and *competing* are necessary if the world is to continue going round.

Because Venus has to do with the need to share, the sign in which it is placed will tell a lot about how you attract people you want to share with. It will also show what attracts you to others. Beyond the love arena, the position of Venus in your horoscope shows your attitudes toward money and personal possessions, creature comforts, and things of beauty. Venus is "feminine" in nature, and women tend to relate to their Venus sign more than men. But for *both* sexes, it is an available energy.

The good side of Venus is:
Sharing, beautifying, peacemaking
The bad side is:
acquisitiveness, self-indulgence, laziness

Because the position of Mars shows how you go about getting what you want, it will tell a lot about your personal drive—how *much* you want what you want. It is the desire principle, and will indicate just how passionate your passions are. Ambition, assertiveness, and anger are just a few steps away from each other, so Mars will also reveal what makes you angry or what gets you going. The planet Mars is "masculine" in nature—highly so—and men will find it easier to get in touch with their Mars energy. However, every woman's got a Mars too, and sooner or later a woman's Mars energy will present itself.

The "good" side of Mars is:
Dynamic energy, courage, sexual drive
The "bad" side is:
manipulation, cowardice, sexual abuse

No matter what area of life you are relating these planets to, it is useful to think of them in sexual terms, and of our human sexual organs. Venus is open and receptive; Mars thrusts forward and penetrates. Because we normally attract someone or are attracted to someone before we get sexually involved, Venus energy precedes Mars energy. In other words, Venus shows how *receptive* you are; Mars shows how *active* you are. Venus also has a lot to do with our ideas and images of romance, our romantic fantasies, while Mars is an indicator of sexual fantasies—which may or may not be acted out, depending on the individual's degree of inhibition.

Just as some combinations of people can coexist in constant harmony while others are in constant conflict,

Venus and Mars in an individual person can work well together, or at cross-purposes. When your Venus doesn't get along well with your Mars, you've got a problem. Sometimes a sexual problem, but always an inner conflict. How can you tell if your Venus and Mars are "friends" or "foes"? First, by looking up the positions of your personal Mars and Venus in the charts provided at the end of this chapter, reading the descriptions of those planets in the signs they fall in for you. But, just to make things a bit clearer, here's a rundown of easy Mars/Venus relationships and difficult ones. (By the way, you can also apply this principle in comparing your Venus/Mars positions to those of someone else, as well.)

Venus and Mars are "at war" when:

- One is in a fire sign, and one is in an earth sign. Here you've got a conflict between the practical and the experimental sides of yourself.
- One is in a fire sign and one is in a water sign. One part of you says "let's do it"; the other side says, "I might get hurt," so you might be stalled.
- One is in an earth sign and one is in an air sign. Air likes to think about things a little; earth needs to know it will work. Once again, it may hold you back.
- One is in an air sign and one is in a water sign. Yours is a conflict between the mental relationship and the emotional one; you may find it hard to decide what you want.

Venus and Mars are on good terms when:

- One is in a fire sign, one is in an air sign.
- One is in an earth sign and one is in a water sign.
- Both are in the same element.

Venus and Mars in The Signs

Venus in Aries (fire element)

While this position of Venus in a man or a woman indicates the kind of person who falls in love impulsively, both sexes want to be conquered, when they have Venus in Aries. They may be outrageously flirtatious, but can lead others on a merry chase before they give in. There is a tendency to look for trouble when Venus is in ths position; actually, it is excitement Venus in Aries people crave. Their personal likes and dislikes will be quite clearly defined, and they will be vocal about them. In matters of taste, there is less refinement than when Venus is in a softer sign. Both the males and the females may play up their sexuality in the way they dress; they like very loud things like rock music and bright colors. There is also an impish charm in these people and a tendency to play love games. The *real* goal is to be swept away by a romantic lover who lives up to a mediaeval code of chivalry and/or chastity.

Mars in Aries (fire element)

This is a highly competitive position for Mars; people with Mars in Aries leave no doubt about the fact that they want it, and they want it *now*—whatever "it" is. Mars in Aries can cut through a lot of life's red tape. When it comes to courtship, Mars in Aries people are equally able to disregard the small talk and get right down to business. However, this position of Mars often makes for a rather selfish lover—one who is so concerned with getting that he/she doesn't do an awful lot of giving. Mars in Aries people are likely to turn off as quickly as they turn on. Passion burns brightly, but is often short-lived. They are highly independent and likely to leave if a romantic partner gets too possessive or demanding. Mars in Aries is also always ready for a fight, so relationships are a bit stormy.

Venus in Taurus (earth element)

This is a highly sensual position for Venus to be in. People with Venus in Taurus are turned on by sweet words and soft music—and any form of touching. They like all kinds of nice and beautiful things, and will be attracted by someone who dresses well and has expensive taste. Venus in Taurus people can be a little self-indulgent, but in the main their desire is to make the object of their affection comfortable. And they will do it in very tangible ways; Venus in Taurus people of both sexes like to do things for others. When someone with Venus in Taurus is attracted, he/she is loyal. Love does not come in a flash, as it does with Venus in Aries people, but when it comes, it usually stays. At least as far as the person with Venus in Taurus is concerned. These people are generally so devoted that a breakup is extremely unsettling. You can always make a Venus in Taurus person happy with candy or flowers. The best kind of love feels good, tastes good, looks good, and smells good.

Mars in Taurus (earth element)

This Mars can express itself as ambition with a definite direction—or as controlled sexuality. Mars in Taurus people of both sexes can appear rather lazy, but actually their slow movements are usually on a deliberate course. Some people with Mars in Taurus are really looking for a safe position in a job or with a partner. Their manner of sexuality is highly sensual though they may be slow to get aroused. When a Mars in Taurus person enters into an affair, however, there is usually the intention to make it a long and serious one. These people are certainly capable of quick affairs, but they generally prefer a comfortable relationship where they do not constantly have to keep proving their love. There is a certain giving quality to Mars in Taurus, and the men are exceptionally considerate lovers. The women are fairly passive, but passionate and giving when they get going.

Venus in Gemini

Venus in Gemini people of both sexes tend to be turned on more by *talk* than by physical stimulation. Relationships have to have a mental dimension in order for them to get involved. In fact, Venus in Gemini people are likely to make better friends than lovers. When their affections *are* engaged, the connection is likely to be a little tenuous, and the Venus in Gemini's feelings may not run as deep as his/her partner's. Fickleness is a reality with these people— they like a lot of changes, and that goes for people as well as environments. Job-hopping is a trait of Venus in Gemini, and so is a constant changing of the guard in their romantic lives. However, Venus in Gemini people make wonderful romantic partners, because they are really *interested* in the people they get involved with. Never tell a Venus in Gemini person to "shut up and make love"; he/she will be very likely to shut the door on the relationship.

Mars in Gemini

Mars in Gemini people assert themselves rather erratically; there isn't a lot of staying power, in jobs or in relationships. The "alternating current" of Mars in Gemini energy makes for a rather on again, off again sexual life. People with Mars in this position are capable of having a number of purely mental relationships in between their sexual ones. These are the kind of people who talk their way into things, including a job and someone's bed. Their approach is a bit on the delicate side, and one may wonder when the Mars in Gemini person is really going to get started. However, once their passion is aroused, Mars in Gemini people like a lot of variety; sex can get quite original with these people. The tendency to bore easily goes both for their attitudes toward their sexual partners and the manner in which they have sex. Both sexes are real charmers, however, and sometimes get their way in a rather devious manner.

Venus in Cancer (water element)

The overriding thing that people with Venus in Cancer want is *security*, really the emotional kind, but since a secure home base goes along with their needs, the material kind is important too. Venus in Cancer people can be highly traditional in their romantic values—home, mother, and apple pie are symbols of the things that turn these people on. If you want to engage the emotions of a Venus in Cancer person, all you have to do is look as if you *need* somebody—preferably a mother. Venus in Cancer people need to be needed, but sometimes can go overboard by totally taking over the other person's life. With Venus in this sign, people respond strongly to all kinds of romantic things, from the card that says "I love you" to a little token of affection for no special occasion. However, Venus in Cancer people are highly self-protective, so you first have to break down their natural reserve and fear of getting hurt. Once you do, you won't find a more faithful lover. Except perhaps Taurus.

Mars in Cancer (water element)

Mars in Cancer people can sneak up on you when they've decided they want you; their approach is a bit sideways, like the locomotion of the crab that is the Cancer symbol. They are soft and subtle lovers and said by some to be among the best sexual partners in the zodiac. However, as sensitive and understanding as they tend to be in the sexual area, they can be overly possessive with people they love, and even turn rather cruel when they are rejected. Cancer is a water sign, and it is as if that water starts boiling—invisibly—then the lid totally pops off when the explosion comes. Mars in Cancer people tend to be a little blind to their sexual/ambition drive and can even pretend to themselves that it doesn't exist. For this reason, they make formidable enemies, because while they look as if they are asking for peace they are really preparing for battle.

Venus in Leo (fire element)

There's a pretty simple way to get a Venus in Leo person to like you. Give him/her a lot of attention—*positive* attention. Venus in Leo people do want love, but they want admiration and adulation to come along with it. A bit like Venus in Aries, Venus in Leo wants a *courtly* lover—someone who will swear absolute loyalty. When it's a Leo sun sign person who also has Venus in Leo, you've got the absolute monarch of them all. Venus in Leo also goes only for the best, and is attracted to what looks expensive or rewarding—in both jobs and people. Venus in Leo expects you to dress and look your best, no matter what the circumstances. It is not a "casual" Venus. Demonstrations of love are very important, too. Words are great, of course, and so is a lot of hugging and the rest of the physical love spectrum. However, candy—or some other tangible token of affection—is expected. Venus in Leo has fierce pride, so if you even slip once and appear not to *respect* this person, he/she is likely to brush you off—with a very grand gesture of course.

Mars in Leo (fire element)

Speaking of grand gestures, Mars in Leo wrote the book. This kind of person is the one who will lavish the object of his/her affection with all kinds of luxurious things. Mars in Leo is a real showy person and expects to be appreciated for it. Both the males and the females are aggressive about going after what they want, and once they are happily ensconced—with a lover or a job—they are loyal and steady. However, the down side of the Mars in Leo position is a violent temper: a *really* violent temper. Both sexes can get quite physical in expressing anger. This is the position of the female who throws plates and the man who slaps his faithless lover on the cheek. Mars in Leo is unrelentingly honest—and will expect you to be too. One devious move, and it's over

Venus in Virgo (earth element)

Venus in Virgo wants a love that *works*. Pure sex or romance may appeal to Virgo's desire for the unadulterated, but there's got to be an element of the practical in it too. People with Venus in Virgo often actually fall in love with their jobs faster than they do with people. When Venus is in the sign, you often find the dedicated, loyal, "number two" person who spends a lifetime catering to the needs of a powerful boss. He/she is likely to be just a little bit in love with that boss too. As for sex, the Venus in Virgo person has a very healthy attitude toward it—possibly too healthy in the sense that it is sometimes regarded as an excellent form of exercise. Venus in Virgo people are not really cold—in fact, when they love someone they can't do enough for them, particularly in attending to their physical comfort. The problem is that this position of Venus makes a person overly analytical in determining what he/she wants. If the Venus in Virgo person keeps his/her mouth shut, and doesn't openly criticize, there is a much better possibility that he/she will make good, solid relationships.

Mars in Virgo (earth element)

Virgo's inventive sexuality is one of the best-kept secrets in the zodiac; Mars in Virgo turns out some of the most experimental and skillful lovers of all. That is, if you can attract one of these people in the first place. Mars in Virgo people are far from promiscuous; in fact, their standards are likely to be a bit too high. They are constantly questioning their *own* desires and drives, picking them apart instead of acting upon them. Mars in Virgo is ideal for success in just about any job or profession. With any sun sign, it adds to the ability to cooly analyze problems and solve them with a reasonable amount of dispatch. When it comes to romantic involvement, this is not one of the more "romantic" Mars positions (unless the sun sign is Libra). You may feel as if your Mars in Virgo lover is checking you over first for anything that might turn him/her off. This is the sign that usually says "let's shower together" before he/she says "let's go to bed."

Venus in Libra (air element)

First off, remember that when the planet Venus is in Libra, it's in its "home sign." When it comes to beauty, harmony, and balance, Venus in Libra people want it all. When Venus is in Libra, the most attractive things in life are the *nicest*—people, places, jobs, clothes, you name it. Venus in Libra people want it nice, but they also want it *easy*. In fact, this sometimes "cold" position of Venus can make for a person who marries for status or money. If you look comfortable in every sense of the word, you've got a shot at attracting that Venus in Libra person who catches your eye. And he/she will, because this position of Venus usually confers a great-looking body. Even if the Venus in Libra person loves or marries for convenience, he/she gives an awful lot in return. Once you've engaged his/her love the Venus in Libra person considers you the best, the most beautiful/handsome, and the brightest person in the universe and will treat you accordingly.

Mars in Libra (air element)

This position of Mars often makes for a passive/aggressive type of individual—a specific psychological pattern. The Mars in Libra person rarely goes directly after what he/she wants, but more or less lingers in front of it, waiting for the other person to make the right move. Mars in Libra people don't get hired as quickly as other types because they don't seem to *care* enough about whether or not they get the job. When it comes to love, Mars in Libra can be quite frustrating. You really don't know what's going on here—does or doesn't he/she want to get involved? This is also a rather "refined" position for brash Mars. Mars in Libra people usually have excellent manners, and never appear to get ruffled. They will just sit and smile while you rant and rave. Suddenly, however, they can turn on their heel and walk out the door. The technique Mars in Libra people use to go about making their subtle conquests is *talk*—but it can easily fool you because it seems so casual.

Venus in Scorpio (water element)

A lot of people with sun sign Scorpio have Venus in Scorpio too; (one's Venus sign is often one's sun sign because Venus is so close to the sun in the solar system). These double-whammy Scorpios are extraordinarily intense in all their emotional needs, but anyone with Venus in Scorpio is going to be touched by the madness of this intense sign. The curious paradox is that Venus in Scorpio people are either totally *turned on* by someone or something—or totally *turned off*. There are very few halfway deals in their lives. Venus in Scorpio can also be highly manipulative, adjusting his/her emotions to suit other needs—like money. When Venus is in Scorpio, people are attracted to what seems mysterious, dangerous, or hard-to-get. They love puzzles, and can be a bit of a puzzle themselves to prospective romantic partners. When they do get involved, however, they have a great deal of staying power—emotionally at least. They can fairly easily separate their physical *actions* from their mental states, however.

Mars in Scorpio (water element)

People with Mars in Scorpio have a very strong "energy field" surrounding them; you can almost see it and feel it. What they want, they want passionately—and will seek in no uncertain terms. They are equally positive about what they *don't* want—so you will know whether you've got a shot with them right away. No waiting with *this* aggressive sign. The legendary supersexuality of Scorpio is real with Mars in Scorpio people. However, they may use their sexual power to control other people and situations. And, if they are rejected against their will (which doesn't happen too often) they are capable of the worst kind of venomous reactions. Jealous lovers who are violent to their former partners are a parody of the Mars in Scorpio type of intensity. One way Mars in Scorpio people can hurt or simply tease others is by withholding their love—and their physical passion. They have great powers of self-control.

Venus in Sagittarius (fire element)

People with Venus in the restless, mobile sign of the Centaur often get the reputation for being fickle, and there is more than a grain of truth in that label. But the reason a Venus in Sagittarius person may move around or not become committed is that he/she is so vulnerable to deceit and dishonesty. As the saying goes, "once burned, twice shy," and openhearted, friendly Sagittarius is likely to get burned very early in life. When Venus in Sagittarius people do get involved, they are absolutely delightful to love. Broadminded, unpossessive, full of fun, they really want to enjoy romance. Sagittarius is also a very intellectual sign, so in order to get Venus in Sagittarius people to stick with you for a while, you've got to keep them interested. Sex is great, but sex with talk is even greater for these people. Venus in Sagittarius is also highly idealistic, so you've got to be a higher type to appeal to someone with Venus in this sign. Love is gallantry and honor and all those things that are so hard to find in life.

Mars in Sagittarius (fire element)

Sagittarius is a sign that thinks in global terms, so when Mars is in the sign of Sagittarius, you find a person who wants it all—and often has to be satisfied with nothing. People with Mars in Sagittarius assert themselves bluntly and get right to the point. However, they tend to be so optimistic in their expectations that they may just as quickly decide they have made a mistake. Better luck next love. Mars in Sagittarius doesn't deliberately hurt people; this sign is kind to all—both animals and humans. Their sexual nature can also be rather "animalistic" because this is a lusty sign, and so fond of all outdoor sports that they often want to do it anywhere, anytime. One way Mars in Sagittarius people get to your heart is through your sense of humor; they really know how to make people laugh. It is a powerful weapon in their professional lives too; it's hard to fire someone who is such a delight to have around—even if he/she isn't around that much. The big problem with Mars in Sagittarius people is that they sometimes don't want to take responsibility for their own actions, and lay things on other people. Even if Mars in Sagittarius is the one to break things up, he/she will somehow or other get you to believe that it's *your* fault.

Venus in Capricorn (earth element)

Appearances count a lot to Venus in Capricorn people—in every sense of the word. In order to appeal to them, you've got to look solid and substantial—and fairly rich as well. Because there is a natural reserve to Capricorn, people with Venus in this sign will dislike public displays of affection; the cooler you are in your approach, the better. Their public image and their private one are not too far apart, either. Not that Venus in Capricorn isn't normal; he/she can be quite passionate in bed. But very, very *serious*, too. If you mistake this sign's sober approach to life for coldness, you will not be the first person who has. Once again, like those with Venus in Virgo, Venus in Capricorn is attracted to *practical* people—people who can really work for them in one way or another. While some do actually consciously go after a financially comfortable marital situation, what the vast majority will settle for is someone who is willing to help handle a lot of the more serious aspects of life. Male or female, Venus in Capricorn people want you to be *useful*. Unfortunately, some people with Venus in this sign have such a low sense of self-worth, that they will try to buy love—or sell it—because they don't feel anyone will accept them for what they are.

Mars in Capricorn (earth element)

Mars in Capricorn people always want to know the rules before they enter the game; they assert themselves with extreme caution. However, when they *know* what they want, they have incredible powers to help them get it. One is patience; Mars in Capricorn can wait very well. Another thing they have going for them is self-control; their timing is excellent because they can hold themselves back when they want to. All this makes for a rather sexually confusing type, and sometimes one who is sexually confused. Mars in Capricorn people can go without sex for amazing lengths of time if nothing seems worth the effort. When they do go for it, their approach can be extremely lusty and earthy, as befits the earth element of Capricorn. Even more than someone with Mars in Scorpio, the person with Mars in Capricorn can be a user. In love or business, he/she can easily fake it to get the carrot on the end of the stick. Then, before you know it, the person who seemed so hot for you has now turned stone cold. Sad, but true.

Venus in Aquarius (air element)

The best way to attract someone with Venus in Aquarius is to be a bit unconventional; these people love anyone or anything that is off-beat. However, you may find that you are considered a specimen rather than a romantic partner—or at least that's how it's likely to feel. People with Venus in Aquarius seem to have a real problem with deep involvement; often they really *want* it, but somehow or other their deepest wells of emotion are very difficult to tap.

Their habitual reaction to love is often "easy come, easy go." Are they cruel people? Generally not, and often Venus in Aquarius people suffer a lot from their difficulty with feeling. They will rarely tell you, however, because there is a real need for distance there. And distance is what they seek in one-on-one relationships. If you become possessive with, or jealous of a person with Venus in Aquarius, you will lose him/her very quickly. As with some of the other mental signs like Gemini and Libra, you have got to keep the affair or the marriage *interesting* in one way or another. This is a Venus position that often likes kinky sex, porno movies, and other forms of artificial stimulation. However, they usually don't care enough about sex-for-the-sake-of-sex to be unfaithful.

Mars in Aquarius (air element)

When Mars is in this erratic sign, people tend to go through periods of feast and famine, largely because they can fluctuate between being extremely assertive and sure about what they want or totally inactive. During the latter periods you could actually call the Mars in Aquarius person lazy. In love, the Mars in Aquarius person tends to go after the unusual or difficult; involvements with people who are already attached are quite common. In many cases it is because the Mars in Aquarius person really is terribly afraid of deep involvement. There is a detachment about Mars in Aquarius people that sometimes works against permanent attachment to people or professional situations. Mars in Aquarius really prefers to go it alone. Perhaps the reason is that they always want to be free to experiment with the new. In sex, the Mars in Aquarius person is hung up on technique; he/she likes intelligent sex, and sometimes wants to prove how clever he/she is via this rather bizarre route.

Venus in Pisces (water element)

For people with Venus in Pisces, what's attractive is often bound up with some kind of sacrifice. This is the position of Venus that leads to martyrdom of all kinds. Some Venus in Pisces people find it impossible to get involved with anything or anyone normal and healthy; their instinctive need is to care for the lame and needy. Therefore, many Venus in Pisces people are rather easily taken advantage of by unscrupulous types who use them or take them for all they're worth. By the same token, Venus in Pisces people can put a real *drain* on the object of their affections—demanding more and more proofs of undying love, soulful demonstrations, sometimes even more tangible support. However, in the broadest, most universal sense of the word, Pisces is the "best" position for Venus as it represents the principle of *true love*. True love is totally unselfish, totally self-sacrificing. Though few normal mortals are capable of such "divine" love, Venus in Pisces people come closest to being able to make it. On the more mundane side, people wth Venus in Pisces are attracted by all kinds of sentimental and often impractical things. They will love you most if you spend your last penny on a bouquet of violets rather than bread for the table. So what? You'll just live on love.

Mars in Pisces *(water element)*

Mars in Pisces people can easily lose their way; the sign of Pisces is not stable enough for the aggressive energy of Mars, so Mars in Pisces people tend to scatter their energies in too many places. On the other hand, they are the most subtle and devious people in the zodiac when it comes to going after what they really *do* want. Their come-on is usually to be rather weak and helpless. Both the males and the females snare you by making you think they really *need* you. There's a lot of poetry to Mars in Pisces people, so the start of an affair is likely to be all moonlight and roses. However, you may find that once you are entangled, you can't get yourself out when you want out. Mars in Pisces people have a way of snarling you up in their webs of erratic energy. Just when they've agreed that you should go, they'll become helpless again and make you feel you have to stay. However, Mars in Pisces people do offer a very wonderful kind of love—soft, sensitive, and caring. The object of their desires is often someone similar or someone involved with art or music in some way. However, Pisces types are best off hooking up with a strong partner—someone who can keep their Mars energy on a straight and even course. The best part of Mars in Pisces people is that they are rarely, if ever, cold.

VENUS SIGN 1910–1975

	Aries	Taurus	Gemini	Cancer	Leo	Virgo
1910	5/7-6/3	6/4-6/29	6/30-7/24	7/25-8/18	8/19-9/12	9/13-10/6
1911	2/28-3/23	3/24-4/17	4/18-5/12	5/13-6/8	6/9-7/7	7/8-11/8
1912	4/13-5/6	5/7-5/31	6/1-6/24	6/24-7/18	7/19-8/12	8/13-9/5
1913	2/3-3/6 5/2-5/30	3/7-5/1 5/31-7/7	7/8-8/5	8/6-8/31	9/1-9/26	9/27-10/20
1914	3/14-4/6	4/7-5/1	5/2-5/25	5/26-6/19	6/20-7/15	7/16-8/10
1915	4/27-5/21	5/22-6/15	6/16-7/10	7/11-8/3	8/4-8/28	8/29-9/21
1916	2/14-3/9	3/10-4/5	4/6-5/5	5/6-9/8	9/9-10/7	10/8-11/2
1917	3/29-4/21	4/22-5/15	5/16-6/9	6/10-7/3	7/4-7/28	7/29-8/21
1918	5/7-6/2	6/3-6/28	6/29-7/24	7/25-8/18	8/19-9/11	9/12-10/5
1919	2/27-3/22	3/23-4/16	4/17-5/12	5/13-6/7	6/8-7/7	7/8-11/8
1920	4/12-5/6	5/7-5/30	5/31-6/23	6/24-7/18	7/19-8/11	8/12-9/4
1921	2/3-3/6 4/26-6/1	3/7-4/25 6/2-7/7	7/8-8/5	8/6-8/31	9/1-9/25	9/26-10/20
1922	3/13-4/6	4/7-4/30	5/1-5/25	5/26-6/19	6/20-7/14	7/15-8/9
1923	4/27-5/21	5/22-6/14	6/15-7/9	7/10-8/3	8/4-8/27	8/28-9/20
1924	2/13-3/8	3/9-4/4	4/5-5/5	5/6-9/8	9/9-10/7	10/8-11/12
1925	3/28-4/20	4/21-5/15	5/16-6/8	6/9-7/3	7/4-7/27	7/28-8/21
1926	5/7-6/2	6/3-6/28	6/29-7/23	7/24-8/17	8/18-9/11	9/12-10/5
1927	2/27-3/22	3/23-4/16	4/17-5/11	5/12-6/7	6/8-7/7	7/8-11/9
1928	4/12-5/5	5/6-5/29	5/30-6/23	6/24-7/17	7/18-8/11	8/12-9/4
1929	2/3-3/7 4/20-6/2	3/8-4/19 6/3-7/7	7/8-8/4	8/5-8/30	8/31-9/25	9/26-10/19
1930	3/13-4/5	4/6-4/30	5/1-5/24	5/25-6/18	6/19-7/14	7/15-8/9
1931	4/26-5/20	5/21-6/13	6/14-7/8	7/9-8/2	8/3-8/26	8/27-9/19

VENUS SIGN 1910-1975

Libra	Scorpio	Sagittarius	Capricorn	Aquarius	Pisces
10/7-10/30	10/31-11/23	11/24-12/17	12/18-12/31	1/1-1/15	1/16-1/28
				1/29-4/4	4/5-5/6
11/19-12/8	12/9-12/31		1/1-1/10	1/11-2/2	2/3-2/27
9/6-9/30	1/1-1/4	1/5-1/29	1/30-2/23	2/24-3/18	3/19-4/12
	10/1-10/24	10/25-11/17	11/18-12/12	12/13-12/31	
10/21-11/13	11/14-12/7	12/8-12/31		1/1-1/6	1/7-2/2
8/11-9/6	9/7-10/9	10/10-12/5	1/1-1/24	1/25-2/17	2/18-3/13
	12-6/12-30	12/31			
9/22-10/15	10/16-11/8	1/1-2/6	2/7-3/6	3/7-4/1	4/2-4/26
		11/9-12/2	12/3-12/26	12/27-12/31	
11/3-11/27	11/28-12/21	12/22-12/31		1/1-1/19	1/20-2/13
8/22-9/16	9/17-10/11	1/1-1/14	1/15-2/7	2/8-3/4	3/5-3/28
		10/12-11/6	11/7-12/5	12/6-12/31	
10/6-10/29	10/30-11/22	11/23-12/16	12/17-12/31	1/1-4/5	4/6-5/6
11/9-12/8	12/9-12/31		1/1-1/9	1/10-2/2	2/3-2/26
9/5-9/30	1/1-1/3	1/4-1/28	1/29-2/22	2/23-3/18	3/19-4/11
	9/31-10/23	10/24-11/17	11/18-12/11	12/12-12/31	
10/21-11/13	11/14-12/7	12/8-12/31		1/1-1/6	1/7-2/2
8/10-9/6	9/7-10/10	10/11-11/28	1/1-1/24	1/25-2/16	2/17-3/12
	11/29-12/31				
9/21-10/14	1/1	1/2-2/6	2/7-3/5	3/6-3/31	4/1-4/26
	10/15-11/7	11/8-12/1	12/2-12/25	12/26-12/31	
11/3-11/26	11/27-12/21	12/22-12/31		1/1-1/19	1/20-2/12
8/22-9/15	9/16-10/11	1/1-1/14	1/15-2/7	2/8-3/3	3/4-3/27
		10-12/11-6	11/7-12/5	12/6-12/31	
10/6-10/29	10/30-11/22	11/23-12/16	12/17-12/31	1/1-4/5	4/6-5/6
11/10-12/8	12/9-12/31	1/1-1/7	1/8	1/9-2/1	2/2-2/26
9/5-9/28	1/1-1/3	1/4-1/28	1/29-2/22	2/23-3/17	3/18-4/11
	9/29-10/23	10/24-11/16	11/17-12/11	12/12-12/31	
10/20-11/12	11/13-12/6	12/7-12/30	12/31	1/1-1/5	1/6-2/2
8/10-9/6	9/7-10/11	10/12-11/21	1/1-1/23	1/24-2/16	2/17-3/12
	11/22-12/31				
9/20-10/13	1/1-1/3	1/4-2/6	2/7-3/4	3/5-3/31	4/1-4/25
	10/14-11/6	11/7-11/30	12/1-12/24	12/25-12/31	

VENUS SIGN 1910–1975

	Aries	Taurus	Gemini	Cancer	Leo	Virgo
1932	2/12-3/8	3/9-4/3	4/4-5/5 7/13-7/27	5/6-7/12 7/28-9/8	9/9-10/6	10/7-11/1
1933	3/27-4/19	4/20-5/28	5/29-6/8	6/9-7/2	7/3-7/26	7/27-8/20
1934	5/6-6/1	6/2-6/27	6/28-7/22	7/23-8/16	8/17-9/10	9/11-10/4
1935	2/26-3/21	3/22-4/15	4/16-5/10	5/11-6/6	6/7-7/6	7/7-11/8
1936	4/11-5/4	5/5-5/28	5/29-6/22	6/23-7/16	7/17-8/10	8/11-9/4
1937	2/2-3/8 4/14-6/3	3/9-4/17 6/4-7/6	7/7-8/3	8/4-8/29	8/30-9/24	9/25-10/18
1938	3/12-4/4	4/5-4/28	4/29-5/23	5/24-6/18	6/19-7/13	7/14-8/8
1939	4-25/5/19	5/20-6/13	6/14-7/8	7/9-8/1	8/2-8/25	8/26-9/19
1940	2/12-3/7	3/8-4/3	4/4-5/5 7/5-7/31	5/6-7/4 8/1-9/8	9/9-10/5	10/6-10/31
1941	3/27-4/19	4/20-5/13	5/14-6/6	6/7-6/1	7/2-7/26	7/27-8/20
1942	5/6-6/1	6/2-6/26	6/27-7/22	7/23-8/16	8/17-9/9	9/10-10/3
1943	2/25-3/20	3/21-4/14	4/15-5/10	5/11-6/6	6/7-7/6	7/7-11/8
1944	4-10/5-3	5/4-5/28	5/29-6/21	6/22-7/16	7/17-8/9	8/10-9/2
1945	2/2-3/10 4/7-6/3	3/11-4/6 6/4-7/6	7/7-8/3	8/4-8/29	8/30-9/23	9/24-10/18
1946	3/11-4/4	4/5-4/28	4/29-5/23	5/24-6/17	6/18-7/12	7/13-8/8
1947	4/25-5/19	5/20-6/12	6/13-7/7	7/8-8/1	8/2-8/25	8/26-9/18
1948	2/11-3/7	3/8-4/3	4/4-5/6 6/29-8/2	5/7-6/28 8/3-9/7	9/8-10/5	10/6-10/31
1949	3/26-4/19	4/20-5/13	5/14-6/6	6/7-6/30	7/1-7/25	7/26-8/19
1950	5/5-5/31	6/1-6/26	6/27-7/21	7/22-8/15	8/16-9/9	9/10-10/3
1951	2/25-3/21	3/22-4/15	4/16-5/10	5/11-6/6	6/7-7/7	7/8-11/9
1952	4/10-5/4	5/5-5/28	5/29-6/21	6/22-7/16	7/17-8/9	8/10-9/3
1953	2/2-3/13 4/1-6/5	3/4-3/31 6/6-7/7	7/8-8/3	8/4-8/29	8/30-9/24	9/25-10/18

VENUS SIGN 1910–1975

Libra	Scorpio	Sagittarius	Capricorn	Aquarius	Pisces
11/2-11/25	11/26-12/20	12/21-12/31		1/1-1/18	1/19-2/11
8/21-9/14	9/15-10/10	1/1-1/13	1/14-2/6	2/7-3/2	3/3-3/26
		10/11-11/5	11/6-12/4	12/5-12/31	
10/5-10/28	10/29-11/21	11/22-12/15	12/16-12/31	1/1-4/5	4/6-5/5
11/9-12/7	12/8-12/31		1/1-1/7	1/8-1/31	2/1-2/25
9/5-9/27	1/1-1/2	1/3-1/27	1/28-2/21	2/22-3/16	3/17-4/10
	9/28-10/22	10/23-11/15	11/16-12/10	12/11-12/31	
10/19-11/11	11/12-12/5	12/6-12/29	12/30-12/31	1/1-1/5	1/6-2/1
8/9-9/6	9/7-10/13	10/14-11/14	1/1-1/22	1/23-2/15	2/16-3/11
	11/15-12/31				
9/20-10/13	1/1-1/3	1/4-2/5	2/6-3/4	3/5-3/30	3/31-4/24
	10/14-11/6	11/7-11/30	12/1-12/24	12/25-12/31	
11/1-11/25	11/26-12/19	12/20-12/31		1/1-1/18	1/19-2/11
8/21-9/14	9/15-10/9	1/1-1/12	1/13-2/5	2/6-3/1	3/2-3/26
		10/10-11/5	11/6-12/4	12/5-12/31	
10/4-10/27	10/28-11/20	11/21-12/14	12/15-12/31	1/1-4/4	4/6-5/5
11/9-12/7	12/8-12/31		1/1-1/7	1/8-1/31	2/1-2/24
9/3-9/27	1/1-1/2	1/3-1/27	1/28-2/20	2/21-3/16	3/17-4/9
	9/28-10/21	10/22-11/15	11/16-12/10	12/11-12/31	
10/19-11/11	11/12-12/5	12/6-12/29	12/30-12/31	1/1-1/4	1/5-2/1
8/9-9/6	9/7-10/15	10/16-11/7	1/1-1/21	1/22-2/14	2/15-3/10
	11/8-12/31				
9/19-10/12	1/1-1/4	1/5-2/5	2/6-3/4	3/5-3/29	3/30-4/24
	10/13-11/5	11/6-11/29	11/30-12/23	12/24-12/31	
11/1-1/25	11/26-12/19	12/20-12/31		1/1-1/17	1/18-2/10
8/20-9/14	9/15-10/9	1/1-1/12	1/13-2/5	2/6-3/1	3/2-3/25
		10/10-11/5	11/6-12/5	12/6-12/31	
10/4-10/27	10/28-11/20	11/21-12/13	12/14-12/31	1/1-4/5	4/6-5/4
11/10-12/7	12/8-12/31		1/1-1/7	1/8-1/31	2/1-2/24
9/4-9/27	1/1-1/2	1/3-1/27	1/28-2/20	2/21-3/16	3/17-4/9
	9/28-10/21	10/22-11/15	11/16-12/10	12/11-12/31	
10/19-11/11	11/12-12/5	12/6-12/29	12/30-12/31	1/1-1/5	1/6-2/1

VENUS SIGN 1910-1975

	Aries	Taurus	Gemini	Cancer	Leo	Virgo
1954	3/12-4/4	4/5-4/28	4/29-5/23	5/24-6/17	6/18-7/13	7/14-8/8
1955	4/25-5/19	5/20-6/13	6/14-7/7	7/8-8/1	8/2-8/25	8/26-9/18
1956	2/12-3/7	3/8-4/4	4/5-5/7 6:24-8/4	5/8-6/23 8/5-9/8	9/9-10/5	10/6-10/31
1957	3-26/4-19	4/20-5/13	5/14-6/6	6/7-7/1	7/2-7/26	7/27-8/19
1958	5-6/5-31	6/1-6/26	6/27-7/22	7/23-8/15	8/16-9/9	9/10-10/3
1959	2-25/3-20	3/21-4/14	4/15-5/10	5/11-6/6	6/7-7/8 9/21-9/24	7/9-9/20 9/25-11/9
1960	4-10/5-3	5/4-5/28	5/29-6/21	6/22-7/15	7/16-8/9	8/10-9/2
1961	2-3/6-5	6/6-7/7	7/8-8/3	8/4-8/29	8/30-9/23	9/24-10/17
1962	3/11-4/3	4/4-4/28	4/29-5/22	5/23-6/17	6/18-7/12	7/13-8/8
1963	4/24-5/18	5/19-6/12	6/13-7/7	7/8-7/31	8/1-8/25	8/26-9/18
1964	2/11-3/7	3/8-4/4	4/5-5/9 6/18-8/5	5/10-6/17 8/6-9/8	9/9-10/5	10/6-10/31
1965	3/26-4/18	4/19-5/12	5/13-6/6	6/7-6/30	7/1-7/25	7/26-8/19
1966	5/6-6/31	6/1-6/26	6/27-7/21	7/22-8/15	8/16-9/8	9/9-10/2
1967	2/24-3/20	3/21-4/14	4/15-5/10	5/11-6/6	6/7-7/8 9/10-10/1	7/9-9/9 10/2-11/9
1968	4/9-5/3	5/4-5/27	5/28-6/20	6/21-7/15	7/16-8/8	8/9-9/2
1969	2/3-6/6	6/7-7/6	7/7-8/3	8/4-8/28	8/29-9/22	9/23-10/17
1970	3/11-4/3	4/4-4/27	4/28-5/22	5/23-6/16	6/17-7/12	7/13-8/8
1971	4/24-5/18	5/19-6/12	6/13-7/6	7/7-7/31	8/1-8/24	8/25-9/17
1972	2/11-3/7	3/8-4/3	4/5-5/10 6/12-8/6	5/11-6/11 8/7-9/8	9/9-10/5	10/6-10/30
1973	3/25-4/18	4/18-5/12	5/13-6/5	6/6-6/29	7/1-7/25	7/26-8/19
1974						
	5/5-5/31	6/1-6/25	6/26-7/21	7/22-8/14	8/15-9/8	9/9-10/2
1975	2/24-3/20	3/21-4/13	4/14-5/9	5/10-6/6	6/7-7/9 9/3-10/4	7/10-9/2 10/5-11/9

VENUS SIGN 1910–1975

Libra	Scorpio	Sagittarius	Capricorn	Aquarius	Pisces
8/9-9/6	9/7-10/22	10/23-10/27	1/1-1/22	1/23-2/15	2/16-3/11
	10/28-12/31				
9/19-10/13	1/1-1/6	1/7-2/5	2/6-3/4	3/5-3/30	3/31-4/24
	10/14-11/5	11/6-11/30	12/1-12/24	12/25-12/31	
11/1-11/25	11/26-12/19	12/20-12/31		1/1-1/17	1/18-2/11
8/20-9/14	9/15-10/9	1/1-1/12	1/13-2/5	2/6-3/1	3/2-3/25
		10/10-11/5	11/6-12/16	12/7-12/31	
10/4-10/27	10/28-11/20	11/21-12/14	12/15-12/31	1/1-4/6	4/7-5/5
11/10-12/7	12/8-12/31		1/1-1/7	1/8-1/31	2/1-2/24
9/3-9/26	1/1-1/2	1/3-1/27	1/28-2/20	2/21-3/15	3/16-4/9
	9/27-10/21	10/22-11/15	11/16-12/10	12/11-12/31	
10/18-11/11	11/12-12/4	12/5-12/28	12/29-12/31	1/1-1/5	1/6-2/2
8/9-9/6	9/7-12/31		1/1-1/21	1/22-2/14	2/15-3/10
9/19-10/12	1/1-1/6	1/7-2/5	2/6-3/4	3/5-3/29	3/30-4/23
	10/13-11/5	11/6-11/29	11/30-12/23	12/24-12/31	
11/1-11/24	11/25-12/19	12/20-12/31		1/1-1/16	1/17-2/10
8/20-9/13	9/14-10/9	1/1-1/12	1/13-2/5	2/6-3/1	3/2-3/25
		10/10-11/5	11/6-12/7	12/8-12/31	
10/3-10/26	10/27-11/19	11/20-12/13	2/7-2/25	1/1-2/6	4/7-5/5
			12/14-12/31	2/26-4/6	
11/10-12/7	12/8-12/23		1/1-1/6	1/7-1/30	1/31-2/23
9/3-9/26	1/1	1/2-1/26	1/27-2/20	2/21-3/15	3/16-4/8
	9/27-10/21	10/22-11/14	11/15-12/9	12/10-12/31	
10/18-11/10	11/11-12/4	12/5-12/28	12/29-12/31	1/1-1/4	1/5-2/2
8/9-9/7	9/8-12/31		1/1-1/21	1/22-2/14	2/15-3/10
9/18-10/11	1/1-1/7	1/8-2/5	2/6-3/4	3/5-3/29	3/30-4/23
	10/12-11/5	11/6-11/29	11/30-12/23	12/24-12/31	
	11/25-12/18	12/19-12/31		1/1-1/16	1/17-2/10
10/31-11/24					
8/20-9/13		1/1-1/12	1/13-2/4	2/5-2/28	3/1-3/24
		10/9-11/5	11/6-12/7	12/8-12/31	
			1/30-2/28	1/1-1/29	
10/3-10/26	10/27-11/19	11/20-12/13	12/14-12/31	3/1-4/6	4/7-5/4
			1/1-1/6	1/7-1/30	1/31-2/23
11/10-12/7	12/8-12/31				

MARS SIGN 1910-1975

Year	Jan.	Feb.	Mar.	Apr.	May	June	July	Aug.	Sept.	Oct.	Nov.	Dec.
1910	AR	TA	GE	GE	CA	CA	LE	VI	VI	LI	SC	SC
1911	SA	CP	AQ	AQ	PI	AR	TA	TA	GE	GE	GE	TA
1912	TA	GE	GE	CA	CA	LE	LE	VI	LI	LI	SC	SA
1913	CP	CP	AQ	PI	AR	AR	TA	GE	CA	CA	CA	CA
1914	CA	CA	CA	CA	LE	LE	VI	LI	LI	SC	SA	SA
1915	CP	AQ	PI	PI	AR	TA	GE	GE	CA	LE	LE	LE
1916	LE	LE	LE	LE	LE	TA	VI	LI	SC	SC	SA	CP
1917	AQ	AQ	PI	AR	AR	TA	GE	CA	LE	LE	SA	VI
1918	LI	LI	VI	VI	TA	GE	CA	LI	SC	SA	VI	CP
1919	AQ	PI	AR	TA	GE	VI	LI	LE	VI	VI	CP	CP
1920	LI	SC	SC	SC	LI	LI	SC	SC	SA	SA	VI	LI
1921	PI	AR	AR	TA	GE	GE	CA	LE	LE	VI	LI	AQ
1922	SC	SC	SA	SA	SA	SA	SA	SA	SA	CP	CP	LI
1923	PI	AR	AR	TA	GE	CA	CA	LE	LE	VI	LI	AQ
1924	SC	SA	CP	CP	AQ	AQ	PI	PI	AQ	AQ	PI	SC
1925	AR	TA	TA	GE	CA	CA	LE	VI	VI	LI	SC	PI
1926	SA	CP	CP	AQ	PI	AR	AR	TA	VI	TA	TA	SC
1927	TA	TA	GE	GE	CA	LE	LE	VI	LI	TA	SC	SA
1928	SA	SA	AQ	PI	PI	AR	TA	GE	GE	CA	CA	CA

76

MARS SIGN 1910–1975

	Jan.	Feb.	Mar.	Apr.	May	June	July	Aug.	Sept.	Oct.	Nov.	Dec.
1929	GE	GE	CA	CA	LE	LE	VI	VI	LI	SC	SC	SA
1930	CP	AQ	AQ	PI	AR	TA	GE	GE	CA	CA	LE	LE
1931	LE	LE	CA	LE	LE	VI	VI	LI	LI	SC	SA	CP
1932	CP	AQ	PI	AR	TA	TA	GE	CA	CA	LE	VI	VI
1933	VI	VI	VI	VI	VI	VI	LI	LI	SC	SA	SA	CP
1934	AQ	PI	AR	AR	TA	GE	GE	CA	LE	LE	VI	LI
1935	LI	LI	LI	LI	LI	LI	CA	SC	SC	SA	CP	AQ
1936	PI	PI	AR	TA	GE	GE	CA	LE	LE	VI	LI	LI
1937	SC	SC	SA	SA	SC	SC	SC	SA	SA	VI	LI	AQ
1938	PI	AR	TA	TA	CP	CA	CA	LE	VI	VI	AQ	AQ
1939	SC	SA	SA	CP	GE	AQ	AQ	CP	CP	AQ	LI	SC
1940	AR	AR	TA	GE	GE	CA	LE	LE	VI	VI	LI	PI
1941	SA	SA	TA	AQ	AQ	PI	AR	AR	AR	AR	AR	SC
1942	TA	TA	CP	GE	CA	LE	LE	VI	VI	LI	SC	AR
1943	SA	CP	GE	AQ	PI	AR	TA	TA	GE	GE	GE	SC
1944	GE	GE	GE	CA	CA	LE	VI	VI	LI	SC	SC	GE
1945	CP	AQ	AQ	PI	AR	TA	TA	GE	CA	CA	LE	SA
1946	CA	CA	CA	CA	LE	LE	VI	LI	LI	SC	SA	LE
1947	CP	AQ	PI	AR	AR	TA	GE	CA	CA	LE	LE	VI

77

MARS SIGN 1910–1975

	Jan.	Feb.	Mar.	Apr.	May	June	July	Aug.	Sept.	Oct.	Nov.	Dec.
1948	VI	LE	LE	LE	LE	VI	VI	LI	SC	SC	SA	CP
1949	AQ	PI	PI	AR	TA	GE	GE	CA	LE	LE	VI	VI
1950	LI	LI	LI	VI	VI	LI	LI	SC	SC	SA	CP	CP
1951	AQ	PI	AR	TA	TA	GE	CA	CA	LE	VI	VI	LI
1952	LI	SC	SC	SC	SC	SC	SC	SC	SA	CP	CP	AQ
1953	AR	AR	AR	TA	GE	GE	CA	LE	LE	VI	LI	LI
1954	SC	SA	SA	CP	CP	CP	SA	SA	SA	VI	AQ	PI
1955	PI	AR	TA	GE	GE	CA	LE	LE	VI	LI	LI	SC
1956	SA	SA	TA	AQ	AQ	PI	PI	PI	PI	PI	PI	AR
1957	AR	TA	TA	GE	CA	CA	LE	VI	VI	LI	SC	SC
1958	SA	CP	CP	AQ	PI	AR	AR	TA	TA	GE	TA	TA
1959	TA	GE	GE	CA	CA	LE	LE	VI	LI	LI	SC	SA
1960	CP	CP	AQ	PI	PI	AR	TA	GE	GE	CA	CA	CA
1961	CA	CA	CA	CA	CA	TA	VI	VI	LI	SC	SA	SA
1962	CP	AQ	PI	PI	AR	TA	GE	VI	CA	LE	LE	LE
1963	LE	LE	LE	LE	LE	VI	VI	SC	SC	SC	SA	CP
1964	AQ	AQ	PI	AR	AR	TA	GE	CA	LE	LE	SA	VI
1965	VI	VI	VI	VI	VI	VI	LE	LI	LE	SA	VI	VI
1966	AQ	PI	AR	AR	TA	GE	CA	CA	LE	VI	VI	LI

MARS SIGN 1910–1975

	Jan.	Feb.	Mar.	Apr.	May	June	July	Aug.	Sept.	Oct.	Nov.	Dec.
1967	LI	SC	SC	LI	LI	LI	LI	SC	SA	SA	CP	AQ
1968	PI	PI	AR	TA	GE	GE	CA	LE	LE	VI	LI	LI
1969	SC	SC	SA	SA	SA	SA	SA	SA	SA	CP	AQ	PI
1970	PI	AR	TA	TA	GE	CA	CA	LE	VI	VI	LI	SC
1971	SC	SA	CP	CP	AQ	AQ	AQ	AQ	AQ	AQ	PI	PI
1972	AR	TA	TA	GE	CA	CA	LE	LE	VI	LI	SC	SC
1973	SA	CP	CP	AQ	PI	PI	AR	TA	TA	TA	AR	AR
1974	TA	TA	GE	GE	CA	LE	LE	VI	LI	LI	SC	SA
1975	SA	CP	AQ	PI	PI	AR	TA	GE	GE	GE	CA	GE

AR—Aries
TA—Taurus
GE—Gemini
CA—Cancer

LE—Leo
VI—Virgo
LI—Libra
SC—Scorpio

SA—Sagittarius
CP—Capricorn
AQ—Aquarius
PI—Pisces

9

The Planets As "Stars"

The Astrological Cast of Characters in Order of Their Appearance

As you learned in the chapter "Defining Terms," the planets are the *sine qua non* of astrology—the factor without which there would be no such study. It is the placement of the planets in the signs of the zodiac that give those signs meaning in human terms, and the placement of the planets in an individual horoscope that "spell out" that individual's character/personality. As for forecasting, it is the movement (transits) of the planets throughout our lifetime that activate one part of our chart or another and bring out certain life conditions.

Those planets are moving bodies and not "stars" in the astrological sense, though they are sometimes referred to with that word. In Shakespeare's play, *Julius Caesar*, Cassius, one of the conspirators, states, "The fault, dear Brutus, is not in our stars but in ourselves that we are underlings." Shakespeare (Cassius) actually knew what he was talking about because astrology was part and parcel of daily life in Elizabethan times when the play was written, as well as in Caesar's ancient Rome. However, Shakespeare seems to have preferred "stars" as a more poetic word than "planets." He also was right about another thing: The "stars" (planets) don't push people around unless you let them. The key is to understand the role each planet plays in your basic astrological makeup through your natal chart and to get to know yourself via this ancient and pragmatic science. Then you will better understand how the transits of the different planets are most likely to affect you.

Though the planets are not stars by astronomical definition (except for the sun), they do play the starring roles in the great cosmic drama that is acted out every day of our lives, and has been since the beginning of life on earth. There are other heavenly bodies—like the asteroids—that play supporting roles, but most astrologers take the Big Ten into consideration when they do a chart or a personal forecast: the sun, the moon, Mercury, Venus, Mars, Jupiter, Saturn, Uranus, Neptune, and Pluto. (Some of these planets, like the Moon, Venus, and Mars, are touched on in other parts of this book, and you may want to read those sections to get a better understanding of their characteristics.)

Each planet rules one or more signs of the zodiac—i.e., is very closely associated with that sign or signs. The one that rules your sun sign is your own personal planet, so to speak, and its description will fill in more of the background of your sign.

The following is a rundown of the planetary cast of characters, presented in their order of appearance, their actual position in our solar system As you know, the sun is the center of our solar system, and the orbits of the planets form rings around it. Looking at the planets this way underscores the fact that the *closer* planets influence us much more strongly as individuals. Planets farther out in the solar system are not only farther away, they also move much more slowly. While a transit of the moon lasts two days, for instance, a transit of Uranus (which takes eighty-four years to circle the zodiac) may influence your life for many months. However, even with these distant planets, their position in a specific *house* of your own horoscope will greatly influence your astrological makeup.

The Sun

Vital Statistics: 864,000 miles in diameter; average distance from earth, 93 million miles; gaseous nature. Appears to circle the zodiac in 365 days.

Rules: The sign of Leo
Fourth period of life: ages 23 to 41
Role: The true "star" ... the male lead ... the doer ... the activator.

Facts and Foibles: The position of the sun in anyone's horoscope is the central fact about that person, astrologically speaking. Your sun sign is your core—your individuality. It is your ego in the best sense of the word, the part of you that moves you in a certain life direction. No matter what your sun sign is, true self-development means developing the highest potential of that sign. People really grow into their sun signs as they mature, and the sun symbolically governs that stage of life (23 to 41) at which we are (or should be) mature individuals who are concerned with creating something in our own right. The sun is considered a masculine planet, because it is the fiery, animating force of life. We are meant to *express* our sun sign; those who do not can literally have a lifeless quality about them.

Those born under the sign of Leo have been said to be favored because of their rulership by the most important "planet" of them all. In ancient times, the sun was often the chief deity and was worshipped for its extraordinary power. It was recognized that without the sun, life on earth could not exist, and the dimming of its light via an eclipse was a terrifying experience for early civilizations that recognized their dependence upon its warmth and vitalizing nature. Whether or not Leo is a special sign is debatable, but there is no doubt that there is a tendency in some Leo sun sign people to become overly self-centered. Perhaps even unconsciously, they sense that it is a heady destiny to be ruled by the sun, but they are unable to handle its tremendous energies properly.

The Moon

Vital Statistics: 238,857 miles from the earth; 2,160 miles in diameter (one-fourth earth's size). Revolves around the earth (circles the zodiac) in about 27 ½ days
Rules: The sign of cancer
The first four years of human life

Role: The leading lady ... the "feeler" ... the mother ... the reactor.

Facts and Foibles: The moon is not exactly a planet, either; it is a satellite of our own planet, earth. However, it is the largest satellite with respect to its parent planet anywhere in the solar system that we know of. It has a tremendous gravitational pull, which is demonstrated on earth by the changing of the tides and other natural phenomena.

The moon has no light of its own, and we can see it shining only because it reflects the sun. Therefore, the moon is considered a *receptive* or "feminine" planet, rather than an active one like the sun. The moon in mythology has always been a woman—often the "Great Mother" to ancient peoples who saw the sun as the "Great Father." Accordingly, the moon rules the first four years of human life, when we are totally dependent on our mothers, and the motherly sign of Cancer, which is closely associated with nurturing and growth. In an individual horoscope, the position of the moon indicates our ability to feel and to respond emotionally. It is our impressionability and sensitivity, i.e., our subjective rather than our objective sign. The moon reacts to experience and remembers it. All our memories are stored in our subconscious, which is the part of the human psyche the moon signifies. In a sense, as the moon rules the night, it rules our dark or hidden side. As it takes some time for us to develop or grow into our sun sign, the moon sign manifests itself much more strongly in young children than the sun sign does. The moon represents the instinctual nature connected with infantile responses; our moon sign acts from habit, often without thinking.

Mercury

Vital Statistics: 36 million miles away from the sun; 2,900 miles in diameter; orbits sun at 108,000 miles per hour; goes through zodiac in 88 days.

Rules: The signs of Gemini and Virgo
Age of curiosity: 4 through 14

Role: The young male lead ... the observer ... the messenger ... the communicator.

Facts and Foibles: Mercury is the hottest, quickest, and smallest of the planets, and is closest to the sun. It is so closely associated with the sun in an astronomical sense, that Mercury is very often in the same sign as the sun in a natal chart. In any horoscope, it is never more than two signs away from your sun sign.

In ancient times Mercury was regarded as the sun's messenger, and the gods with whom it was associated always had some kind of communicating function. In Egypt, Mercury was Thoth—scribe to the gods, keeper of the divine books. The Greeks called him Hermes, the messenger; the Romans renamed him Mercury, but assigned similar functions. Hermes/Mercury always had a golden tongue, and was regarded as the great persuader. Quickness and deftness also associate Mercury with all kinds of human skills requiring manual and mental dexterity.

Mercury has a double role to play as ruler of the signs of Gemini and Virgo. In a sense, Mercury is two-faced; the communicative side in Gemini, his precise specialist side in Virgo. No matter what your sun sign is, in your horoscope Mercury symbolizes your style of thinking and communicating—not so much how intelligent you are as how you tend to put things together mentally.

Mercury is a very human planet, and has a very human foible; occasionally he gets things all mixed up and causes a lot of trouble. About three times a year, for about three weeks at a time, Mercury seems to be going *backwards*. (That appearance is caused by the varying rates of speed of various planets—like two trains traveling in the same direction that can seem as if they are traveling in two different directions.) During these periods Mercury is said to be *retrograde*, it is known to cause problems in all kinds of human interactions. People get the wrong message, or don't get it at all. People who are supposed to meet on a street corner never find each other. Trains and planes are missed, luggage is lost, orders simply never get transmitted or seem to vanish in thin air. There has been quite a bit of research on Mercury retrograde, and it all proves out. Even if people don't know *why* retrograde Mercury

makes things go wrong, they sure know it does. In 1986 Mercury will be retrograde during these periods:
March 7 through March 30.
July 9 through August 3.
November 2 through November 22.

Venus

Vital Statistics: 67.2 million miles from the sun; 26 million to 160 million miles from earth; approximately the same size and volume as earth. Goes through all twelve signs of the zodiac in about 225 days.
Rules: The signs of Taurus and Libra
Period of developing sexuality: ages 14 to 21
Role: The young, nubile female lead . . . the love interest . . . the artist.
Facts and Foibles: Like Mercury, Venus follows the sun very closely, so in anyone's horoscope it is never very far away from your sun sign. Symbolically, Venus represents your capacity to love and relate, and the capacity to appreciate beauty. In ancient myth, Venus was seen as the daughter of the moon, a feminine planet associated with many of the earthly things traditionally associated with women: the providing of food and shelter, the beautifying of the home, the harmonizing of opposites and settler of strife. Venus is a peaceful planet in every sense of the word. Aphrodite to the Greeks, Venus to the Romans, this goddess/planet was seen as the bounteous giver of life's gifts and pleasures—the personification of beauty. She is supposed to inspire us with the desire for both material and spiritual growth.

Like Mercury, Venus has two faces, but, strangely, one rules a feminine sign, Taurus, and one rules a masculine sign, Libra. In Taurus, Venus shows her earthier side, more concerned with creature comforts, sex, and material prosperity. In Libra, a more refined Venus shines forth as the graceful "hostess," the one who beautifies things and relates to others.

Though most Libra males are quite virile, their rulership by the planet Venus often manifests itself in extremely good looks and a great appreciation of beauty. The virile male hairdresser or interior decorator is the personification of this side of Venus. Because Venus seeks peace rather than war, harmony rather than discord, she rules lawyers, mediators, and arbitrators.

Since Venus rules one feminine earth sign and one masculine air sign, she is sometimes seen as a symbol for the fact that all things in the universe can be made to work in harmony—even the incompatible elements of air (Libra) and earth (Taurus) and the often antagonistic principles of male and female—in real life as in astrology. Divorce courts come under the rulership of Venus.

Mars

Vital Statistics: 14 million miles from the sun; 35 million miles from earth; 10 percent of earth's size; circles the zodiac in about 687 days.
Rules: The sign of Aries
Ages 42 to 56
Role: The virile male antagonist ... the lover ... the warrior.
Facts and foibles: Mars is a rather small planet and has sometimes been called "Earth's little brother." However, since ancient times Mars has been attributed with great powers—possibly because of its fiery red color. Even the earliest peoples associated Mars with strife and sex and a warriorlike attitude. In fact, Mars has had a rather bad reputation in astrology and was sometimes known as the "lesser malefic." But some groups assigned Mars another role and gave him a different dimension. The Egyptians called Mars Artes, and connected him with personal creative expression; to the Hebrews he played a similar role. When you think about it, sex, strife, and creative expression are only a few steps away from each other. Certainly, the act of procreation is a creative one, as it gives new life. War and strife are divisive, but often a new order comes out of them as well.

Mars is pure masculine energy—sometimes a bit rough, but always determined. In a personal horoscope, the sign position of Mars tells how you tend to assert yourself, how aggressive you are likely to be when going after what you want, even how much you will want it. Mars is our desire nature. (See the chapter on Venus and Mars to find out more about Mars in your own horoscope.) As the god of war, Mars is associated with courage and bravery, traits that are available to the Aries sun sign person if he/she cares to develop them. Mars is moral courage too, and the Mars-ruled Aries sun sign person at his/her best will never desert a cause or a person—no matter how rough the going gets.

About once every two years Mars returns to the same place it occupied on the day of your birth; to astrologers this is known as the "Mars return." It is a period of time during which one can make great strides, because Mars is stimulating that area of the natal chart connected with taking on the world. People often feel a great surge of energy during their Mars return, but if that energy is not directed in a productive channel, it can cause a lot of problems in relationships. You are far better taking out your Mars return aggressiveness on another job or another creative project rather than another person.

Jupiter

Vital Statistics: Largest planet in the solar system, 318 times larger than earth; 365 million to 600 million miles from earth; gaseous nature; circles the zodiac in about 12 years.

Rules: The sign of Sagittarius
        Ages 57 to 68

Role: The hero ... the "father confessor" ... the one who saves the day.

Facts and Foibles: From earliest times, Jupiter was assigned a role in the "cosmic drama" almost as important as that of the sun. Huge and luminous, Jupiter was easily visible to the naked eye eons before the age of the telescope. The sun may have been god in the all-encompassing sense, but Jupiter was *the* god who could make things happen, even interfere in human affairs if he was needed. And he has always been a "good guy." The Hindus, whose roots lie in antiquity, call him Vishnu, the preserver. To the Greeks, he was Zeus, the god who reigned supreme on Mount Olympus; he became Jupiter under the Romans. The important thing about this masculine god-planet is that it has always been very godly but very human at the same time. Zeus frequently came down from Mount Olympus to bestow his favors on people—particularly women who caught his fancy (causing his wife Hera to become jealous). Jupiter-Zeus is the god who keeps one foot in heaven and one foot firmly planted on the earth. Since the planet itself is large and impressive-looking, it has always been associated with benevolence and expansiveness. Our English word "jovial" has its roots in the name Jove, by which name Jupiter was sometimes called.

Joviality is one of the characteristics that is available to people born under the sign of Sagittarius, which Jupiter rules. Some Sagittarians are jovial, they spend all their money and all their energy on making life one long party.

But Jupiter has a serious side, too. Jupiter is associated with the divine law, and the ability to make that law known to men on earth. The higher Sagittarian, ruled by Jupiter, has a sense of this mission, and often takes the real-life role of priest-missionary or teacher of higher studies. While Venus and Libra, the sign Venus rules, are associated with the *practice* of law, Jupiter and Sagittarius are connected with the *making* and *interpretation* of laws.

Saturn

Vital Statistics: 75,000 miles in diameter, 95 times as big as earth; 886 million miles from the sun; takes 29 years to circle the zodiac.
Rules: The sign of Capricorn
Ages 68 on
Role: The "older man" ... the taskmaster ... the disciplining father.
Facts and Foibles: Like Jupiter, Saturn is so large it can be seen with the naked eye from earth and was watched carefully by early peoples. It was quickly observed that certain transits of Saturn brought trials and troubles on earth and so the planet earned itself the name of the

"greater malefic" by the time astrologers had begun to record their findings. Is Saturn really a "bad guy" as so many astrology books will tell you? There is no question that Saturn represents the principle of limitation; when you go too far out on a limb or get over expansive, Saturn is always there to teach you that there are rules and restrictions. However, as Saturn also represents the principle of contraction, this planet can and does bring periods of time in which we can consolidate our forces and make a secure place for ourselves in this world.

Saturn is also sometimes called the "lord of Karma." Translated into human terms, that means that Saturn represents our inevitable responsibilities, our "fated" duties in this world. Once again, there is a positive side. When Saturn is strongly placed in an individual's chart, that individual is exceptionally able to handle responsibility and achieve worldly success. As ruler of the sign of Capricorn, Saturn brings to that sign an extraordinary talent for working long and hard as well as reaping the material rewards that come with dedication to a task.

Kronos (or Chronos) was the ancient Greek god who is generally regarded as the prototype for Saturn's particular personality or role, and his story sheds a lot of light on the perceptions of this planet. Kronos was born to the very highest ancient god, Ouranos, and to the original earth mother, Ge. Kronos got a little carried away with this position and overthrew his father (castrating him) to take over the throne. When Kronos was told one of his own children would do the same to him, he swallowed them all—except Zeus, who was miraculously saved and became the "avenger." Later on, Zeus banished Kronos into exile. We know Kronos as Father Time—that shadowy old man who reminds us that it's later than we think. Kronos/Saturn also cautions against runaway ambitions, which is often punished by a downfall like his.

One of the most fascinating aspects of Saturn is that it is an uncannily accurate cosmic clock. Taking about 29 years to make a full circle of the zodiac, Saturn returns to the same place it occupied in your horoscope at your birth when you are about 29 years old. The "Saturn return" is regarded by astrologers as the true end of childhood (astrology is kind to us weak mortals by giving us more time to "grow up" than conventional earthly wisdom does). When Saturn begins to creep up on us in our late twenties, we generally begin to feel that it's time to settle down and do something big in the way of taking on earthly responsibility. Many people go through a "life crisis" at this time, because they feel the push that Saturn is giving them, but have trouble knowing what to do about it. Many, many people resolve the dilemma by getting married, buying a home, having a child, or getting divorced. The point is that it is time to *do something decisive* and to take responsibility for our own lives and actions. There are an incredible number of "Saturn return babies" because having a child is probably the most joyful as well as the biggest responsibility a person can assume.

On its second return—at about the human age of 58—people are generally ready to start relaxing their responsibilities and enjoying the fruits of their labors. It is a wise precaution to make ready for the second Saturn return, because just as Saturn tells us we have to *work*, he also tells us when it is time to *stop* working. But remain a productive human being, with real interests and the wherewithal to pursue them.

Uranus

Vital Statistics: 1.7 billion miles from earth; 29,300 miles in diameter, 15 times larger than earth; takes 84 years to circle the zodiac; has an erratic orbit.
Rules: The sign of Aquarius
Teenagers
Role: The rebel ... the home-wrecker ... the visionary.
Facts and Foibles: Uranus is the first of the "modern" planets, i.e., those unknown to the ancients, and only discovered via the telescope. Uranus, the first planet to be discovered in this manner, was thus a shock to both astronomers and astrologers. Both groups believed the orbit of Saturn defined the limits of our solar system,

and both had to revise their thinking at this discovery. Astrologers took things in their stride by calling Uranus a "planet of the higher octave" and interpreting it as a breakthrough from the realm of purely earthly influences (with Saturn as the dividing line) to the "cosmic" or "higher" order of things. They decided that Uranus—an unconventional planet in many respects—must be the ruler of the quirky sign of Aquarius (which had been formerly ruled by Saturn). In a way it is uncanny that the sudden discovery of Uranus in 1781 heralded all the breakthrough discoveries of the 19th and 20th centuries. In a sense, Uranus ushered in the modern world; it also rules our current Age of Aquarius. As that age (approximately 2000 years long) will continue to shock us with discovery after discovery, it hopefully will also bring us the sense of brotherhood of humanity that is the hallmark of the sign of Aquarius.

As Uranus takes 84 years to circle the zodiac, it stays in each sign about seven years. (It is currently about two-thirds of the way through the sign of Sagittarius.) Whatever Uranus touches as it transits a person's natal chart gets a real jolt. Sometimes very suddenly. Uranus hates the status quo and almost always shakes it up. That means that a lot of changes take place when Uranus comes along, but for most people those changes are eventually positive ones. Uranus gets you out of whatever rut you happen to be in and does it quite forcefully. However, those who resist the changes Uranus "suggests" can cause themselves a lot of trouble. If you aren't willing to bend, Uranus can really "break you up."

Uranus is appropriately associated with the teen years, during which young people are often in a state of rebellion. However, here too, it is a *necessary* fact of life that people must eventually rebel against the strictures of childhood in order to become separate individual human beings. Uranus is associated not only with teenagers, but also with many of the things that represent their rebellion, like rock music, blaring radios, and all that goes with them. In essence, Uranus is the symbol of the electronic modern world.

Neptune

Vital Statistics: 2.6 billion miles from earth; 2.7 billion miles from the sun; takes about 165 years to circle the zodiac.

Rules: The sign of Pisces
No specific age.

Role: The fascinating stranger ... the poet ... the one who confuses the issue... the dreamer of great dreams.

Facts and Foibles: As it is difficult to get a handle on people heavily influenced by Neptune (like Pisceans), it took astronomers a while to figure out what Neptune really was. At first they observed nothing but some rather weird abberations in the orbit of Uranus as they began to plot that planet's orbit. In the early 1840s, some of them proved mathematically that there *must* be another planet out there, although it couldn't be seen. Finally, using all the data at hand, a German astronomer spotted Neptune in 1846.

There is a rather "sneaky" character to Neptune, but what this nebulous planet really symbolizes is the love that passes all understanding, the all-encompassing universal love that is virtually impossible for mortals to feel and give. Venus represents two-way love, the sharing kind. Neptune's love goes only in one direction. Neptune gives in a sense of self-sacrifice, and takes nothing in return.

There is evidence that even though no one really *saw* Neptune until 1846, the ancients knew all about its principles, and embodied them in the mythical figure of Poseidon (later called Neptune), the lord of the seas, master of the deep. When you think that more than three-quarters of the earth's surface is covered by water, you realize that Neptune was pretty important in the overall scheme of things. In fact, according to the Greeks, when the universe was created, it was divided among Zeus-Jupiter, who took the heavens, Hades-Pluto who took the underworld, and Poseidon-Neptune who took the oceans.

Just as water is difficult to contain, it is difficult for many people to get in touch with Neptune's higher qualities in their own charts. Water is soul and spirit, metaphysically speaking, so Neptune should make us aspire to much higher things. Not only universal love, but poetry, music and art in its purest forms. However, what Neptune touches in most people's natal charts often turns into an area of confusion rather than creativity. Neptune rules liquid in all its forms and, unfortunately, some people react to Neptune's confusing vibes by turning to alcohol or drugs. For many drug and alcohol abusers, however, the real goal of their vice is to attain a kind of "cosmic consciousness" which is the real realm of Neptune.

Since Neptune takes 165 years to circle the zodiac, it stays in one sign for 13 years or more. Therefore, it is the zodiacal *sign* Neptune makes to the "personal planets" in your chart that really count. People positively influenced by Neptune make the true artists and poets of this world—as well as the visionaries who interpret its meaning in more philosophical and metaphysical terms.

Pluto

Vital Statistics: 3,666 billion miles from the sun; takes about 242 years to circle the zodiac.
Rules: The sign of Scorpio
            Prenatal
Role: The "heavy" ... the transformer ... the tragic hero.
Facts and Foibles: As you will note, Pluto is a little light on vital statistics. That's because this immensely distant planet, only discovered in 1930, has yet to reveal some of its secrets to astronomers. Like Neptune, it was discovered only because of the erratic nature of the orbit of Uranus. But, even when Pluto was conclusively sighted in 1930, its small size relative to its extremely strong gravitational pull didn't make sense to astronomers. Either Pluto is much larger than we now think or it is so dense that it exerts a force much greater than its size should account for.

Either way, there's no doubt that Pluto represents *power*. In fact, many astrologers connect the discovery of Pluto with the discovery by man of the extraordinary power in matter itself—the power of the atom. As with Neptune, Pluto's "realm" had been staked out in myth and astrology long before its actual discovery. Pluto is Hades, lord of the underworld—the place of darkness that all men fear. However, since most older religions regard life and death as a cycle, Pluto represents rebirth as well. We die only to be reborn. One of the symbols for Pluto is the Phoenix that rises triumphantly from its own ashes. Pluto—and the sign of Scorpio that it rules—hold onto their secrets, but have an incredible power to endure and triumph over life's circumstances. The extremes of life and death that Pluto/Scorpio is associated with connect neatly with the extremism of this astrological sign. "Plutonic" Scorpios often regard the world as totally black and white, with very few grays in between. They can also be the "best" of people, like reformers and religious leaders, or the "worst" of people, like criminals and those who manipulate others for their own purposes.

10

Astrotrivia

How Do You Rate in the Best Game in Town?

The ancient art of astrology is loaded with bits and pieces of miscellaneous information—all of it fascinating, and some of it more useful than you may think. For instance, did you know that every zodiac sign has a special day of the week and certain colors assigned to it? And, how good are you at guessing sun signs of celebrities—those larger-than-life models of sun signs in the flesh? The Astrotrivia that follows is partly in quiz form, partly in short-take astrological facts. In the first part, you can test your own astrological perceptivity; in the second, you can add a lot to your fund of astrological information—and maybe even learn a few things, you can use in your daily life.

Astrotrivia Part I
Sun Signs of the Rich and Famous

Try to answer the following questions yourself; if you're stumped you'll find the answers on page 103–104.

1. What famous stripper and the famous actress who played her mother in a Broadway show have the sign of Capricorn in common?

2. What two show biz buddies—who run in the same pack—are both Sagittarians?

3. What do these people have in common: Joseph Stalin, Richard Nixon, Herman Goering, Al Capone, and Mao Tse Tung?

4. What two handsome male movie stars, both known for their progressive ideas, have the same sun sign? And, what is it?

5. What highly Scorpionic actor had an on-again, off-again lifetime romance with a glamourous Pisces actress?

6. What two female tennis pros are both athletic Sagittarians?

7. What U.S. president had a "show-me-I'm-from-Missouri" personality, and what was his sun sign?

8. What two famous "lonely hearts" columnists get their soft Cancerian shoulders cried on all the time?

9. What two "greats" of American popular music were both thoroughly American, and both born on the Fourth of July?

10. Under what sign were these warrior peacemakers all born: Dwight D. Eisenhower, David Ben Gurion, Jimmy Carter, Mohandus Ghandi, and Eleanor Roosevelt?

11. What anti-American villainess of World War II was born on the Fourth of July?

12. What sun sign do these people have in common: Oscar Wilde, Truman Capote, and Gore Vidal?

13. What two famous rock stars—one early, one late—were born not only under the same sign, but on the same day?

14. Which of the following is/was not a Scorpio?
    Charles Manson   Robert Kennedy
    Bo Derek   Pablo Picasso
    Katherine Hepburn   Indira Ghandi
    Princess Grace   Johnny Carson
    Henry Kissinger   Billy Graham

15. All of the following were born under the two most musical signs of the zodiac. What are they?

Judy Collins	Michael Jackson
Barbra Steisand	George Gershwin
Stevie Wonder	Luciano Pavarotti
Fred Astaire	Paul Simon
Irving Berlin	Julie Andrews
Bing Crosby	Anthony Newly
Beverly Sills	John Lennon
Bobby Darin	Guiseppe Verdi

16. All the following ladies of the stage and screen are masters of their craft. Which craftsman-like sun sign were they all born under?

Lauren Bacall	Celeste Holm
Anne Bancroft	Greer Garson
Ingrid Bergman	Twiggy
Greta Garbo	Jo Ann Worley
Sophia Loren	Claudette Colbert
Lilly Tomlin	Raquel Welch

17. What sun sign do the following famous rebels and rule-breakers have in common: Marlon Brando, Warren Beatty, Eddie Murphy, Charlie Chaplin, Hugh Hefner?

18. What sun sign do these medical and research geniuses have in common: Madame Curie, Jonas Salk, Christian Bernard?

19. What present-day famous Leo "princess" lived in Camelot with her Gemini "prince"?

20. What two great ballet stars were both born in the same country, and share the graceful sun sign, Pisces?

Answers on p. 103–104

Astrotrivia Part II
More Celebrity Sun Sign Lore

Just a handful of the many, many stage/screen-struck Leos:

Robert DeNiro	Julia Child
Mike Jagger	Arlene Dahl
Lucille Ball	Alfred Hitchcock
Dustin Hoffman	Mae West
Cecil B. Demille	George Bernard Shaw
John Derek	Dino D. Laurentis
Mike Douglas	Robert Mitchum
Robert Redford	Peter O'Toole
Jason Robards Jr.	Roman Polanski
Esther Williams	Jill St. John
Stanley Kubrick	Robert Taylor
Shelly Winters	Keenan Wynn

And here are some Leos who make/made the international scene their stage:

Fidel Castro	Henry Ford
Jackie Onassis	Alex Haley
Coco Chanel	Lawrence of Arabia
Benito Mussolini	Mata Hari
Rasputin	Napoleon
Neil Armstrong	Andy Warhol
Mike Conners	

Librans are often lovely, like Catherine Deneuve and Brigitte Bardot. Barbara Walters is the ultimate "cool" Libra.

Cancer is the second fame sign, because Cancer rules the public. Cancers who have made it somehow or other are:

Bill Cosby	Ringo Starr
Jimmy Cagney	John Glenn
Ernest Hemingway	Arthur Ashe
Gerald Ford	The Mayo brothers
	(of the Mayo clinic)

Some outspoken, inventive Aquarians whose opinions have not always been popular, but were always ahead of their time:

Norman Mailer   Ralph Nader
Charles Darwin Thomas Edison
Jules Verne   Betty Friedan
Ayn Rand   Vanessa Redgrave
Galileo   Franklin D. Roosevelt

Astrotrivia Part III
Fascinating Facts About the Signs

Here are the colors that, by tradition, match each of the signs of the zodiac:

1. Aries: bright red, scarlet, magenta

2. Taurus: pastels in most shades, especially pink and turquoise

3. Gemini: beiges and light gray

4. Cancer: shimmery and irridescent shades of gray and silver; anything luminous

5. Leo: bright golds and yellows

6. Virgo: dark navy, brown, gray

7. Libra: cloudy pales, especially blue-green

8. Scorpio: murky colors, especially blood red and black

9. Sagittarius: rich blues, purples, greens

10. Capricorn: black, "no-color" colors

11. Aquarius: checks, stripes, patterns, electric blue

12. Pisces: deep lilac, mauve, sea green

Each Sign/Planet owns a day of the week:

Sunday = Sun/Leo

Monday = Moon/Cancer

Tuesday = Mars/Aries, Mars/Scorpio

Wednesday = Mercury/Gemini, Mercury/Virgo

Thursday = Jupiter/Sagittarius, Neptune/Pisces

Friday = Venus/Taurus, Venus/Libra

Saturday = Saturn/Capricorn, Saturn/Aquarius

(Since there are only seven days and twelve signs, some of the signs double up. Also, since the ancients only knew seven planets, there are only enough days to match seven of the ten planets we now recognize.)

Astrotrivia Part IV
Where Do You Belong?

Each sign is said to have certain places where it belongs. Long ago, the world was divided up according to astrological tradition, so there are certain countries, cities, and areas that have the vibrations of certain signs. Tradition divides up other kinds of spaces, too, as you will see.

- *Aries places:* In the world: Birmingham, Oldman, Leicester, and Blackburn, *England* ... Florence, Naples, Verona and Padua *Italy* ... Marseilles and Burgundy *France* ... *Denmark, Germany, Palestine, Syria, Japan.*

    Anywhere: sheepfolds, forges, tool houses, fireplaces, on sandy soil, kilns, ceilings, fire houses, emergency rooms.

- *Taurus places:* In the world: Dublin, *Ireland* ... Mantua, Parma, Palermo, *Italy* ... St. Louis, *U.S.A.* ... *The Greek Islands, Asia Minor,* the *Caucasus.*

    Anywhere: banks, dairies, pastures, shady places, corn fields, middle rooms of houses, altars, maypoles.

- *Gemini places:* In the world: San Francisco, *U.S.A.* ... London and Plymouth, *England* ... Bruges, *Belgium* ... Versailles and Louvaine, *France* ... Nurenburg, *Germany* ... *Lower Egypt, Armenia, Wales.*

    Anywhere: buildings with pillars, bookcases, hills and mountains, upper back rooms, graineries.

- *Cancer places:* In the world; St. Andrews, *Scotland* ... Amsterdam, *Holland* ... New York City, *U.S.A.* ... Stockholm, *Sweden* ... Genoa, Venice, Milan, *Italy* ... *Paraguay, North and West Africa.*

Anywhere: lakes and brooks, salt marshes, pubs, kitchens, cellars, corner houses facing north.
- *Sagittarius places:* In the world: Avignon, *France* ... Stuttgart, Cologne, *Germany* ... Nottingham, Sheffield, Bradford, *England* ... Provence, *France* ... *Hungary, Arabia, Tuscany.*

  Anywhere: highest place around, topmost room in house, stables for racing horses, obelisks, places near fire, where incense is burned.
- *Capricorn places:* In the world: Brussels, *Belgium* ... Port Said, *Egypt* ... *India, Afghanistan, Mexico, Lithuania, Orkney Islands, Macedonia.*

  Anywhere: vaults, convents, thick forests, gates and hinges, old trees, jails, cattle barns, door knockers, game preserves.
- *Aquarius places:* In the world: Brighton and Trent, *England* ... Salzsburg, *Austria* ... Hamburg, *Germany* ... the Piedmont, *Italy* ... *Prussia, Red Russia, Westphalia.*

  Anywhere: buses, bridges, ladders, garages, airplanes, power transmitters, fountains, springs and streams, sleds, ice caps.
- *Pisces places:* In the world; Alexandria, *Egypt* ... Seville, *Spain* ... Southport, Lancaster, Bournemouth, Tiverton, *England* ... *Portugal, Calabria, Normandy, Sahara.*

  Anywhere: fish ponds, oceans, oil fields, submarines, séances, flooded areas, bars, aquariums, boat yards, swimming pools, hospitals.
- *Leo Places:* In the world: Rome, Ravenna, *Italy* ... Bath, Bristol, Portsmouth, Blackpool, *England* ... Philadelphia, Chicago, *U.S.A.* ... *Bohemia, Sicily, the Alps, Damascus.*

  Anywhere: wild animal preserves, deserts and forests, castles, furnaces, gold mines, porches, forts.
- *Virgo places:* In the world: Paris, Lyons, Toulouse, *France* ... Boston, Los Angeles, *U.S.A.* ... Heidelberg, *Germany* ... *Turkey, West Indies, Brazil, Silesia, Switzerland.*

  Anywhere: pantries, restaurants, refrigerators, medicine cabinets, desks, malt houses.

- *Libra places:* In the world: Dover, Liverpool, Newcastle, *England* ... Messina, *Italy* ... Halifax, *Nova Scotia* ... *China, Norway, The Transvaal, the Barbary coast.*

    Anywhere: windmills, wood sheds, harbors, tops of mountains, garrets and lofts, guest rooms, tops of dressers, domed buildings.
- *Scorpio places:* In the world: Copenhagen, *Denmark* ... Leeds, Nottingham, *England* ... Johannesburg, *South Africa* ... Burma, *India* ... *Tibet, North China, Argentina.*

    Anywhere: junk yards, meat markets, laboratories, low gardens and streams, vineyards, deepest part of ocean.

Astrotrivia Part V
Which Animal Best Suits You?

Each sign is said to have an affinity with certain kinds of pets. Here's the rundown.

Aries: No animal that needs a lot of taking care of; but if Aries has one pet, he/she will usually have two, so the animals can take care of each other.

Taurus: Almost any kind of soft, warm creature. Taurus is a great nature lover, so even a skunk would be welcome.

Gemini: Anything with fascinating habits, like bees or ants, or anything that talks, like a parrot or a minah bird.

Cancer: Anything in need of a mother is welcome in Cancer's house, no matter how sloppy or in need of care.

Leo: Cats, of course, preferably with good breeding. Peacocks or anything with bright colors or plumage are fine too.

Virgo: Cats are preferable, because they are clean animals, but any animal in distress brings out Virgo's warmth.

Libra: This sign would just as soon do without, but if a pet is preferred, it's the perfectly groomed poodle or other refined breed of dog or cat.

Scorpio: This sign goes for rather dangerous pets, such as snakes, or anything with a sting. Basically, animals are creatures to be observed, not coddled.

Sagittarius: Horses—at home or at the race track. Any very large dog in the city, almost anything of immense size in the country.

Capricorn: Capricorns *need* pets to help pull them out of their frequent depressions. The friendliest kind of animals are the best bet, like sheepdogs.

Aquarius: This sign needs a very smart animal, so is picky about the breed of dog or cat. Actually, birds are preferable to this cool sign.

Pisces: Many people born under this sign will take in any stray that strays into their path, no matter how scraggly or ugly. They often put animals before humans in their scheme of things.

Astrotrivia Part I answers

1. Gypsy Rose Lee and Ethel Merman (who played Gypsy's mother in *Gypsy*).
2. Frank Sinatra and Sammie Davis, Jr.
3. They were all born under the calculating sign of Capricorn.
4. Paul Newman and Alan Alda were both born under the sign of Aquarius.
5. Richard Burton was the Scorpio; Liz Taylor the Pisces.
6. Billie Jean King and Chris Evert.
7. Harry S. Truman, a Taurus.
8. Abigail Van Buren ("Dear Abby") and Ann Landers.

9. George M. Cohan ("Yankee Doodle Dandy") and Louis "Satchmo" Armstrong.
10. Libra.
11. Tokyo Rose.
12. Libra.
13. Elvis Presley and David Bowie (January 5—Capricorn).
14. Henry Kissinger. He's a wily Gemini, but he could easily fool you, because his moon sign is Scorpio.
15. The column on the left are Taureans; those on the right are Librans.
16. Virgo.
17. Aries.
18. Scorpio.
19. Jackie Kennedy Onassis is a Leo; John F. Kennedy was a Gemini.
20. Rudolph Nureyev and Vaslav Nijinsky.

11

Sun Sign Changes. 1920–1975

If you were born "on the cusp" (very near the end or the beginning of a sign) you can find out what your sign really is by using the chart that follows. Many people do not realize that the sun does not "change signs" on the same day every year—or, for that matter, at the same time. For this reason the chart of sun sign changes is calculated to the minute.

How to Use the Chart

Locate your year of birth, then the month in which you were born. Let's say you were born in April of 1942. In the box for that month and year you will see

20–Tau
12:30 P.M.

That means if you are born *after* 12:30 p.m. on April 20 in 1942, you are a Taurus. If you were born before that date and time, your sun sign is the preceding one, Aries.

In this chart (as well as in the rising-sign chart) the signs are abbreviated as follows:

Ar = Aries
Tau = Taurus
Gem = Gemini
Can = Cancer
Leo = Leo
Vir = Virgo
Lib = Libra
Sc = Scorpio

Sag = Sagittarius
Cap = Capricorn
Aq = Aquarius
Pis = Pisces

NOTE: All times given in the sun sign changes chart are Eastern Standard. You must correct for daylight savings time (subtract one hour) and for time zone. For Central Standard Time subtract one hour; for Mountain Standard Time subtract two hours; for Pacific Standard Time subtract three hours.

	1920	1921	1922	1923	1924	1925	1926	1927	1928	1929
Jan	21–Aq 4:05 am	20–Aq 8:55 am	20–Aq 2:48 pm	20–Aq 8:35 pm	21–Aq 2:29 am	20–Aq 8:20 am	20–Aq 2:13 pm	20–Aq 8:12 pm	21–Aq 1:57 am	20–Aq 7:42 am
Feb	19–Pis 5:29 pm	18–Pis 11:21 pm	19–Pis 5:16 am	19–Pis 11:00 am	19–Pis 4:51 pm	18–Pis 11:43 pm	18–Pis 4:35 am	19–Pis 10:35 am	19–Pis 4:20 pm	18–Pis 10:07 pm
Mar	20–Ar 5:00 pm	20–Ar 10:51 pm	21–Ar 4:49 am	21–Ar 10:29 am	20–Ar 4:20 pm	20–Ar 11:13 pm	21–Ar 4:01 am	21–Ar 11:59 am	20–Ar 3:44 pm	20–Ar 9:35 pm
Apr	20–Tau 4:39 am	20–Tau 10:32 am	20–Tau 4:29 am	20–Tau 10:06 pm	20–Tau 3:59 am	20–Tau 10:51 pm	20–Tau 3:36 pm	20–Tau 9:32 pm	20–Tau 3:17 am	20–Tau 8:11 am
May	21–Gem 4:22 am	21–Gem 10:17 am	21–Gem 9:11 pm	22–Gem 9:45 pm	21–Gem 3:41 am	21–Gem 10:33 am	21–Gem 3:15 pm	21–Gem 9:08 pm	21–Gem 2:53 am	21–Gem 8:48 am
June	21–Can	21–Can 6:36 pm	22–Can 12:27 pm	22–Can 6:03 am	21–Can 12:noon	21–Can 5:50 pm	21–Can 5:21 pm	22–Can 11:30 pm	21–Can 11:07 am	21–Can 5:01 pm
July	22–Leo 12:40pm	23–Leo 5:31 pm	23–Leo 11:20 pm	23–Leo 5:01 pm	22–Leo 11:58 pm	23–Leo 4:45 pm	23–Leo 10:25 pm	23–Leo 4:17 pm	22–Leo 11:02 pm	23–Leo 3:54 pm
Aug	23–Vir 11:40 pm	23–Vir	23–Vir	23–Vir 11:52 pm	23–Vir 5:48 am	23–Vir 11:33 am	23–Vir 5:14 pm	23–Vir 11:06 pm	23–Vir 4:53 am	23–Vir 10:41 am
Sept	23–Lib 6:22 am	23–Lib 12:15 pm	23–Lib 6:04 pm	23–Lib	23–Lib	23–Lib	23–Lib	23–Lib	23–Lib	23–Lib
Oct	23–Sc 3:25 am	23–Sc 11:20 am	23–Sc 5:10 am	24–Sc 9:04 pm	23–Sc 2:58 am	23–Sc 8:43 am	23–Sc 2:25 pm	24–Sc 8:17 pm	23–Sc 2:36 am	23–Sc 7:52 am
Nov	22–Sag 12:31 pm	22–Sag 6:03 pm	22–Sag 11:53 pm	23–Sag 5:51 am	22–Sag 11:44 am	22–Sag 5:31 pm	22–Sag 11:18 pm	23–Sag 5:07 am	22–Sag 10:55 am	22–Sag 4:41 pm
	22–Sag 9:15 am	22–Sag 3:21 pm	22–Sag 8:55 pm	23–Sag 2:54 am	22–Sag 8:46 am	22–Sag 2:36 pm	22–Sag 8:28 pm	23–Sag 2:14 pm	22–Sag 8:00 pm	22–Sag 1:48 pm
Dec	21–Cap 10:17 pm	22–Cap 4:08 am	22–Cap 9:57 pm	22–Cap 3:53 pm	21–Cap 10:45 pm	22–Cap 3:37 am	22–Cap 9:34 am	22–cap 3:18 pm	21–Cap 9:04 pm	22–Cap 2:53 am

	1930	1931	1932	1933	1934	1935	1936	1937	1938	1939
Jan	20–Aq 1:33 pm	21–Aq 7:18 pm	20–Aq 1:07 pm	20–Aq 6:53 pm	20–Aq 10:37 am	20–Aq 6:29 pm	21–Aq 12:12am	20–Aq 6:01 am	20–Aq 11:59 am	20–Aq 5:51 pm
Feb	19–Pis 4:00 am	19–Pis 9:06 am	19–Pis 3:29 am	19–Pis 9:16 am	19–Pis 3:02 am	19–Pis 8:52 am	19–Pis 2:33 pm	18–Pis 3:21 pm	19–Pis 2:20 am	19–Pis 8:10 pm
Mar	21–Ar 3:30 am	21–Ar 9:40 am	20–Ar 2:54 pm	21–Ar 8:43 pm	21–Ar 2:28 am	21–Ar 8:19 am	20–Ar 1:58 pm	20–Ar 7:45 pm	21–Ar 1:43 am	21–Ar 7:29 am
Apr	20–Tau 3:06 pm	20–Tau 8:40 pm	20–Tau 2:28 am	20–Tau 8:19 am	20–Tau 2:00 pm	20–Tau 7:50 pm	20–Tau 1:31 am	20–Tau 7:20 am	20–Tau 1:15 pm	20–Tau 6:55 pm
May	21–Gem 2:42 pm	21–Gem 8:15 pm	21–Gem 2:07 am	21–Gem 7:57 am	21–Gem 1:35 pm	21–Gem 7:25 pm	21–Gem 1:08 am	21–Gem 6:57 am	21–Gem 12:51 pm	21–Gem 6:27 pm
June	21–Can 11:53 pm	23–Can 4:28 am	21–Can 10:23 am	21–Can 4:12 pm	21–Can 9:48 pm	22–Can 3:32 am	21–Can 9:22 am	21–Can 3:12 pm	21–Can 9:04 pm	22–Can 2:40 am
July	23–Leo 10:42 am	23–Leo 3:21 pm	22–Leo 9:18 pm	23–Leo 3:06 am	23–Leo 8:42 am	23–Leo 2:33 pm	22–Leo 8:18 pm	23–Leo 2:07 am	23–Leo 7:57 am	23–Leo 1:37 pm
Aug	23–Vir 4:27 pm	23–Vir 10:10 pm	23–Vir 4:06 am	23–Vir 9:53 am	23–Vir 3:32 pm	23–Vir 9:24 pm	23–Vir 3:11 am	23–Vir 8:58 am	23–Vir 2:46 pm	23–Vir 8:31 pm
Sept	23–Lib 1:35 pm	23–Lib 7:23 pm	23–Lib 1:16 am	23–Lib 7:01 am	23–Lib 10:45 am	23–Lib 6:38 pm	23–Lib 12:26 am	23–Lib 6:13 am	23–Lib 12:noon	23–Lib 5:50 pm
Oct	23–Sc 11:25 pm	24–Sc 4:15 am	23–Sc 10:04 am	23–Sc 3:48 pm	23–Sc 9:35 pm	24–Sc 3:29 am	23–Sc 10:18 am	23–Sc 3:06 pm	23–Sc 8:54 pm	24–Sc 2:46 am
Nov	22–Sag 7:34 pm	23–Sag 1:25 pm	22–Sag 7:10 pm	22–Sag 10:53 pm	22–Sag 6:44 pm	23–Sag 12:35 am	22–Sag 6:25 pm	22–Sag 12:17 pm	22–Sag 6:06 pm	22–Sag 11:59 pm
Dec	22–Cap 8:40 am	22–Cap 2:30 pm	21–Cap 8:14 pm	22–Cap 1:58 am	22–Cap 5:49 pm	22–Cap 1:37 pm	21–Cap 7:27 pm	22–Cap 1:22 am	22–Cap 7:13 am	22–Cap 1:05 pm

	1940	1941	1942	1943	1944	1945	1946	1947	1948
Jan	20—Aq 11:44 pm	20—Aq 5:34 am	20—Aq 11:16 am	20—Aq 5:20 pm	20—Aq 11:09 pm	20—Aq 4:55 am	20—Aq 10:44 am	20—Aq 4:23 pm	20—Aq 10:18 pm
Feb	19—Pis 2:04 pm	18—Pis 7:59 pm	19—Pis 1:39 am	19—Pis 7:41 am	19—Pis 1:28 pm	18—Pis 7:15 pm	19—Pis 1:10 am	19—Pis 6:53 am	19—Pis 12:37 pm
Mar	20—Ar 1:24 am	20—Ar 7:21 am	21—Ar 1:03 am	21—Ar 7:03 am	21—Ar 12:49 pm	20—Ar 6:38 pm	21—Ar 12:34 am	21—Ar 6:13 am	20—Ar 11:57 am
Apr	20—Tau 12:51 am	20—Tau 6:51 am	20—Tau 12:30 pm	20—Tau 6:32 pm	20—Tau 12:18 am	20—Tau 6:08 am	20—Tau 12:03 pm	20—Tau 5:40 pm	19—Tau 11:25 pm
May	21—Gem 12:23 am	21—Gem 6:23 am	21—Gem 12:01 pm	21—Gem 6:03 pm	20—Gem 11:51 pm	22—Gem 5:41 am	21—Gem 1:34 am	21—Gem 5:04 pm	20—Gem 10:58 pm
June	21—Can 8:37 am	21—Can 2:33 am	21—Can 8:08 pm	22—Can 2:13 am	21—Can 9:03 am	21—Can 1:52 pm	21—Can 7:45 pm	22—Can 1:19 am	21—Can 7:11 am
July	22—Leo 7:34 pm	23—Leo 1:26 am	23—Leo 6:59 am	23—Leo 1:05 pm	22—Leo 6:55 pm	23—Leo 12:48 am	23—Leo 6:37 am	23—Leo 12:12 pm	22—Leo 6:06 pm
Aug	23—Vir 2:21 am	23—Vir 8:30 am	23—Vir 1:50 pm	23—Vir 7:55 pm	23—Vir 1:47 am	23—Vir 7:36 am	23—Vir 1:23 pm	23—Vir 7:09 pm	23—Vir 1:03 am
Sept	22—Lib 11:46 pm	23—Lib 5:33 am	23—Lib 11:10 am	23—Lib 5:12 pm	22—Lib 11:02 pm	23—Lib 4:50 am	23—Lib 10:41 am	23—Lib 4:29 pm	22—Lib 10:22 pm
Oct	23—Sc 8:39 am	23—Sc 2:22 pm	22—Sc 8:01 pm	24—Sc 2:09 am	23—Sc 7:57 am	20—Sc 1:45 pm	23—Sc 7:37 pm	24—Sc 1:27 am	23—Sc 7:19 am
Nov	22—Sag 5:49 am	22—Sag 11:38 am	22—Sag 5:23 pm	22—Sag 11:22 pm	22—Sag 5:09 am	22—Sag 10:56 am	22—Sag 4:47 pm	22—Sag 10:38 pm	22—Sag 4:29 am
Dec	21—Cap 6:55 pm	22—Cap 12:44 am	22—Cap 6:31 am	22—Cap 12:30 pm	21—Cap 6:15 pm	22—Cap 12:04 am	22—Cap 5:54 am	22—Cap 11:44 am	21—Cap 5:23 pm

	1949	1950	1951	1952	1953	1954	1955	1956	1957
Jan	20–Aq 4:11 am	20–Aq 10:00 am	20–Aq 3:53 pm	20–Aq 9:38 pm	20–Aq 3:22 am	20–Aq 9:14 am	20–Aq 3:03 pm	20–Aq 8:49 pm	20–Aq 2:43 am
Feb	18–Pis 6:27 pm	19–Pis 12:16 am	19–Pis 6:10 am	19–Pis 11:57 am	18–Pis 5:41 pm	19–Pis 11:33 pm	19–Pis 5:19 am	19–Pis 11:05 am	18–Pis 5:01 pm
Mar	20–Ar 5:49 pm	20–Ar 11:30 pm	21–Ar 5:26 am	20–Ar 11:14 am	20–Ar 5:01 pm	20–Ar 10:54 pm	21–Ar 4:36 am	20–Ar 10:21 am	20–Ar 4:17 pm
Apr	20–Tau 5:18 am	20–Tau 11:00 am	20–Tau 4:49 pm	20–Tau 10:37 pm	19–Tau 4:26 am	20–Tau 10:20 am	20–Tau 3:58 pm	19–Tau 9:44 pm	20–Tau 3:45 am
May	21–Gem 4:51 am	21–Gem 10:27 am	21–Gem 4:15 pm	20–Gem 10:04 pm	21–Gem 3:53 am	21–Gem 9:48 am	21–Gem 3:25 pm	20–Gem 9:13 pm	21–Gem 3:09 am
June	21–Can 1:03 pm	21–Can 6:37 pm	22–Can 12:25 am	21–Can 6:13 am	21–Can 12:noon	21–Can 5:55 pm	21–Can 11:32 pm	21–Can 5:24 am	21–Can 11:21 am
July	22–Leo 1:58 pm	23–Leo 5:30 am	23–Leo 11:29 am	22–Leo 5:05 pm	22–Leo 10:53 pm	23–Leo 4:45 am	23–Leo 10:25 am	22–Leo 4:20 pm	22–Leo 10:13 pm
Aug	23–Vir 6:49 pm	23–Vir 12:24 pm	23–Vir 6:22 pm	23–Vir 12:03 am	23–Vir 5:46 am	23–Vir 11:37 am	23–Vir 5:19 pm	22–Vir 11:15 pm	23–Vir 5:07 am
Sept	23–Lib 4:05 am	23–Lib 9:44 am	23–Lib 3:38 pm	22–Lib 9:24 pm	23–Lib 3:07 am	23–Lib 8:56 am	23–Lib 2:42 pm	22–Lib 8:30 pm	23–Lib 2:27 am
Oct	23–Sc 1:04 pm	23–Sc 6:48 pm	23–Sc 12:37 am	23–Sc 6:22 am	23–Sc 12:07 pm	23–Sc 5:58 pm	22–Sc 11:44 pm	23–Sc 5:35 am	23–Sc 11:33 am
Nov	22–Sag 10:17 am	22–Sag 4:03 pm	22–Sag 9:52 pm	22–Sag 3:36 am	22–Sag 9:23 am	22–Sag 3:14 pm	22–Sag 9:02 pm	22–Sag 2:51 am	22–Sag 8:45 am
Dec	21–Cap 11:24 am	22–Cap 5:14 am	22–Cap 11:01 am	21–Cap 4:44 pm	21–Cap 10:22 pm	22–Cap 4:25 am	22–Cap 10:12 am	21–Cap 4:00 pm	21–Cap 9:49 pm

	1958	1959	1960	1961	1962	1963	1964	1965	1966
Jan	20—Aq 2:20 pm	20—Aq 2:20 pm	20—Aq 8:11 pm	20—Aq 2:02 am	20—Aq 7:49 am	20—Aq 1:55 pm	19—Aq 7:43 pm	20—Aq 1:30 am	20—Aq 8:21 am
Feb	18—Pis 10:49 pm	19—Pis 4:38 pm	19—Pis 10:26 am	18—Pis 6:27 pm	18—Pis 10:16 pm	19—Pis 4:09 am	19—Pis 10:25 am	18—Pis 3:49 pm	18—Pis 9:39 pm
Mar	20—Ar 10:06 pm	21—Ar 3:55 am	20—Ar 9:43 am	20—Ar 5:27 am	20—Ar 9:30 am	21—Ar 3:20 am	20—Ar 9:43 am	20—Ar 3:05 am	20—Ar 8:53 am
Apr	20—Tau 9:28 am	20—Tau 3:17 pm	20—Tau 10:06 pm	20—Tau 2:33 am	20—Tau 8:51 am	20—Tau 2:37 pm	19—Tau 9:00 pm	20—Tau 2:27 am	20—Tau 8:12 am
May	21—Gem 8:52 am	21—Gem 2:38 pm	20—Gem 8:33 pm	21—Gem 1:51 am	21—Gem 8:17 am	21—Gem 1:59 pm	20—Gem 8:33 pm	21—Gem 1:27 am	21—Gem 7:33 am
June	21—Can 4:57 pm	21—Can 10:50 pm	21—Can 4:43 am	21—Can 10:12 am	21—Can 4:24 pm	21—Can 11:04 pm	21—Can 4:43 am	21—Can 9:56 am	21—Can 3:33 pm
July	23—Leo 3:51 am	23—Leo 9:45 am	22—Leo 5:38 pm	22—Leo 9:12 pm	23—Leo 3:19 am	23—Leo 9:00 am	22—Leo 3:38 pm	22—Leo 8:49 pm	23—Leo 2:24 am
Aug	23—Vir 10:47 am	23—Vir 4:44 pm	22—Vir 10:35 pm	23—Vir 3:46 am	23—Vir 10:13 am	23—Vir 3:58 pm	22—Vir 10:35 pm	23—Vir 3:43 am	23—Vir 9:18 am
Sept	23—Lib 5:10 am	23—Lib 2:09 pm	22—Lib 8:00 pm	23—Lib 1:26 am	23—Lib 7:35 am	23—Lib 1:24 pm	22—Lib 8:00 pm	23—Lib 1:06 am	23—Lib 6:43 am
Oct	23—Sc	23—Sc 11:12 pm	23—Sc 5:03 am	23—Sc 10:46 am	23—Sc 4:41 pm	23—Sc 11:30 pm	23—Sc 5:03 am	23—Sc 10:11 am	23—Sc 3:52 pm
Nov	22—Sag 2:30 am	22—Sag 8:23 pm	22—Sag 2:19 am	22—Sag 8:10 am	22—Sag 2:02 pm	22—Sag 7:50 pm	22—Sag 2:19 am	22—Sag 7:30 am	22—Sag 1:15 pm
Dec	22—Cap 3:40 am	22—Cap 9:35 am	21—Cap 5:27 pm	21—Cap 9:25 pm	22—Cap 3:15 am	22—Cap 9:02 am	21—Cap 3:27 pm	21—Cap 8:41 pm	22—Cap 2:29 pm

	1967	1968	1969	1970	1971	1972	1973	1974	1975
Jan	20–Aq 1:05 pm	20–Aq 6:54 pm	20–Aq 12:30 am	20–Aq 6:25 am	20–Aq 12:14 pm	20–Aq 6:00 pm	19–Aq 11:49 pm	20–Aq 5:47 am	20–Aq 11:37 am
Feb	19–Pis	19–Pis 9:11 am	18–Pis 2:47 pm	18–Pis 8:43 pm	19–Pis 2:28 am	19–Pis 8:12am	18–Pis 2:02 pm	18–Pis 8:00 pm	19–Pis 1:51 am
Mar	3:25 am								
	21–Ar 2:37 am	20–Ar 8:22 am	20–Ar 2:08 pm	20–Ar 7:59 pm	21–Ar 1:28 am	20–Ar 7:22 am	20–Ar 1:13 pm	20–Ar 7:08 pm	21–Ar 12:58 am
Apr	20–Tau 1:56 am	19–Tau 7:42 pm	20–Tau 1:18 am	20–Tau 5:16 am	20–Tau 12:54 pm	19–Tau 6:38 pm	20–Tau 12:31 am	20–Tau 5:19 am	20–Tau 12:08 pm
May	21–Gem 1:19 pm	20–Gem 7:07 pm	21–Gem 12:41 am	21–Gem 6:32 am	21–Gem 12:16 pm	20–Gem 6:00 pm	20–Gem 11:54 pm	21–Gem 5:37 am	21–Gem 1:25 pm
June	21–Can 4:23 pm	21–Can 1:13 am	21–Can 6:55 am	21–Can 2:43 pm	21–Can 8:21 pm	21–Can 2:07 am	21–Can 8:01 am	21–Can 1:38 pm	21–Can 7:27 pm
July	23–Leo 8:16 am	22–Leo 2:13 pm	22–Leo 8:05 pm	23–Leo 1:38 am	23–Leo 7:15 am	22–Leo 1:03 pm	22–Leo 6:56 pm	23–Leo 12:30 am	23–Leo 7:23 am
Aug	23–Vir 3:13 pm	23–Vir 9:52 pm	23–Vir 2:35 am	23–Vir 6:35 am	23–Vir 2:16 pm	22–Vir 8:04 pm	23–Vir 1:55 am	23–Vir 7:29 am	23–Vir 1:24 pm
Sept	23–Lib 12:38 pm	22–Lib 6:26 pm	23–Lib 12:07 pm	23–Lib 5:59 am	23–Lib 11:47 am	22–Lib 5:34 pm	22–Lib 11:22 pm	23–Lib 4:59 am	23–Lib 10:56 am
Oct	23–Sc	23–Sc 1:30 am	23–Sc 9:03 am	23–Sc 3:05 pm	22–Sc 8:53 pm	23–Sc 2:42 am	23–Sc 8:31 am	23–Sc 2:12 pm	23–Sc 8:07 pm
Nov	22–Sag 7:05 pm	22–Sag 12:59 am	22–Sag 6:23 am	22–Sag 12:25 pm	22–Sag 6:15 pm	22–Sag 12:04 am	22–Sag 5:55 am	22–Sag 11:39 am	22–Sag 5:32 pm
Dec	22–Cap 8:17 am	21–Cap 2:00 pm	21–Cap 7:44 pm	22–Cap 1:36 am	22–Cap 5:26 am	21–Cap 1:14 pm	21–Cap 7:09 pm	22–Cap 12:57 am	22–Cap 7:47 am

12

Taurus: The Big Picture

Because the twelve signs of the zodiac represent twelve ways of being in the world, you will know more about yourself and why you tend toward certain types of behavior and attitudes by knowing more about Taurus. If you read about the elements and qualities in "Defining Terms," for instance, you'll find out that you are one of the solid, practical *earth signs*, and, as one of the *fixed signs*, you have a lot of staying power. You can meet yourself in the Taurus prototype described in "Twelve Places at the Table," and your lovely planetary ruler, Venus, provides some excellent clues about the Taurus style.

However, even with these broad brush strokes, your Taurus portrait is still a bit abstract; to see yourself in totality, you need more of the background filled in. That means going back to some very important basics: your second-place position in the zodiac, your picture/symbol, the bull, and the "shorthand figure," or glyph, that astrologers use to indicate Taurus when they draw up a horoscope. In Taurus, as in every astrological sign, these three factors link together, forming a strong chain of meaning that holds together everything that is Taurus.

When the sun passes out of Aries, the first sign of the zodiac, about April 20, it enters Taurus, and stays there until about May 20. This is the period of the earth's year that is "full spring"—the month that falls between the beginning spring of Aries and the late spring of Gemini. Leaves are their greenest, flowers are in full bloom, and all around are reminders of the fertile, creative force of nature and the power to endure and bloom again after the long winter. As the sign connected with this period, Taurus is the earthiest of the earth signs, and the softest one as well; the ground must be warm and moist in order for green things to flourish.

Taurus' second-place position in the zodiac makes it one of the fixed signs, the logical follower to cardinal sign Aries, the initiator. Taurus consolidates what Aries has started, bringing about the stable conditions necessary for things to come to completion. It is the role of Taurus to exhibit patience, to stay put, to provide a bulwark for others to lean on. Some might say Taurus' role in the zodiac is not as exciting as Aries'; perhaps not, but it is an essential one if anything in this world is ever going to get done.

In ancient times the sun's entry into Taurus was celebrated as a Feast of Maya, what we now call May Day, with a procession headed by the Sun, represented as a white bull with a golden disk between his horns, followed by a retinue of virgins. The symbolism of fertility and fecundity is fairly obvious. It still exists in our own May Day, though much of the original meaning is obscured. Taurus means fertility in every sense of the word. Taurus is the original earth mother, and—regardless of gender—Taureans have a nurturing, protective attitude toward others. They also generally have a very healthy sexual appetite.

As for the famous bull that is Taurus' picture symbol, bull worship was an important part of a number of ancient cultures, including the Egyptian. It was said that the bull (particularly the white bull) represented Osiris, the Egyptians' most important god, the one life force. During life bulls were treated with reverence. When a sacred bull died, the whole nation went into mourning. Some of the symbols used in the cult of Osiris remain with us today. If you look at the back of a one-dollar bill, you will see an eye above a pyramid. The eye is Osiris, the pyramid represents permanence, and the symbol means our currency is stable. Like the ideal Taurus.

The bull was also notorious for its sexuality in Greek and Roman mythology. The great god Zeus, maddened by love for Europa, took the form of a gentle bull. Drawn to the bull because of its tameness, Europa ended up succumbing to the bull's sexual charms and running off with Zeus to bear the famous King Minos of Crete. In Taurus, too, the themes of fertility and sexuality are intertwined and inseparable.

The glyph used by astrologers (see illustration) looks very much like what most people say it represents—the bull's face and horns. There are other interpretations, however, which are useful in explaining the astrological sign of Taurus. For one thing, it is the first letter of the Hebrew alphabet—Aleph, or Alpha (as in Alpha and Omega, the beginning and the end). At one time in prehistory, when the constellations were most important, Taurus was said to be the first sign of the zodiac. A fact some shyer, gentler Taurus types should remember.

Also revealing is the reading that says the symbol is the full moon with a crescent moon attached to it. The moon in ancient times was the celestial mother, the one of great strength who protected her creatures and helped them grow, a role Taureans of either sex tend to play. The sign of Taurus is sometimes connected with earthly wealth; it is possible that the real wealth of Taurus is this sign's ability to be sensitive and compassionate to the needs of others.

13

Taurus: Objectives and Obstacles

A Game Plan for Being the Most Successful Taurus Under the Sun

Every astrological sign is a set of possibilities; being born under a particular sign does not guarantee you *are* or *will be* all those things that sign is capable of being. Nor would you want to. There are positive characteristics to be cultivated, as well as negative ones you can avoid or overcome. Living "à la carte"—selecting what you want from all the options available—is open to you, within the overall context of your sign.

You can, of course, order the "prix fixe" dinner by living your life as it comes without attempting to direct it. The choice is yours, which is one good reason it is incorrect to regard your astrological destiny as preordained. You are responsible for how you embody your sign, and what results from that embodiment.

Astrologically speaking, your life as a sign is a journey with a starting point, the raw, or primitive end of the side, and a destination, the evolved or ideal realization of that sign. Once again, you don't have to take the full trip; there are plenty of exits if you choose to use them, and few people are ever totally "finished." But if you at least know where you are going, and what potential booby traps lie along the way, you will be way ahead of the game.

Regard the following as a map and use it in charting your course. The most successful way to be the best of your astrological sign is to work with it, in full knowledge of its up side and its down side. The most successful and happy people of any astrological sign are those who aim high and are not afraid to stretch their understanding of themselves in order to reach their goal.

Where Taurus Starts

Taurus is an exhausting sign, with its sometimes brute force and ceaseless activity. Taurus comes next in the zodiac, and quite naturally seeks peace and quiet. At its best, their Taurean tendency makes for the strong, silent type, people who are patient and helpful. However, in the primitive Taurean, the peace that is sought is simply lack of activity. Bluntly, Taureans can be lazy. If not lazy in body, then lazy in mind. Some people accuse Taurus of having no imagination; the real problem is that being original requires a lot of effort that Taurus is not always willing to make. Taurus is also a creature of habit, and many of those habits can be quite self-indulgent ones in the unevolved Taurus. Not a few Taureans have serious weight problems, and some overindulge in alcohol. At their very worst, Taureans can be greedy, and that trait, greed, often manifests itself by a desire to accumulate money and things just for their own sake, resulting in an overly materialistic view of life. The famous Taurean sexuality is also real, and can even lead to promiscuity as Taurus lets it get out of control.

Here are some buzz words by which you can recognize the primitive Taurus type:

Greedy	Boring
Obstinate	Obsessive
Cloddish	Resentful
Materialistic	Self-indulgent
Possessive	Lazy

Where Taurus Can Go

An easy acceptance of life, a mature understanding of what it means simply "to be,"—serene, without conflict, without confusion—and yet to do one's useful work in this world; this is what Taurus can achieve if he/she is willing to rise above primitive status. Serenity does not mean passivity, however. The truly evolved Taurean is a "builder" in the best sense of the word because

Taurean activity is constructive activity and is approached with a practical sense of what the world needs. There are many successful Taureans in the business world, and not a few of them have attained great financial worth. When a Taurus knows where he/she is going, and the place Taurus is aiming for is high in terms of its human value, there is almost nothing this strong sign cannot achieve. And—if Taurus really reaches maturity and has learned self-control—the sign can have a wealth of material goods while remaining sublimely detached from his/her possessions. The obstinacy of the primitive Taurean can be totally transformed into a positive confidence and determination. When Taurus grows into the best of his/her sign, he/she is self-assured rather than stubborn; at peace with him-/herself and the rest of the world. The ferocious bull is replaced by the gentle Ferdinand who quietly enjoys pleasures of this earth and doesn't like to fight. Some buzz words to recognize the evolved Taurus type:

Loyal	Nurturing/helpful
Practical	Calm
Tenacious	Patient
Fertile mind	Good values
Sensitive	Affectionate

How Taurus Can Get There

There is a part of Taurus that demands performance and stability; change is not only frightening, it is profoundly unsettling. The challenge for the Taurus who wants to succeed is to avoid remaining static. It's very hard to go places if you don't put yourself in the path of opportunity. Naturally, it is unlike Taurus to seek out high risk occupations—not simply those that require physical courage, like skydiving, but even those relatively sedentary jobs where nerves of steel are essential. It is possible for Taurus to compromise, however, by simply testing the waters. Some Taureans must literally force change on themselves, so the idea is to start with little things, like changing your daily routine, trying out a new method of doing something familiar.

Then Taurus can take the next step by asking for more responsibility and new duties on the job. It's not the *amount* of work that's likely to frighten Taurus; it's the necessity to switch gears and start traveling down a new path. Taurus should keep reminding him-/herself that the more things change, the more they remain the same. You'll be surprised at how many familiar landmarks you will find along the way. Don't hesitate to reach out for the brass ring; you can keep lots of things the same—like steady relationships and a secure domestic life—and still make a lot of progress through change.

Potential Pitfalls

The Taurean appetite for good things of the senses is not exaggerated. Scratch the surface of even the most spartan Taurus and you will find that he/she has a secret (and usually excessive) self-indulgence. Taurus' extreme sensibility can be an asset, however; there are many professions in which a good ear, a good eye, and a well-honed sense of touch are the secret of success. And it is from this fact that the usual Taurus can get an excellent clue for pampering him-/herself without overdoing. When Taurus gets the itch that signifies inner turmoil (usually the root of the problem) one sure cure is music. If you immerse yourself in the sounds you most enjoy, regardless of style, you will find that the inner you calms down, and is better able to accept the bustle of the outside world. Any art form is good for Taurus—especially sculpture, which can be very soothing because it is a hands-on activity.

Another two-edged sword the Taurus sun sign carries around is a love of simplicity. At its best, this tendency means you can cut through a lot of extraneous matters and get to the root of a problem. However, it also can mean that Taurus takes the easy way out (for "easy" read "unimaginative"). Sooner or later the same old way of doing things may still be a snap, but will have outlived its usefulness. And people will start calling Taurus "stubborn" for sticking to it. Be willing to take those leaps that allow you to be a lot more creative and interesting.

14

Pairing Off with Taurus

Your Compatibility with Other Signs of the Zodiac

Since there are only twelve signs of the zodiac, it would be unusual to go through life without having to interact with each of them at one time or another. Obviously, your astrological makeup is more complex than your Taurus sun sign, but there are some basic truths about how you tend to react when face to face with someone of another sun sign. If you have read about "The Geometry of Relationships," you already know that being an earth sign means Taurus relates more easily to certain elements than to others. Now, getting more specific, you will see what the odds are on your match-ups with each of the other signs, including your own.

When people talk about "relationships," they are usually referring to the romantic kind, and there is no doubt that since time immemorial love has been observed to have a great deal to do with keeping the earth revolving in its orbit. However, we also have a lot of other interpersonal interactions, from important ones, like boss-employee and parent-child to more casual ones, like waitress-patron, cabdriver-rider, and buddy-buddy. The general rules that follow apply in all cases; just change the language a little and do a bit of interpretation. You will find that there is more truth than poetry in the matter of astrological compatibility.

Taurus with Aries This could be a battle of wills at the start, but Aries' fresh charm and enthusiasm could win you over in the end, and it would be a good thing for you. Aries is far more adventurous than you, in love as well as other aspects of life (though you are more so in the sexual area). You can let your hair down with an Aries without feeling foolish and admit to those deep-down needs for security; and you could provide Aries with the firm foundation the sign often needs. This relationship is possible—but not probable. In the long run, your essential differences will come out and take over.

Taurus with Taurus   Mutual respect could draw you together and possibly make the bond a permanent one. However, unless one or both of you has some fire in your astrological makeup, the whole thing could get rather dull. The two of you might become overly intense about the material aspects of life, as well. It is true that like attracts like, and you two would be *simpático* in many areas. Sex, for instance, could be phenomenal. But it is most likely that each of you will realize you're better off with a different astrological partner.

Taurus with Gemini   This could be simply a mad affair, but one you should try not to miss. There is a flexibility in Gemini that would be excellent for you to observe and emulate. When you think there is no question about something, Gemini will introduce you to a totally different side of the issue. Gemini is stimulating in every way, including sexually. And under that possibly flighty exterior, Gemini sess the world as realistically as you do. Be warned, however, that if you want this sign, you are going to have to work for it—Gemini will not stick around if you don't.

Taurus with Cancer   When you try to dominate Cancer, you will quickly find that he/she will refuse to move an inch. In fact, you may get a big surprise when you discover that underneath Cancer's soft exterior beats a heart that is even more determined than your own. But you need Cancer, so this sign should make you open up the floodgates of your own softness and sweetness. Cancer should respond to you in every way. In the end it's not a question of who wins—you both do.

Taurus with Leo   Leo is a fixed sign, like you, but

that fact won't take this relationship very far. In fact, it could lead to a royal battle to see who will budge first. You might enjoy Leo's playful outlook on life, but you also might end up finding out that you are just a game of the moment. Don't get too involved with Leo, or you may find yourself hurt. You shouldn't let the loss of Leo get you down. This likable, friendly sign can't give you the depth that you need to feel secure. There are much better mates in the zodiac for you.

Taurus with Virgo Because you are both earth signs, there will be an immediate affinity, but it is Virgo who may be the more attracted. You are much less nervous than Virgo, and your outward placidity is like balm to that sign's often jangled spirits. This is a relationship that could work, but it could be a little on the workaday side as well. If you both feel you get enough kicks together, then get together for life. In business this works well if Taurus is the boss and structures things for Virgo.

Taurus with Libra Libra will charm you, delight you, provide you with a safe haven where life could be beautiful. However, you must be willing to accept the fact that you may be the stronger partner. You both look at life logically, which is another check in the positive column, and both of you seek out beauty in everything. The big negative is that you both can be extremely lazy; not in the physical sense so much as the mental one. You might end up in the same place you start. You might want to look for more positive energy in a partner.

Taurus with Scorpio This could be a match made in heaven—or hell. You are polar opposites in the zodiac, and will naturally gravitate toward each other. In a romantic relationship, the sex could be extraordinary. In a business relationship you would make powerful partners. However, Taurus runs the risk of being totally swallowed up by Scorpio's tremendous intensity. If you seek peace, as many Taureans do, you won't find it in a relationship with Scorpio. If you end up in one, be prepared for lots of action—and not a few life changes.

Taurus with Sagittarius Sagittarius takes life in great strides and doesn't like to stay in one place too long. Taurus might find it a rather peculiar way to live, since you most often like to know exactly where you're going. On the other hand, you could provide Sagittarius with a center they want and you could get the stimulation you need in Sagittarius' stimulating mentality. Don't walk away from this one until you've examined all the options. Sometimes earth and fire make an unbeatable combination.

Taurus with Capricorn As plausible relationship as they may seem on the surface (earth with earth), Capricorn is a bit too self-sufficient to need you as much as you want to be needed. Your worldly values should coincide, but Capricorn looks for more show than domesticated Taurus has. On the other hand, it is a slow and steady pace that both of you are comfortable with, so on certain levels this relationship is very productive. You certainly could warm up occasionally cold Capricorn—especially in the sexual area.

Taurus with Aquarius Aquarius could come off as a strange bird to predictable Taurus. Who knows where this one is coming from? Also, Aquarius is too removed for Taurus, who generally likes romance that's a bit on the intimate side. Actually, it's really too bad you two don't get together—at least for a while. Aquarius could provide you with the broader mental outlook you need; you could teach Aquarius some valuable lessons in the art of down-to-earth relationships. In business or friendship this should be a good team.

Taurus with Pisces Here is someone who needs your understanding and solidity to such a degree that you may find a good reason for total surrender. You may also have to abandon some cherished practical values, however, because Pisces values "higher" things. If you run across a Pisces who seems interested, go for it! Pisces can add a lot to your stature as a whole person, and you could be just the anchor this watery, sometimes scattered person requires. Pisces simply won't let you be pedestrian in your outlook.

15

The Taurus Sex Role Dilemma

One of the most important ways in which the twelve signs of the zodiac are divided is into "masculine" signs and "feminine" signs, and there are six of each. The reason is simple: As one sign follows the other in the zodiac, they alternate energies, much like the Yin/Yang principle of eastern philosophy. The universe is made up of opposites that complement each other: light and dark, hot and cold, black and white, hard and soft. One is not better than the other; rather, each is essential to the existence of its opposite. In other words, you can't have one without the other.

The six fire and air signs are "masculine," since fire and air are connected with *active, assertive, outgoing* energy.

Aries	Gemini
Leo	Libra
Sagittarius	Aquarius

The six water and earth signs are "feminine," because water and earth represent *reactive, inner-directed, receptive* energy.

Taurus	Cancer
Virgo	Scorpio
Capricorn	Pisces

To put it simply, *the masculine fire and air signs are positive, while the earth and water signs are negative.* To remain neutral and avoid placing a higher value on one or the other kind of energy (or sign) it is useful to think of a battery with positive and negative poles. Without both, it simply doesn't work.

Though the masculine/feminine division of the signs has nothing whatever to do with human physical sexuality or sexual preference, it has very important implications for human behavior. Bluntly put, women born into male signs can be more "masculine"/achieving/competitive than men born into female signs. On the other hand, men born in female signs can be more "feminine"/nurturing/cooperative than women born into male signs. Both men and women born into signs that match their own sex may overemphasize the behavior and attitudes connected with that gender. The ideal person, psychologically and metaphysically speaking, has a healthy mix of both masculine and feminine attitudes. Without at least some of both, we cannot be whole people, able to encompass and understand the total range of human emotions, desires, drives, and goals. Since none of us is perfect, just about everyone could stand a bit more gender blending. Your astrological sign offers some excellent clues about how you can accomplish that.

Since Taurus is a feminine sign, the women born into it are generally comfortable with themselves but often unduly passive. Taurus men, on the other hand, find it easier than many other males to be tender and caring, but they do not always like to show it for fear they may look like pushovers, both in love and business. The Taurus sex role dilemma is clear: A Taurus woman who wants to achieve masculine goals must learn to become more self-assertive. Taurus men should *not* repress their soft side but rather learn to use it to their advantage. Keep these things in mind as you read the following Taurus portraits, and you will better understand the why of your Taurus behavior.

16

The Taurus Female

Salt of the Earth

The sign of Taurus turns out some of the strongest women in the zodiac—yet some of the softest as well. It is one of the best signs for a woman to be born into, especially at this particular point in time. The Taurus woman can feel free to develop her talents in any competitive field without fear of losing her femininity. It is so firmly ingrained that it would be very difficult for her to do so. Yet, Taurus women are perfectly able to go it alone, and be both productive and happy without a partner in their personal lives. Catherine the Great was a Taurus, as is Queen Elizabeth II, and there is no doubt there is something queenly about a mature Taurean female. However, the Taurus woman very often grows up in a female-dominated household, where her mother was the stronger of her two parents—at least in her eyes. It is highly likely she had a mother who bore a great deal of responsibility, while her father was more passive. In some ways, this creates problems for the Taurus woman who seeks an equal partnership with a mate, because she does not always respect the masculine principle in its pure form.

As a child, the Taurus girl is usually a fairly docile type. Many Taurus children of both sexes are a bit repressed because it is not in their natures to fight back against parental orders. However, the Taurus girl learns early that if she digs in her heels and refuses to budge, she can wear out the opposition. The Taurus girl is rarely as spontaneous a leader as her peers of other signs, though she's not exactly a follower either. If what her playmates want to do doesn't suit her mood of the moment, she will rarely suggest or insist on doing something else. She will simply retire into her own little world where she feels peaceful and secure. Once again, she will win in her own way. Though the Taurus girl is often mothered to death by the parent of her same sex, she usually feels in sympathy with her father. She can team up with him against her mother—emotionally speaking, at least—whom she sees as rather heavy-handed with her father too. Taurus girls, unless there is some other strong astrological influence, are "all-girl." Even if they try to hide it, as some tomboy types do, there is no mistaking the feminine heart that beats inside that nicely shaped little body.

As a young woman, Taurus is able to negotiate the twin roads of work and romance without going overboard in either direction. Taureans of both sexes tend to marry late, probably out of a natural sense of caution and the intuitive knowledge that the only kind of relationship that makes sense for them is the one that is for keeps. Many Taurus women choose careers in the arts or something related to them under the impression—mistaken perhaps—that there is less dog-eat-dog competition. The fashion and beauty fields appeal to them too, because they are by their very nature feminine pursuits. However, Taurus comes by a good head for business so naturally that many Taurus women find themselves running the show before they know it.

Meanwhile, in their personal lives, they are trying to make an accommodation between their strong desires for physical passion and mothering and their equally strong fear of getting stuck with the wrong person. Many young Taurean women try live-in arrangements—which are best for them—only to find they are so deeply entrenched in that way of life that the breakup is totally devastating. When the Taurus woman loses her man, she loses her warm cocoon, her emotional security, and everything that goes with it. Some get so hurt so early that they literally try to live without love; convents are very Taurean. In her sexual life, the Taurean woman has natural instincts that make her very direct and very spontaneous. Taurus is also loyal by nature, and the

Taurus woman may suffer deep guilt when she's the one to call it quits in a nonmarital relationship.

As a mate, the Taurus woman is just about the best wife in the zodiac, in the good old-fashioned sense of the word. When she settles down, she is really determined to make a warm and happy home for her husband. She may well continue in her career, because she is intensely practical and eager to own the finer things. But, no matter how far she goes in the business world, her home will be where her heart really is. The Taurus woman likes to care for her husband, and will also provide him with a quiet but receptive sounding board for his troubles in the outer world. Is she perfect? Hardly, because it is the Taurus woman who runs almost the greatest risk of turning into the slightly sloppy housekeeper who's also a bit overweight and likes nothing better than to sit home by the fire. Some men might not notice, but most men will, and the Taurus woman must keep ever alert. If she goes that route, she could lose her man, whom she loves more than anything else in the world.

As a mother, the Taurus woman plays the role very well, and she may secretly love her children more than she loves her man. But it is as a parent that the Taurus woman faces her biggest challenge, because she can become the classic, overprotective, possessive, dominating mother, even though she saw and disliked such things in her own childhood. Suddenly she starts remembering how wonderful it was to be pampered, to be taken care of, fed too much and too well, and begins the same pattern with her own children. Though the Taurus woman is not particularly independent, she is very strong. But if she isn't careful, she will *not* pass on that strength to her children, but turn them into the type of people who go through life looking for a mommy. "Live and let live" should be the Taurus mother's motto.

17

The Taurus Male

Raging Bull/Sweet Romantic

The Taurus male has a great shot at becoming "androgynous" in the best sense of the word. His astrological heritage gives him the solidity and building power of the earth element *plus* the soft side a feminine sign confers. If he plays his cards right, there is little he cannot accomplish in love and in business. However, the Taurus male does not always know how to go about getting it together, because he's a little mixed up about his own sexuality. Like the Taurus female, he most often grew up in an atmosphere where mommy was strong—almost frighteningly so. He adored her, but feared her as well. Daddy wasn't too much help because he had a bit of trouble understanding his sweet little boy, and nobody in the family talked about their feelings. However, the Taurus male who's taken the trouble to get to know himself is quite comfortable with the fact that he likes to bake bread as much as he likes to close a business deal or build a house. It is all constructive activity, which is essential to the Taurean nature, and he satisfies both parts of his androgynous soul. Taurus men can be sweet one minute, sexy the next, and totally involved in worldly affairs immediately following that.

As a child, the Taurus boy can confound his parents by switching from patient, peace-loving Ferdinand the Bull into the classic snorting, dangerous beast right before their eyes. Sooner or later they will get the clue; never, *never* tell Taurus to do something "because I say so." The young Taurus male—like his female counterpart—will be utterly reasonable, as long as you are too. Early in life the Taurus male starts exhibiting some of the traits that will serve him well in the business world. If you explain *why*, he will listen patiently, consider your argument, and make a fair decision—at least in his own mind. All Taurus children are sturdy and active; it is only later that they slow down to a walk. The Taurus boy is likely to excel in sports that require strength and endurance. However, his parents should recognize that under his "all-male" exterior, there is a sweet and loving child who wants to be hugged. Taurus males who are denied tactile love early in life are the ones who have the hardest time with their own sexuality.

As a young man, Taurus starts out on the right foot by exhibiting a built-in sense of responsibility, which immediately earns him points on the job. His conscientiousness may not be backed up by burning ambition, however, unless something excites him. Many Taurus men are caretakers rather than entrepreneurs, being happier with what's safe and steady than with what's risky. The same pattern applies in his single, romantic life, which is likely to go on into his mid-thirties. Like his Taurus sister, he can't be rushed into anything permanent. However, his affairs are likely to be sweet, but not short. The Taurus man likes to be settled, and the arrangement that most resembles a marriage will be the most comfortable for him. If he has the bad luck to choose a live-in companion who bores easily, before long he will be cooking dinner for one.

Most Taureans are wonderful lovers, and the young male Taurus combines sweetness with sexiness in a way many women find hard to resist. He is also considerate and romantic at the same time. However, if he sounds like a paragon, consider this: When the male Taurus finally decides to choose a wife, he is deadly serious and sometimes dangerous. A thwarted, jilted Taurean suffers intensely—and loudly.

As a mate, the Taurus male is generally a classic good husband, similar to his female counterpart. He is a good breadwinner who will always provide and never complain about working hard. He is so loyal and faithful that he is likely to become blind to the lure of other females. Even the thought of divorce is anathema. The Taurean male is totally devoted to wife, home, and family: He may be sloppy, but he is sweet, and he likes to help around the house. Naturally, there is a twist to this arrangement: The Taurus male is determined to take care of his woman *totally,* so if she wants to work and prove herself in her own right, she usually has a battle on her hands. Eventually the Taurus male will give in, but woe to the woman who lets her outside job interfere with her "real job,"—which is what her Taurus husband considers her home duties and responsibilities. She can expect either sullen silence or a full-scale stampede by the raging bull. The best Taurus husbands are those who are comfortable enough with their masculinity to let their wives express their own achieving side. Then you've got a great combination: a man who's proud of his wife and passionate about her as well.

As a father, the Taurus male generally excels. In fact, most Taurus fathers are excellent "mothers," better than many women, especially those born into masculine signs. If the Taurus father is typical, he may want more than fifty percent of the responsibility for his children. He will be interested in and oversee their lives at school, their lessons (generally music) and their budding social lives. In fact, Taurus fathers can be a bit overbearing—particularly for a fire-sign child. The loving Taurus father may also expect all his children to be as reasonable and malleable as he was. Nonetheless, his children will grow up with wonderful memories of a gentle dad who was never ashamed to roll up his sleeves and give them a bath and read to them before bed. Taurus fathers, Taurus mothers, instinctively know what makes children feel warm and secure.

18

Taurus Help Wanted

Selecting a Career/Your On-the-Job Style

A vitally important aspect of your successful Taurus game plan is making sure you land in the "right" job or career—i.e., the one that best suits your native talents and tendencies. It is more than a truism that people perform better doing what comes naturally. There are some natural careers for Taurus, and they all have several common denominators. It is not possible to list *all* the specific jobs a Taurus should do well at, but there are some Taurus images that provide useful guidelines. Though you may not literally end up *doing* any of these things, conjure up an idea of what it takes to do the following jobs, and you'll have a better handle on what kind of inner resources Taurus people have available to them for career success.

Accountant	Banker/investment counselor
Botanist	Construction worker/architect
Baker/chef	Fashion designer
Stock breeder	Gynecologist/obstetrician
Interior decorator	Real Estate
Muscian/music teacher	Nurse

Equally important to finding the best job slot for you is understanding how your Taurus sun sign affects your modus operandi on the job. And your potential for moving up. Every sun sign has certain success skills that can smooth and widen the career path, as well as blind spots that can cause roadblocks. The more you know about both, the better off you will be.

Taurus has all the basic equipment to make an excellent executive. This sign's fixity of purpose makes up for what can sometimes be inertia or lack of ambition. This is often the scenario: The Taurus employee does a good, steady careful job, and keeps a low profile. However, his/her sense of responsibility and generally good performance eventually gets noticed, and Taurus is singled out for promotion. This money-loving sign will be delighted with a boost in pay, but will have grave doubts about moving up the ladder into new territory. Many a successful Taurus executive has been *dragged* to the top of the heap, kicking and screaming all the way.

Taurus people can always be counted on to conserve, to consolidate, and to organize resources for the long haul. They can withstand shocks and stress far better than they can tolerate going out on a limb, however. The result may seem like a lack of imagination; more often it is a better-safe-than-sorry attitude about life in general.

The Taurus boss can be a harridan, demanding and rigid. He/she wants it this way, and that's that. The Taurean way of managing is very autocratic. However, Taurus has very soft shoulders, and is always willing to help and listen to those who work for him/her. Taurus will be understanding about personal problems and eager to help. However, Taurus has little tolerance for those who chronically complain. Life is real, life is earnest, and there are few good excuses for not performing.

Excellent judgment, an intense sense of responsibility, and a practical approach to the most knotty problems are attributes that should take Taurus far in any career he/she chooses, as long as it has a Taurean twist. For best success, look for fields in which you take care of others or have the opportunity to utilize your extremely strong sensibilities and your delight in the creature comforts.

19

How "Pure" a Taurus Are You?

Your Moon Sign ... Your Rising Sign

No one is a pure Taurus—or pure anything for that matter—when it comes to astrological signs. As you will learn when you read "Defining Terms," there are many other factors in a horoscope that add up to the total person that is you. Yes, there are twelve basic personality types according to the zodiac, but within those broad groups there are almost infinite variations.

Though you are a Taurus at the core, and can count on the portrait of your sun sign to define you in essence, the two other horoscope factors that count most are in your personality profile: your moon sign and your rising sign. Many people know their moon sign; anyone can quickly determine it via an ephemeris. If you know your birth time at least within one hour, you can use the table in this book to find out what your rising sign is.

The Moon—Your "Dark Side"

Almost more than your sun sign, your moon sign indicates what makes you run. Most of the time, you do not know it yourself, because the moon is your subconscious, your "dark side" not because it is bad, but because it is hidden. When the meaning of your moon sign is added to your Taurus sun sign, it is a fuller picture and a better indicator of your probable personality. Here's how a Taurus sun sign mixes with each of the moon signs.

Taurus sun sign/Aries moon sign With this moon sign, you should have lots more drive than the typical

Taurus—but you could drive some people crazy. You are a fanatic organizer who believes everyone but everyone should see it and do it your way. You are also more independent than the norm, which is excellent in terms of your business life. It could also make you a bit less domesticated in your personal life, which is not a bad thing.

Taurus sun sign/Taurus moon sign   You are solid oak in terms of your dependability and high sense of responsibility. It is almost impossible for you not to follow through on what you promise. However, it is almost equally impossible for you to change your course once you have determined it. Rigidity and a refusal to see change when it is on the horizon are traits you should attempt to overcome.

Taurus sun sign/Gemini moon sign   A great combination, because your directional sun sign gives your directionless moon sign a straight line to follow. You are generally more imaginative than the typical Taurus, but may hesitate to express your ideas. Put them in writing, because your verbal skills should be excellent. You could be something of a flirt.

Taurus sun sign/Cancer moon sign   You run the risk of being a sensationalist who constantly seeks new thrills for the body and to a certain degree for the mind. Put the tendency to good use and avoid overindulgence. You also tend to be ultrasensitive, and even timid. However, your imagination is greater than the typical Taurean's.

Taurus sun sign/Leo moon sign   You are a very loving lover but an equally hating hater; all your emotions and opinions tend to be extreme. You are quite sound, of body as well as of mind, and this sun/moon combination could take you far. If you don't watch it, you could go overboard and turn into a self-pampering sybarite. Your love life will be especially stormy.

Taurus sun sign/Virgo moon sign   The good part is that you are generally more adaptable than the typical Taurus, easily reacting more positively to the suggestions of others. The bad part is that you can be overly demanding and critical of others. You may even run the risk of being somewhat self-righteous—especially about your hard-working attitude. Lighten up.

Taurus sun sign/Libra moon sign Stubbornness is increased in this combination, often to a real fault. Your feelings may dominate your reasons, so that when you dig your heels in, you can't even give others a good reason why. This is a particularly sensuous pairing of sun and moon, and you are highly emotional and romantic. It is wise to attempt to develop your logical side so that you will not be led astray by your own emotion or by other people.

Taurus sun sign/Scorpio moon sign Vanity, ultra-conservatism and secretiveness come along with this sun/moon pairing, as do possessiveness, jealousy and high appetites. More than many—and especially more than many Taureans—you will have to learn self-control if you are to live a productive and happy life. On the positive side, you have enough drive to take yourself to the heights of success.

Taurus sun sign/Sagittarius moon sign You talk a lot faster and act a lot more impulsively than others of your sign. You are quite optimistic and have a high energy level. However, you may promise more than you deliver because you can waste a lot of that energy in meaningless fits of overwork. Try to develop a slower but steadier modus operandi. Let your Taurus sun be your guide.

Taurus sun sign/Capricorn moon sign With this combination, you are capable of not only making carefully laid and highly ambitious plans, but of carrying them out as well. You should be an exemplary person who wants to uplift everyone else as well. On the less positive side, you could be extremely materialistic and conventional to the point of dullness. Broaden your horizons.

Taurus sun sign/Aquarius moon sign Practical and prudent, you are also totally sincere in your desire to help others. Your keen mind is firmly ensconced in a constructively work-oriented body. However, you may lack some of the softness and sweetness of the typical Taurean. It is a sense of duty more than a sentimental urge that leads you to take others under your wing.

Taurus sun sign/Pisces moon sign   This is an ultra-receptive combination—receptive both to people you love, and those you hardly know. You love nothing more than peace and harmony—unless perhaps good food, good drink, and good living. Don't always be as kind to yourself as you are to others, and don't be such a pushover for compliments.

Your Rising Sign—Know Your Cover

The third of the "big three" astrological factors is your rising sign, which you can think of as an *overlay* to your sun sign. Although it does not carry the psychological weight your moon sign does, your rising sign is also unconscious because it is a mode of external behavior that comes so naturally to you you may not be aware of it. In a sense, your rising sign is your cover. It can never totally obscure the real you of your sun sign, but it can temporarily mask that sign, especially when people first meet you. Here's what happens to Taurus when you lay a rising sign over typical Taurus behavior:

Taurus with Aries rising   You appear to be more energetic and assertive than you are. People are surprised when they find out how relaxed you can be.

Taurus with Taurus rising   You are a true pleasure-loving type, and you may look it as well. People are instantly attracted by your warmth.

Taurus with Gemini rising   There's real substance in what you say, even though you may talk too much. Often about money.

Taurus with Cancer rising   Male or female, your sexuality really shines through. The opposite sex finds it hard to resist.

Taurus with Leo rising   Your enthusiasm is refreshing, and you often turn out to be the life of the party.

Taurus with Virgo rising There is a natural shyness in you that people may take for standoffishness. Practice being more outgoing.

Taurus with Libra rising It's possible you are very easy on the eyes—and on other people. You are the perfect host or hostess.

Taurus with Scorpio rising You may appear tougher to deal with than you really are, and this works to your benefit. Stick with it.

Taurus with Sagittarius rising You are among the more jovial of God's creatures. Your apparent interest in others turns out to be real.

Taurus with Capricorn rising Though at first you seem to fight, you quickly join. Be careful not to come off as crusty.

Taurus with Aquarius rising You are not as freewheeling as you seem. You surprise people by backing up your wild ideas with practical good sense.

Taurus with Pisces rising Your charm is great, but could be too much. Try not to be too effusive on first meeting someone.

20

Find Your Rising Sign

It is easier than many people think to find out your rising sign. One reason is that it is based on "universal" or "sidereal" time—the measure used in space travel. To ascertain your rising sign, look through the following chart and locate the birthdate nearest your birthdate; look across and locate the time nearest your birth time. Remember that if daylight saving time was in effect at your birth, you must subtract one hour from the time stated on your birth certificate. In the section for your date and time, you will find an abbreviation for the sign that was rising when you were born. For instance, if your birthdate is June 12 at 9:30 a.m., your rising sign is Leo; if you were born on the same date at 9:30 p.m., your rising sign is Capricorn.

You will notice that the *year* you were born does not affect your rising sign. However, the geographical latitude does. These tables are calculated for the middle latitudes of the United States. If you were born far to the south, it is wise to look at the sign that *follows* your rising sign as well. If you were born far to the north, check out the *previous* sign.

Rising Signs—A.M. Births

	1 AM	2 AM	3 AM	4 AM	5 AM	6 AM	7 AM	8 AM	9 AM	10 AM	11 AM	12 NOON
Jan 1	Lib	Sc	Sc	Sc	Sag	Sag	Cap	Cap	Aq	Aq	Pis	Ar
Jan 9	Lib	Sc	Sc	Sag	Sag	Sag	Cap	Cap	Aq	Pis	Ar	Tau
Jan 17	Sc	Sc	Sc	Sag	Sag	Cap	Cap	Aq	Aq	Pis	Ar	Tau
Jan 25	Sc	Sc	Sag	Sag	Sag	Cap	Cap	Aq	Pis	Ar	Tau	Tau
Feb 2	Sc	Sc	Sag	Sag	Cap	Cap	Aq	Pis	Pis	Ar	Tau	Gem
Feb 10	Sc	Sag	Sag	Sag	Cap	Cap	Aq	Pis	Ar	Tau	Tau	Gem
Feb 18	Sc	Sag	Sag	Cap	Cap	Aq	Pis	Pis	Ar	Tau	Gem	Gem
Feb 26	Sag	Sag	Sag	Cap	Aq	Aq	Pis	Ar	Tau	Tau	Gem	Gem
Mar 6	Sag	Sag	Cap	Cap	Aq	Pis	Pis	Ar	Tau	Gem	Gem	Can
Mar 14	Sag	Cap	Cap	Aq	Aq	Pis	Ar	Tau	Tau	Gem	Gem	Can
Mar 22	Sag	Cap	Cap	Aq	Pis	Ar	Ar	Tau	Gem	Gem	Can	Can
Mar 30	Cap	Cap	Aq	Pis	Pis	Ar	Tau	Tau	Gem	Can	Can	Can
Apr 7	Cap	Cap	Aq	Pis	Ar	Ar	Tau	Gem	Gem	Can	Can	Leo
Apr 14	Cap	Aq	Aq	Pis	Ar	Tau	Tau	Gem	Gem	Can	Can	Leo
Apr 22	Cap	Aq	Pis	Ar	Ar	Tau	Gem	Gem	Can	Can	Leo	Leo
Apr 30	Aq	Aq	Pis	Ar	Tau	Tau	Gem	Can	Can	Can	Leo	Leo
May 8	Aq	Pis	Ar	Ar	Tau	Gem	Gem	Can	Can	Leo	Leo	Leo
May 16	Aq	Pis	Ar	Tau	Gem	Gem	Can	Can	Can	Leo	Leo	Vir
May 24	Pis	Ar	Ar	Tau	Gem	Can	Can	Can	Leo	Leo	Leo	Vir
June 1	Pis	Ar	Tau	Gem	Gem	Can	Can	Can	Leo	Leo	Vir	Vir
June 9	Ar	Ar	Tau	Gem	Gem	Can	Can	Leo	Leo	Leo	Vir	Vir
June 17	Ar	Tau	Gem	Gem	Can	Can	Can	Leo	Leo	Vir	Vir	Vir
June 25	Tau	Tau	Gem	Gem	Can	Can	Leo	Leo	Leo	Vir	Vir	Lib
July 3	Tau	Gem	Gem	Can	Can	Can	Leo	Leo	Vir	Vir	Vir	Lib
July 11	Tau	Gem	Gem	Can	Can	Leo	Leo	Leo	Vir	Vir	Lib	Lib
July 18	Gem	Gem	Can	Can	Can	Leo	Leo	Vir	Vir	Vir	Lib	Lib
July 26	Gem	Gem	Can	Can	Leo	Leo	Vir	Vir	Vir	Lib	Lib	Lib
Aug 3	Gem	Can	Can	Can	Leo	Leo	Vir	Vir	Vir	Lib	Lib	Sc
Aug 11	Gem	Can	Can	Leo	Leo	Leo	Vir	Vir	Lib	Lib	Lib	Sc
Aug 18	Can	Can	Can	Leo	Leo	Vir	Vir	Vir	Lib	Lib	Sc	Sc
Aug 27	Can	Can	Leo	Leo	Leo	Vir	Vir	Lib	Lib	Lib	Sc	Sc
Sept 4	Can	Can	Leo	Leo	Leo	Vir	Vir	Vir	Lib	Lib	Sc	Sc
Sept 12	Can	Leo	Leo	Leo	Vir	Vir	Lib	Lib	Lib	Sc	Sc	Sag
Sept 30	Leo	Leo	Leo	Vir	Vir	Vir	Lib	Lib	Sc	Sc	Sc	Sag
Sept 28	Leo	Leo	Leo	Vir	Vir	Lib	Lib	Lib	Sc	Sc	Sag	Sag
Oct 6	Leo	Leo	Vir	Vir	Vir	Lib	Lib	Sc	Sc	Sc	Sag	Sag
Oct 14	Leo	Vir	Vir	Vir	Lib	Lib	Lib	Sc	Sc	Sag	Sag	Cap
Oct 22	Leo	Vir	Vir	Lib	Lib	Lib	Sc	Sc	Sc	Sag	Sag	Cap
Oct 30	Vir	Vir	Vir	Lib	Lib	Sc	Sc	Sc	Sag	Sag	Cap	Cap
Nov 7	Vir	Vir	Lib	Lib	Lib	Sc	Sc	Sc	Sag	Sag	Cap	Cap
Nov 15	Vir	Vir	Lib	Lib	Sc	Sc	Sc	Sag	Sag	Cap	Cap	Aq
Nov 23	Vir	Lib	Lib	Lib	Sc	Sc	Sag	Sag	Sag	Cap	Cap	Aq
Dec 1	Vir	Lib	Lib	Sc	Sc	Sc	Sag	Sag	Cap	Cap	Aq	Aq
Dec 9	Lib	Lib	Lib	Sc	Sc	Sag	Sag	Sag	Cap	Cap	Aq	Pis
Dec 18	Lib	Lib	Sc	Sc	Sc	Sag	Sag	Cap	Cap	Aq	Aq	Pis
Dec 28	Lib	Lib	Sc	Sc	Sag	Sag	Sag	Cap	Cap	Aq	Pis	Ar

Rising Signs—P.M. Births

	1 PM	2 PM	3 PM	4 PM	5 PM	6 PM	7 PM	8 PM	9 PM	10 PM	11 PM	12 MIDNIGHT
Jan 1	Tau	Gem	Gem	Can	Can	Can	Leo	Leo	Vir	Vir	Vir	Lib
Jan 9	Tau	Gem	Gem	Can	Can	Leo	Leo	Leo	Vir	Vir	Vir	Lib
Jan 17	Gem	Gem	Can	Can	Can	Leo	Leo	Vir	Vir	Vir	Lib	Lib
Jan 25	Gem	Gem	Can	Can	Leo	Leo	Leo	Vir	Vir	Lib	Lib	Lib
Feb 2	Gem	Can	Can	Can	Leo	Leo	Vir	Vir	Vir	Lib	Lib	Sc
Feb 10	Gem	Can	Can	Leo	Leo	Leo	Vir	Vir	Lib	Lib	Lib	Sc
Feb 18	Can	Can	Can	Leo	Leo	Vir	Vir	Vir	Lib	Lib	Sc	Sc
Feb 26	Can	Can	Leo	Leo	Leo	Vir	Vir	Lib	Lib	Lib	Sc	Sc
Mar 6	Can	Leo	Leo	Leo	Vir	Vir	Vir	Lib	Lib	Sc	Sc	Sc
Mar 14	Can	Leo	Leo	Vir	Vir	Vir	Lib	Lib	Lib	Sc	Sc	Sag
Mar 22	Leo	Leo	Leo	Vir	Vir	Lib	Lib	Lib	Sc	Sc	Sc	Sag
Mar 30	Leo	Leo	Vir	Vir	Vir	Lib	Lib	Sc	Sc	Sc	Sag	Sag
Apr 7	Leo	Leo	Vir	Vir	Lib	Lib	Lib	Sc	Sc	Sc	Sag	Sag
Apr 14	Leo	Vir	Vir	Vir	Lib	Lib	Sc	Sc	Sc	Sag	Sag	Cap
Apr 22	Leo	Vir	Vir	Lib	Lib	Lib	Sc	Sc	Sag	Sag	Sag	Cap
Apr 30	Vir	Vir	Vir	Lib	Lib	Sc	Sc	Sc	Sag	Sag	Cap	Cap
May 8	Vir	Vir	Lib	Lib	Lib	Sc	Sc	Sag	Sag	Sag	Cap	Cap
May 16	Vir	Vir	Lib	Lib	Sc	Sc	Sc	Sag	Sag	Cap	Cap	Aq
May 24	Vir	Lib	Lib	Lib	Sc	Sc	Sag	Sag	Sag	Cap	Cap	Aq
June 1	Vir	Lib	Lib	Sc	Sc	Sc	Sag	Sag	Cap	Cap	Aq	Aq
June 9	Lib	Lib	Lib	Sc	Sc	Sag	Sag	Sag	Cap	Cap	Aq	Pis
June 17	Lib	Lib	Sc	Sc	Sc	Sag	Sag	Cap	Cap	Aq	Aq	Pis
June 25	Lib	Lib	Sc	Sc	Sag	Sag	Sag	Cap	Cap	Aq	Pis	Ar
July 3	Lib	Sc	Sc	Sc	Sag	Sag	Cap	Cap	Aq	Aq	Pis	Ar
July 11	Lib	Sc	Sc	Sag	Sag	Sag	Cap	Cap	Aq	Pis	Ar	Tau
July 18	Sc	Sc	Sc	Sag	Sag	Cap	Cap	Aq	Aq	Pis	Ar	Tau
July 26	Sc	Sc	Sag	Sag	Sag	Cap	Cap	Aq	Pis	Ar	Tau	Tau
Aug 3	Sc	Sc	Sag	Sag	Cap	Cap	Aq	Aq	Pis	Ar	Tau	Gem
Aug 11	Sc	Sag	Sag	Sag	Cap	Cap	Aq	Pis	Ar	Tau	Tau	Gem
Aug 18	Sc	Sag	Sag	Cap	Cap	Aq	Pis	Pis	Ar	Tau	Gem	Gem
Aug 27	Sag	Sag	Sag	Cap	Cap	Aq	Pis	Ar	Tau	Tau	Gem	Gem
Sept 4	Sag	Sag	Cap	Cap	Aq	Pis	Pis	Ar	Tau	Gem	Gem	Can
Sept 12	Sag	Sag	Cap	Aq	Aq	Pis	Ar	Tau	Tau	Gem	Gem	Can
Sept 20	Sag	Cap	Cap	Aq	Pis	Pis	Ar	Tau	Gem	Gem	Can	Can
Sept 28	Cap	Cap	Aq	Aq	Pis	Ar	Tau	Tau	Gem	Gem	Can	Can
Oct 6	Cap	Cap	Aq	Pis	Ar	Ar	Tau	Gem	Gem	Can	Can	Leo
Oct 14	Cap	Aq	Aq	Pis	Ar	Tau	Tau	Gem	Can	Can	Can	Leo
Oct 22	Cap	Aq	Pis	Ar	Ar	Tau	Gem	Gem	Can	Can	Leo	Leo
Oct 30	Aq	Aq	Pis	Ar	Tau	Tau	Gem	Can	Can	Can	Leo	Leo
Nov 7	Aq	Aq	Pis	Ar	Tau	Tau	Gem	Can	Can	Can	Leo	Leo
Nov 15	Aq	Pis	Ar	Tau	Gem	Gem	Can	Can	Can	Leo	Leo	Vir
Nov 23	Pis	Ar	Ar	Tau	Gem	Gem	Can	Can	Leo	Leo	Leo	Vir
Dec 1	Pis	Ar	Tau	Gem	Gem	Can	Can	Can	Leo	Leo	Vir	Vir
Dec 9	Ar	Tau	Tau	Gem	Gem	Can	Can	Leo	Leo	Leo	Vir	Vir
Dec 18	Ar	Tau	Gem	Gem	Can	Can	Leo	Leo	Leo	Vir	Vir	Vir
Dec 28	Tau	Tau	Gem	Gem	Can	Can	Leo	Leo	Vir	Vir	Vir	Lib

21

Taurus Astro-Outlook for 1986

This is a year of renewed energy and a return of the fires of ambition for you, Taurus. The year 1986 could be a highly significant year because a lot of possibilities are out there for substantial moves ahead—in love, business, or any personal enterprise. Just show your willingness to make a big commitment, and big things can happen.

You are going to have to come to terms with your attitude toward spending and saving, and alter your style a bit in that area. Though there are indications that a windfall might come through in the nick of time for you after a big splurge, you are wise not to count on it. Better to work out a new and more solid plan for budgeting what you've got, saving and/or investing your money.

Though the sun appears to be shining brightly in your career life, there may be a few storms on the personal relationship front. If you're settled, don't unsettle things by giving in to an urge to argue, or by allowing minor tiffs to turn into highly charged conflicts. For some Taureans, the pressure will be on from a romantic partner—for marriage or a deeper, more passionate relationship. Selectivity is the key to success in this life area. Whatever you do, don't let a rocky relationship interfere with fulfilling those high ambitions of yours.

February's your best month to take a big leap forward—in love or business. April and June are great for just plain fun, and in July, a major change could occur in your domestic sphere (possibly marriage). For a more detailed map of your astro-outlook for the year, consult the day-by-day forecasts that follow.

22

Fifteen Months of Day-by-Day Predictions

OCTOBER 1985

Tuesday, October 1 (Moon in Taurus) You are at your most "Taurean" today—in every sense of the word. One thing that means is that you will be particularly susceptible to the lures of good food and good drink. Remember that there is a lot of work to be done—and that you are in great shape to do it. When a member of the opposite sex—or a business associate—indicates that you are being a bit stubborn, be willing to bend a little. You can impose your will rather easily, but it may not be the thing to do right now.

Wednesday, October 2 (Moon in Taurus) You are still riding high as the moon makes its monthly pass through your sign. Don't hesitate to step right up and make yourself heard; a lot of people should be willing to listen to what you have to say. However, take care not to be the ultimate Taurus when a situation arises that arouses your anger; try to be flexible enough to see that there is another point of view possible.

Thursday, October 3 (Moon Taurus to Gemini 8:26 a.m.) Your social instinct should be particularly strong today, and you may feel like spending some money so that a good time can be had by all. Great—as long as you don't overdo your generosity. Someone may offer you a deal that sounds absolutely terrific, but don't jump into it until you have checked out all the fine points. You may not be taking all the possibilities into consideration, and you could find yourself feeling as if you've been "taken in."

Friday, October 4 (Moon in Gemini) Today, you may find yourself doing a lot of thinking about what is most important to you; a recent setback may have made you realize that money isn't everything. You are on the right track, and you should take someone close to you into your confidence—and possibly arrive at a new outlook on income versus outgo. A Scorpio could be a good advisor in your current situation.

Saturday, October 5 (Moon Gemini to Cancer 8:42 p.m.) This is a good day to stick close to home—possibly sorting out some "memorabilia." You may get a bit nostalgic, however, so keep a tissue handy—and be prepared to get sentimental with someone you love. He/she will love you all the more for your "soft side." If you feel like taking a chance today, you could have some luck with the number 4.

Sunday, October 6 (Moon in Cancer) This is a day to put out the welcome mat for friends and relatives. If you don't entertain on your own home ground, you should get a lot of pleasure out of making a visit nearby. Whatever happens, you should have a warm glow of "family feeling"—no matter who you interact with. Be aware that you could overdo in the food or drink department; moderation should be a goal today.

Monday, October 7 (Moon in Cancer) You should start out the work week feeling rather "together." Throw yourself into a task that requires both diligence and sensitivity. Those you work with may be feeling a bit out of sorts, and you may be the one to let them know that it isn't wise to get overly emotional about the day-to-day routine. You may also have to remind yourself that it's a good idea to keep a positive outlook. The lucky number is 6.

Tuesday, October 8 (Moon Cancer to Leo 6:38 a.m.) Today, you would fight to the death to protect you and yours. Whatever situation arises, realize that you may overreact and make something rather small into a "cause célèbre." It is admirable to defend those you love, but it is foolish to "tilt with windmills." You are far better off doing something tangible to make your home base a pleasanter and more luxurious place to live—for everyone.

Wednesday, October 9 (Moon in Leo) If you dig in your heels today, you are going to run head-on into someone just as stubborn as you are. Even if you have to force yourself, keep an open attitude and be willing to compromise. Pride is an excellent thing, but it can be carried to excess. In your work situation, you should be able to exhibit your wonderful qualities of leadership. Take the praise that comes with a clear idea of how much you are worth.

Thursday, October 10 (Moon Leo to Virgo 1:24 p.m.) You could be particularly efficient and effective today; don't waste it on unimportant projects. Take advantage of your ability to concentrate and catch up on details. You could get a lot of satisfaction for yourself—and score some big points with those who count. Later on, take some time out for relaxation with someone you care about a lot. The lucky number is 9 today.

Friday, October 11 (Moon in Virgo) You wind up the week very much in the mood to indulge yourself. Go ahead—as long as it isn't excessive. Someone may try to appeal to your "soft side" and get you to put yourself out more than you are willing to do; realize that it is not necessary. Just think of how many times you have been the one to go more than halfway, and you will know that it is someone else's turn.

Saturday, October 12 (Moon Virgo to Libra 2:38 p.m.) It's inspiration you need today, and you could find it in some creative or artistic activity. Give in to that urge to express yourself—even if it is simply through making a few changes in your home environment. You may also feel like spending some money in a rather self-indulgent way. Realize that you deserve a certain amount of pampering—as long as you take others into consideration, too.

Sunday, October 13 (Moon in Libra) Take care not to tangle with someone today. You will not be the aggressor, but someone may take you to task in a way that you find unfair. If you can't reason with the person, just smile and say "you're right." Tomorrow is another day, and you can prove your point then. Meanwhile, you can spend a very productive day and end it with a real feeling of accomplishment.

Monday, October 14 (Moon Libra to Scorpio 2:50 p.m.) As hard as you try, you may find that the ball is in someone else's court today. If you feel as if you are running into obstacles, take the line of least resistance; realize that emotions are running rather high. Keep a low profile and try not to rock the boat more than someone else is doing. Some of you may find today brings a sensational emotional/sexual interlude. Enjoy!

Tuesday, October 15 (Moon in Scorpio) This is an excellent time to cooperate with others toward a mutual goal—one that both sides find equally important and involving. You may be particularly emotional about what you want, and what you want to get across to others. You can be very eloquent, as long as you keep your arguments reasonable. It is a day in which you can exercise a lot of power simply by being you.

Wednesday, October 16 (Moon Scorpio to Sagittarius 2:25 p.m.) Finances can sometimes take over for you, and this may be one of those days. Do not let your vision be clouded by economic issues, no matter how important they seem. The broad view and the long perspective are what is needed now. In fact, if you are willing to give up immediate gratification for future gain, you could make an absolute "killing" at this time. The lucky number is 6 today.

Thursday, October 17 (Moon in Sagittarius) For some Taureans, this could be a day when jealousy and possessiveness threaten to sabotage a relationship. Realize that your emotions are a bit out of control and a bit exaggerated. Step back and look at things as they really are, and you will discover the real truth. On the other hand, for some of you this could be a particularly creative time in which you are able to get in touch with some special talents. Stick with it!

Friday, October 18 (Moon Sagittarius to Capricorn 3:37 p.m.) You may be thinking rather "lofty" thoughts today—especially for someone with your practical turn of mind. Take advantage of it by gazing at the future with open eyes and an open mind. You may be amazed at the possibilities you see there. Meanwhile, don't neglect someone who wants to talk about a travel plan.

Saturday, October 19 (Moon in Capricorn) Yesterday's experiences make you think about what means most to you today. As you weigh things in the balance, you realize that personal relationships are the most important to you—followed quickly by your need to know and to go on with your education. You will talk with a number of people about this and consult them about a plan that will help you realize your goals. Start studying a foreign language; you might as well be ready.

Sunday, October 20 (Moon Capricorn to Aquarius 8:04 p.m.) Now you have a really clear, sharp focus on your long-range plans. You have found a couple of good advisors who are giving you sincere back-up in your search for guidance. The most constructive thing you can do today is to catch up on correspondence. There are people out there who are waiting to hear from you—and whose advice could be very helpful in your current situation.

Monday, October 21 (Moon in Aquarius) Everyday matters pull you in one direction—your new interests pull you in another. The best course today is to stick with the familiar and not branch out too far. Let a loved one know that domestic security faces no threat. Someone who has been a "teacher" in the past is available again; this is the person you should ask questions of, and confide your dilemma to.

Tuesday, October 22 (Moon in Aquarius) Today, you may look at yourself in the mirror and realize you've been neglecting something—yourself. As you become aware of your body image, you may decide to embark on a whole new program which includes proper diet, proper exercise, proper everything. You don't have to do it alone, however. There are lots of special services available that can help you in this new endeavor. Listen to a Gemini who has been through it. The lucky number today is 3.

Wednesday, October 23 (Moon Aquarius to Pisces 3:35 a.m.) You may be feeling a little bit dreamy today and the focus may be on romance—real or imagined. What you want most is emotional fulfillment, and it will come your way after a slight delay. Financial matters are an intrusion, but a necessary one. Pay attention to a Scorpio or a Leo who has a lot to say that is worth listening to.

Thursday, October 24 (Moon in Pisces) Your dreamy feelings are gone and you have every reason to be optimistic again. In fact, your desire for romance may be fulfilled. At any rate, you will feel extraordinarily creative today and you will easily be able to make your mark; the good impression you leave should enhance your sense of self-worth, and that is not all bad. For extra good feeling, try your luck with number 5.

Friday, October 25 (Moon Pisces to Aries 2:09 p.m.) Today, you get a second chance to prove yourself—don't knock it. Not only is it a rare occurrence; you also have the solid support of your family behind you. When you succeed, you will be in a mood to celebrate. When you gather friends together, don't forget a Libra or a Sagittarius who could be the life of the party. Your lucky number today is 6.

Saturday, October 26 (Moon in Aries) You are content to be alone today. Far from being lonely, the temporary seclusion gives you a chance to meditate. It's nice to retreat once in a while and realize there is a haven in the world. Have a quiet meeting later on with someone who appreciates you. Think about just how lucky you are.

Sunday, October 27 (Moon in Aries) This is the second day of a rather quiet weekend, and one that helps you restore your energy and your confidence. Someone you love underlines your feeling that you are on the brink of a major breakthrough. Don't be afraid to make big plans, because you can be more independent and have greater freedom of thought and action than you have right now. It's important to keep the faith.

Monday, October 28 (Moon Aries to Taurus 2:11 a.m.) This is the most important full moon of the year for you, Taurus. It should make you realize why you have had to go through what you have gone through recently. The result now is significant progress—especially in the area of communication with people who have been rather distant from you recently. In another matter, you are totally vindicated, and you could feel rather smug. Don't. Be grateful for the good things you have—including the fact that you are rid of an unnecessary burden. Don't be surprised if more people are listening to you now.

Tuesday, October 29 (Moon in Taurus) The influence of the full moon in Taurus continues, and you should be ready for a whole new start. It is time to lead rather than follow, and you may find you are catapulted into the leadership position. Don't hesitate to trust your own judgment; others will be embarrassed by their previous lack of confidence in you when they see you dancing to your own tune.

Wednesday, October 30 (Moon Taurus to Gemini 2:36 p.m.) You may come down off your "full moon high" today, but it will be with a gentle thump. The most comfortable base is your own home. Some good news will put the topping on a wonderful, comfortable scenario. A Cancer or an Aquarian may provide some excitement, but in the main things are smooth and unruffled. Indulge that urge to contact someone who has been rather elusive lately.

Thursday, October 31 (Moon in Gemini) Some nice things that have happened recently may make you feel like going out and celebrating. One way you could indulge that feeling is by buying some new things to wear. That way you will be ready when some more good news comes your way—in the form of a request that is finally granted. Celebrate with some fun friends, possibly a Gemini or a Sagittarian may be among them. Reserve some time for children on this trick-or-treat holiday.

NOVEMBER 1985

Friday, November 1 (Moon in Gemini) It is important to be very direct today when you must approach someone on a rather delicate subject. It is the only way to break the code of silence and find out what you have to know. Make it clear that your inquiries are meant in the most kindly way possible. In fact, the other person may benefit as much as you. Get a few tips from a Leo or an Aquarius who knows how these things go. The lucky number today is 1.

Saturday, November 2 (Moon Gemini to Cancer 3:12 a.m.) You may be a bit touchy today and feel like mourning over what you think is a lost cause. Your spirits should quickly revive when you realize you have an unexpected second chance to make it work. You may have to justify certain things and prove that you know you are on the right track. After that, it's smooth sailing. Call or drop in on someone you've been wanting to talk to for a while. You've got some pretty good things to talk about.

Sunday, November 3 (Moon in Cancer) This is far from a dull Sunday, and far from what you expected. You will find yourself with some very interesting people who have interesting things to say—even though they may challenge some of your most cherished beliefs. Keep an open mind and you will really learn something. You might even be asked to participate in a fascinating activity. The subject could be travel. Keep your sense of humor, and try your luck with number 3.

Monday, November 4 (Moon Cancer to Leo 3:12 a.m.) Don't get rattled when you have to make a quick change today—the word may come in a telephone call or letter. Understand that it is better to dump some plans you've made in favor of some that have a much stronger foundation. You don't have any choice anyway. The person you are dealing with—possibly another Taurus or Scorpio—is just as hardheaded as you are, and a lot more determined about this one. Relax, you'll love it.

Tuesday, November 5 (Moon in Leo) It's time to call in the experts; you can't always rely on yourself, even though you are rather savvy in these matters. This is a matter of property, and a rather important one. Listen carefully—it may make you realize you are being asked to give up something for nothing. On a lighter note, you may have a very exciting encounter with someone who makes you feel really good about yourself. Enjoy the feeling, and decide whether you want to pursue this.

Wednesday, November 6 (Moon Leo to Virgo 9:34 p.m.) There may be a mild uproar on the home front today—or tonight. You are going to have to deal with the fact that someone wants a greater say in certain matters. If you are smart, you will make some intelligent concessions—without giving away the store. Everyone has to adjust occasionally, even you.

Thursday, November 7 (Moon in Virgo) Your popularity may go to your head today. While you are having fun, look at people and things in a realistic light. It would be too easy for you to see the world through a romantic haze at this time. Enjoy the mood of the moment—and the fact that you could actually win something today. But recognize it for what it is. The lucky number today is 7.

Friday, November 8 (Moon in Virgo) Now you are coming down off your dizzying toboggan slide. You felt far more adventurous yesterday than you do today, which is just as well. You are going to have to have some emotional stability to deal with the demands that some people put on you today—perhaps some very young people who need a lot of guidance. Spend some time doing creative thinking, however, because you are particularly able to find unusual answers today.

Saturday, November 9 (Moon Virgo to Libra 1:14 a.m.) This may be a self-help weekend for you. First of all, you finish up a job you should have finished long ago. Then, you decide to spend some time working out a new diet which will make you look better and feel better. You may even make a new work schedule which tells you what you are going to do when; if you do, resolve to stick to it. Also on the positive side, you may no longer be burdened by someone who takes but never gives. You are well rid of him/her.

Sunday, November 10 (Moon in Libra) A dynamic person may come along today and give you a lot of encouragement about your new diet/exercise routine. In fact, it is such a constructive day for you that you may begin to feel a little smug. Realize that while *you* feel rather good about yourself, other people may not be of the same opinion. You may have to come down to earth and relate to people on their level. A Leo or an Aquarius could give you a run for your money.

Monday, November 11 (Moon Libra to Scorpio 1:53 a.m.) You may find it rather annoying today when a family member becomes overly protective of you. Could it be that you've been acting as if you need it? Resolve to put hypochondria aside and look at your health in a realistic way. There is nothing wrong with you that your new resolutions about diet and exercise will not cure. The lucky number today is 2.

Tuesday, November 12 (Moon in Scorpio) It is not too late to make some revisions in a contractual agreement. Be absolutely clear about what changes you want, and make them known to the people who can do something about it. You have every right to have your own ideas listened to—submit them in writing. You can get what you want without pushing today, because your public relations ability should be working quite well. That means you should be able to avoid a clash on the home scene.

Wednesday, November 13 (Moon Scorpio to Sagittarius 1:12 a.m.) You may be brave enough to get into an emotional battle today; it's been coming for a while, but you have not been able to face it until now. You may come out a bit bruised, but you will have made your point. Pay some attention to some more practical matters, too, like a loan you need and should be thinking about. You should not have any problems, because people see you as stable.

Thursday, November 14 (Moon in Sagittarius) Don't take anything for granted today and you will not be disappointed. Read between the lines and analyze someone's behavior; if you are persistent, you will reach the truth. It may not be all that bad, but you are better off knowing it. Listen to an associate who gives you some rather sound financial advice.

Friday, November 15 (Moon Sagittarius to Capricorn 1:10 a.m.) A moral issue surfaces and you cannot ignore it. It is a question of values—yours versus someone else's. You may realize that someone else is right, and that you are wrong. Take it with good grace, and realize that you have learned something. On a lighter note, discuss your holiday or vacation plans with those who will be part of them. Make sure everybody is in sync. The lucky number today is 6.

Saturday, November 16 (Moon in Capricorn) Today, it is easier for you to understand what really happened yesterday. Now you can put things in proper perspective and see where you were wrong. The good result of all of this is that you are now able to communicate much more easily with another person; you understand each other on new terms. You are inclined to reach higher in terms of your thinking than you have done before. A Pisces who discusses, may be instrumental in this.

Sunday, November 17 (Moon Capricorn to Aquarius 3:54 a.m.) In general, you are rather self-reliant, but today someone shows you up. The example makes you willing to accept more responsibility, not just because it is good for you, but because it makes you come out ahead in the long run. Because you are a practical person, you know there is more than one kind of reward. It is nice to be able to look in the mirror and smile, but it is equally nice to realize that there is more money in the bank. Your prestige is rising.

Monday, November 18 (Moon in Aquarius) It is easy for you to deal with a superior today. Your new approach proves very constructive, because it is both direct and creative. You show your independence and your ability to state your case in a confident manner. Take some time to relax later and have an intimate discussion with someone who loves you; there is no better listener. The lucky number today is 9.

Tuesday, November 19 (Moon Aquarius to Pisces 10:04 a.m.) Today, you realize there is a big wide world out there and that you can explore a bigger part of it. A new situation or a promotion puts you in a position where you will be doing just that. You may be a bit surprised when a member of the opposite sex tells you how interested he/she is in getting to know you better. Wait and watch this one; it is not wise to take anything for granted. A Leo may play a big role today.

Wednesday, November 20 (Moon in Pisces) A pleasure principle is emphasized today, as if you needed it emphasized! More than usual, you may be in a mood to celebrate with good food, good drink, and good friends. Better to indulge yourself that way than in emotionalism about a slight problem that arises. Realize that you are not altogether logical today. A family member helps you make a strong wish come true. Reciprocate if you can.

Thursday, November 21 (Moon Pisces to Aries 8:00 p.m.) Someone may get a bit mushy today and sing your praises too loudly. If you find it embarrassing, be sure to say so. Your own powers of persuasion are running particularly high and you could sell just about anything. Or anyone, and that includes a romantic partner. A recent career or business move has you feeling on top of the world. Take a risk and try your luck with number 3.

Friday, November 22 (Moon in Aries) Something or someone makes it necessary for you to pull in your horns today. It is only temporary, and the delay will work in your favor. Use this quiet time to keep a promise to someone who is not as able to get around as you are. Be patient and savor your privacy now; soon you will realize how precious it is.

Saturday, November 23 (Moon in Aries) It is better to lie back than to act right now; that would be premature. Bide your time and enjoy a romantic interlude. You may be swept up in some behind-the-scenes activities or meetings. Enjoy the feeling of being in on the know. Don't be tempted to do things the old way today; shopworn procedures are not what is needed now.

Sunday, November 24 (Moon Aries to Taurus 8:37 a.m.) You should be feeling a lot more secure with the moon now going into your sign. The frustration of the past several days is over, and you are glad to be rid of it. Things seem a lot brighter, and you even get some help from someone who helped you a long time ago, but whom you never thought that you would see again—at least in this role. It's possible that an unexpected gift will even come your way. Enjoy this rather special day. The lucky number is 6.

Monday, November 25 (Moon in Taurus) The chance you have been waiting for finally arrives today. Now you are ready to step forward into the spotlight, and start doing your very own thing. Whatever else happens today, you will be presented with an opportunity for a major advancement, and you should not overlook it. Listen carefully when you talk to someone—possibly a Pisces or a Virgo—who seems to know what is really going on.

Tuesday, November 26 (Moon Taurus to Gemini 9:02 p.m.) The pressure is building, but you should be welcoming the challenge. You've got what it takes at this time to make it where money and love are concerned. Suddenly you find yourself with the authority to make some changes; don't forget those plans you've been wanting to put into action. As you display your talents, people are noticing—possibly a Cancer or a

Capricorn who has great relevance to what can happen to you in the future. The lucky number is 8.

Wednesday, November 27 (Moon in Gemini) This full moon shines brightly in your house of money. Interpret that according to your current situation. If you are using your talents properly, it should mean some kind of increase in your income. If nothing else, by the end of this day you should find something you thought had been lost. On an equally mundane level, you could be finished with a task and rid of an unnecessary expense. An Aries, a Leo, or a Libra could be very prominent in the scenario today.

Thursday, November 28 (Moon in Gemini) The focus of the day is again on financial matters; don't expect to make a fortune, but use this time to make the most of your current assets. You should be feeling particularly adventurous, and willing to take the pioneer position in a project. A new relationship is on the threshold of change, and if you want to, you can really get those changes on the road today. The lucky number today is 1.

Friday, November 29 (Moon Gemini to Cancer 8:59 a.m.) The pieces of the puzzle are beginning to fall into place. Trust the conclusions you are arriving at now—as long as you have been properly analytical. You should feel confident and not lapse into self-doubt and brooding. Trust the reaction you get from some conservative people who admire your stability, and realize what you are worth.

Saturday, November 30 (Moon in Cancer) You are going to feel like you are all over the place today, no matter what you do. You'll have lots of little things to tend to and lots of messages to get across. The telephone may be your very best friend. This evening, be sure to attend a social event where you are invited. It may shake you up a bit, but you will be extremely entertained. And—believe it or not—rather relaxed. The lucky number today is 3.

DECEMBER 1985

Sunday, December 1 (Moon Cancer to Leo 8:04 p.m.) You may have felt a bit emotionally off-balance recently. Today, you recover your sense of standing on solid ground, and it may be through the help of someone who loves you very much. You can help yourself by retiring into some quiet meditation. It could work wonders, and let you see where you are at this point in time. If you must deal with others, make sure they are substantial people. One may be a Cancer or a Capricorn; listen, and heed this person's word.

Monday, December 2 (Moon in Leo) The thinking you did yesterday should set you on the right course today. You know you must look beyond the immediate, and make some plans for the future. The important thing is to give yourself lots of room; you don't need to tie yourself down right now. A commitment will wait. You may get the pleasant surprise that something you own is worth a lot more than you thought. Try your luck with number 3.

Tuesday, December 3 (Moon in Leo) You should prepare yourself to rebuild; something is resting on a rather flimsy foundation. If necessary, get professional advice. You could spend time very productively today going over some papers and seeing what is really there. With your temperament, it will make you feel a lot more safe and secure. You may receive additional support from an Aquarian, a Scorpio, or a Leo. The lucky number today is 4.

Wednesday, December 4 (Moon Leo to Virgo 4:38 a.m.) Today, you feel like kicking over the traces and having some fun. There is no reason why you shouldn't—particularly since you have been working so hard lately. Do whatever turns you on, from romping with children to expressing your creative talents. For some of you, romance may be right there—are you ready for it? Even if you are not, it's nice to know that someone finds you attractive.

Thursday, December 5 (Moon in Virgo) You are

going to have to adjust to others today, even if it is not to your liking. Console yourself by listening to a younger person who has some wonderful suggestions about how things can be made nicer to live with. You are a constructive type, so you should enjoy receiving constructive suggestions. The most helpful person on the scene today may be a Libra or another Taurus. Your lucky number today is 6.

Friday, December 6 (Moon Virgo to Libra 9:44 a.m.) Don't let wishful thinking fog your view today. Make sure you are really seeing what you think you see. If you define terms and set the record straight, you will cut through a lot of red tape and accomplish what needs to be done. Be diplomatic, however; if you force issues, you will intimidate others. Be the sweet rather than a stubborn Taurus today.

Saturday, December 7 (Moon in Libra) You have more power than you think in this situation. Remember that when you have to oversee what some other people do today; don't come down too hard. Your temper may not be the best, because there are so many things and people that demand your attention. Don't overreact to a reasonable request that comes from a relative. Relax, and try your luck with number 8.

Sunday, December 8 (Moon Libra to Scorpio 1:05 p.m.) Now you feel as if you are out of the woods, and you should be relieved. You seem to get along better with everyone today, even those at your own home base. In fact, a family member feels so comfortable with you that he/she confides a problem. Listen sympathetically, even if you are not totally sympathetic. We all have our foolish moments—even you.

Monday, December 9 (Moon in Scorpio) You are off and running today, ready for a new challenge, and perhaps a whole new start. Though you are feeling rather independent, you should make an effort to give your all to cooperative efforts today. Be willing to give, and you will get. As a reward, you may have a rather interesting encounter with somebody rather exciting. He/she is a welcome addition to your scene.

Tuesday, December 10 (Moon Scorpio to Sagittarius 1:11 p.m.) Lie low, go slow. Don't try to take the lead today, or you will end up losing everything. Make it a time to gather all the facts you need and get your ducks in a row; your cycle will rise very soon. In your patient mood, you may have to exercise particular patience with another Taurus or possibly a Leo. Realize that either one is equal to you in determination.

Wednesday, December 11 (Moon in Sagittarius) Try to shake off some potentially bitter feelings about a former friend—at least you thought that he/she was a friend. Look into the future and see what better things lie there. You may be feeling rather intrigued by the occult right now; allow yourself to investigate things that presently are beyond your understanding. You may find it an enlightening experience.

Thursday, December 12 (Moon Sagittarius to Capricorn 1:03 p.m.) Today, you make some sort of breakthrough—even though it may not be a major one, it gives you great satisfaction. For one thing, you may now have access to information that was previously withheld from you. It is almost amazing how you are able to put it to work for you now. You are a thrifty soul, and it makes you feel good to be able to salvage something you thought might have to be thrown away. Your lucky number is 4.

Friday, December 13 (Moon in Capricorn) The moon position puts you in the mood for adventure and change. Good for you! Explore as many new prospects as you can find, and don't be afraid to roam around new territory. Your judgment is right on target, so you can easily discern the motives of some people you get involved with today. However, with the quick-thinking type—possibly a Gemini or a Sagittarian—you should realize that you are over-matched.

Saturday, December 14 (Moon Capricorn to Aquarius 1:39 p.m.) You may not be in the mood for it when a family member brings up matters of money and budget—and the need to stretch things a bit in order to buy some needed items; take a deep breath, and make some concessions. Don't risk disturbing your peace; you know how much you love sweet harmony at home. Send your mind on a trip into the future—possibly with thoughts of a trip you would like to take. The number you should try today is 6.

Sunday, December 15 (Moon in Aquarius) Be ready for someone to give you a rather tough time today; don't bend when he/she tests you. If you stand your ground, you will find this person makes a turnabout that ultimately says you are okay. Though you may resent the experience, realize that it elevates your prestige and strengthens your standing in the community—whatever community of interest that is. Be tough yourself, and look behind the scenes where you will find more than superficial explanations. This is not a day to be shy; you may be on display more than you like.

Monday, December 16 (Moon Aquarius to Pisces 6:21 p.m.) You've got the power today; be sure you use it constructively. One way could be in making a relationship grow stronger. You are well able to influence the "other" at this time. A slight problem may arrive in your mailbox, but you should be able to handle it quite easily. If it's a matter of money and/or taxes, get the advice of someone rather good in that area—possibly a Cancer or a Capricorn. The lucky number today is 8.

Tuesday, December 17 (Moon in Pisces) Something comes from out of the blue today, and it fulfills one of your fondest dreams. It could be in tangible form—i.e., money or a gift—or it could be in the form of something you no longer have to do. If that is the case, you will breathe a big sigh of relief and you may find that you can use your new-found time to great advantage. Why not spend at least some of it having just plain fun? You also might try your luck with number 9 today.

Wednesday, December 18 (Moon in Pisces) You may feel as if you are a character in a spy thriller today. If you feel rather guilty about making some clandestine arrangement, remember that sometimes what people don't know won't hurt them. In another area, be open and direct and ready to state your views in a very positive manner. Someone else may do that to you today—and it could be a member of the opposite sex who tells you in no uncertain terms how attractive he/she finds you.

Thursday, December 19 (Moon Pisces to Aries 2:55 a.m.) You may be asked to give your opinion on a rather weighty subject today. Be prepared to probe inside yourself for the real answers. Realize this is no small matter, and what you say or do now will have great impact in the future. Someone with lots of energy gets you going today—and becomes a great new pal. Together you should be able to work wonders.

Friday, December 20 (Moon in Aries) You just know you are on the brink of something big. When someone makes you an offer, you sense that it is quite valid. It may be, but you should not hesitate to ask all the questions you have. An interesting friend may ask you to get together with him/her and plan a rather fun party. Let your imagination run wild, as it can sometime, and you will be able to cook up something great.

Saturday, December 21 (Moon Aries to Taurus 3:09 p.m.) Your sense of drama is running high today and you may find yourself playing a principal role in a rather intense scenario. Glamour and intrigue color your day. Don't let it distract you from things that need to be done, including a letter to be written or a call to be made. There is someone somewhere waiting to hear from you, and you feel a bit guilty about it. Another Taurus may be a good partner today.

Sunday, December 22 (Moon in Taurus) Now you feel the full force of the moon in your sign. Significant things could happen today, and they should all be in your favor. Your feelings are dominated by energy and optimism—and it feels good to be able to dance to your own tune. You are able to cut through things today and make quite accurate judgments. Don't miss any opportunities—including trying your luck with number 5.

Monday, December 23 (Moon in Taurus) You should look great and feel it today. In fact, you may be so aware of your image that you decide to do something about improving it. It may be exactly the right time to try that new diet. Your personality wins the day today, and you may be able to convince someone else to do something that you'd rather not do yourself. Don't get lazy!

Tuesday, December 24 (Moon Taurus to Gemini 3:46 a.m.) This should be a lovely holiday, in many respects. As you count your blessings, look back over this year and think about the number of people who have been good to you. Realize also that you deserve it—you sometimes take yourself for granted. Someone gives you a gift that is worth far more than its actual price, because it shows how much the giver really thinks of you.

Wednesday, December 25 (Moon in Gemini) Aside from all of the other wonderful things that happen today, someone who has been rather indifferent and even a touch cold lately will now come much closer and even confide a personal problem. Be willing to forget the past and to do what you can to help. When some minor things don't get done exactly the way you want them to, don't let it mar your holiday spirits. Today is not a day to be Taurean-perfect.

Thursday, December 26 (Moon Gemini to Cancer 3:41 p.m.) You realize that your money situation is more flexible than you thought; it's comfortable to feel comfortable and pleased with your assets. Just make sure holiday spirits do not cloud your perception of a situation. The best way to deal with it is to state your own intentions quite clearly. The lucky number is 9.

Friday, December 27 (Moon in Cancer) This full moon falls in the sector of your chart that has to do with communication with those right around you. It may highlight the necessity for a new approach. Don't get rattled when someone tries to pin you down about some plans; simply state what you'd like to do but indicate that you are willing to compromise. A fiery type—possibly a Leo or an Aries—will attempt to get you going today. Don't overreact.

Saturday, December 28 (Moon in Cancer) Today, you may focus on some things that need doing. Suddenly something looks quite threadbare and you see how it could be improved vastly. It's worth the expense. Before you do anything, consult an older individual who has dealt with this sort of thing before. He/she could be extremely helpful. The lucky number today is 2.

Sunday, December 29 (Moon Cancer to Leo 1:51 a.m.) If someone tries to back you against the wall today, refuse to be crowded. You may also have to restrain yourself from making some undiplomatic remarks. Focus on your own plans for the future, and realize you are not trapped—even if you may feel so now. Get out and get around with some spirited people who can lift your spirits.

Monday, December 30 (Moon in Leo) As you look back over this past year, you are able to see a total picture. Some things that were unclear at the time, now are defined for you. As a result, you feel stronger and more optimistic about the coming year. You might think about getting much more involved in some community or political activities you dipped your toe into this year. It could be a great outlet for your energy. If you are inclined to speculate today, a lucky number is 4.

Tuesday, December 31 (Moon Leo to Virgo 10:06 a.m.) Home is the place to celebrate this New Year's Eve, and those close to you probably agree. You may even have to dodge an invitation from someone who may be fun—but only in small doses. Don't get so mellow that you make a promise you may be sorry for later. As you wind up the year, be nice to yourself, but realize some things could stand improvement. Set realistic goals for yourself when you make your resolutions—but resolve to stick to them. Happy New Year!

JANUARY 1986

Wednesday, January 1 (Moon in Virgo) This is an excellent day to start off the New Year with. No matter what your activities today, you will do them with great style—and pleasure. For some, a new romance may be starting; for others, someone declares him-/herself and lets you know what his/her true feelings are. You can have a ball with a Leo or an Aquarian today.

Thursday, January 2 (Moon Virgo to Libra 3:45 p.m.) Your creative juices continue to flow today, and some may use them to "psych out" someone who is a bit difficult to understand. Your character analysis will be quite correct. This is a time to spend some serious thought on family relationships and matters of what belongs to whom. Try to think in the long term. A hunch you have now is very likely to be on target. The lucky number is 2.

Friday, January 3 (Moon in Libra) Once again you must use your analytical powers to take apart a person—or a situation. That may be the only way that you get to accomplish what needs accomplishing today. Diplomacy and humor would also be excellent weapons to keep at hand. Don't be too proud to ask someone for help; he/she is much closer to your point of view than you may think. Get set for an interesting weekend, and try your luck with number 3.

Saturday, January 4 (Moon Libra to Scorpio 7:44 p.m.) The bits and pieces are beginning to fall into place now, and you can see your way clear to completing something or building it from the ground up. What you build may not necessarily be a physical construction; it may be a whole new attitude or relationship. On a less lofty scale, many will have to put the nose to the grindstone today and get some nitty-gritty responsibilities out of the way. Others may be relying on your judgment now, and you should make sure it is as unbiased as possible. Surprisingly it is a Scorpio who would be the best one to consult in a rather touchy matter.

Sunday, January 5 (Moon in Scorpio) Your views may contrast sharply with someone else's today and the result could be an explosion. Try to see it coming, and possibly head it off. In everything, it is wise to go slowly today and check your facts at every stage. For some, it may be your most significant relationship—possibly your marriage—which is up for scrutiny now. For a lighter touch, have some fun with a Gemini or a Sagittarian. The lucky number today is 5.

Monday, January 6 (Moon Scorpio to Sagittarius 9:47 p.m.) Someone tries to rain on your parade today, but you come through beautifully. As a matter of fact, you surprise others by your remarkable resiliency—and your ability to make a comeback. In the process, you attract some new friends and allies who are drawn to your rather special way of doing things. They also are impressed at your having the courage of your convictions.

Tuesday, January 7 (Moon in Sagittarius) Continue to protect your flanks today, because there may be some offstage maneuvering going on. You are not usually a patsy, but you may have to take special care to protect your rights right now. If necessary, get legal counsel. A lighter scenario shows you hitting the jackpot—at least in terms of finding what you need to make the progress you want. It is not wise to take anything for granted today, however, because a bit of deception is in the air.

Wednesday, January 8 (Moon Sagittarius to Capricorn 10:42 p.m.) Now you are out of the woods, and your position is much stronger. As a matter of fact, someone may make a "settlement" that favors you. For some, the subject could actually be a legal one. Take some time out to examine your investment opportunities; you may find that you have resources you weren't even aware of. They could be financial—or they could lie right within your own tremendous capabilities. Talk it over with a Cancer or a Capricorn, for either one could be the key to some kind of a windfall. The lucky number today is 8.

Thursday, January 9 (Moon in Capricorn) Your

thoughts may go soaring off into the stratosphere today if you do not hold them down to earth. Stick with the work at hand, but do not totally suppress your vision of the future. For some, that could mean travel plans. By applying a bit of creative thinking you could get a messy project taken off your plate—and put on to someone else's. Don't feel guilty; you are right. The lucky number today is 9.

Friday, January 10 (Moon in Capricorn) Once again your thoughts should be riding high—and so should you. Grab at an opportunity to take the initiative and break new ground; you may surprise some people. Let them know you can be a leader as well as a follower. You will be feeling particularly industrious, but do not overdo in any area.

Saturday, January 11 (Moon Capricorn to Aquarius 12:01 a.m.) It is possible to take a giant step forward now. For some, that will mean a tangible change; for others, the advancement could be purely mental. Either way, things come out in your favor and you achieve a significant victory. Another aspect of the scenario indicates you should do some catching up on bookkeeping now; you might even need some help from an expert. Enjoy an invitation.

Sunday, January 12 (Moon in Aquarius) If you do not have some exciting plans for today, make some. It's a wonderful time to get out, get around, and zap up your social life. For some of you, this will bring an awareness of body image, and every aspect of personal appearance. If you are considering some personal overhauling, the timing is right now.

Monday, January 13 (Moon Aquarius to Pisces 3:39 a.m.) Don't dig in your Taurus hills when someone asks you to be flexible today; realize it is an intelligent concession you are being asked to make. In fact, you may find that the new regime enhances your pleasure as well. For some, creative pursuits could be particularly fulfilling today. It doesn't much matter what you do as long as you do it with gusto. A fond wish may come true—and you are the one who makes it so.

Tuesday, January 14 (Moon in Pisces) Someone around you could be very intense today, and express his/her feelings in a rather dramatic fashion. Don't let it throw you. Realize that there is some exaggeration in what he/she says. Physical attraction could play a large part in today's scenario; enjoy, but don't get carried away. A change comes about literally out of the blue—and it should be to your benefit. Have some fun with a Gemini or a Sagittarian.

Wednesday, January 15 (Moon Pisces to Aries 11:03 a.m.) Romance for some is the major theme today. It could be underscored by a gift with great sentimental value. For other Taureans, it is a day to enhance your physical surroundings—and possibly make a luxury purchase. Before buying, consult with another person who has a "good eye" like yours. It could be a Libra or another Taurus.

Thursday, January 16 (Moon in Aries) Some threads continue through this day. That means there is an aspect of bedazzlement which could cloud your vision; rub your eyes and see things clearly. Some will gain access to confidential information and should understand the necessity to be discreet. It could be a good day to try your luck with number 7.

Friday, January 17 (Moon Aries to Taurus 10:14 p.m.) For some, the pressure is really on and this day might be more full of responsibilities than you would like. In fact, some may be asked to do more than usual. Take it in your stride, and realize that rewards are highly possible. Some will be dealing with older people who have been there before; listen carefully and take the benefit of their experience to heart. The moon position highlights secrecy—possibly even confinement. A lighter time is coming.

Saturday, January 18 (Moon in Taurus) As the moon moves into your sign, your cycle swings upward. If you found it difficult to be heard yesterday, today you can state your views with authority—and a certainty that they will hit the mark. A stroke of light puts some in the right place at exactly the right time. Most will have reason to celebrate, and should do so with moderation. Steer clear of playmates who could lead you astray. The lucky number is 9.

Sunday, January 19 (Moon in Taurus) This is a day to express feelings openly; that applies to you as well as someone very important to you. No matter what the outcome, cherish the fact that you are getting to the heart of matters. Some will get an unexpected second chance to right something that has gone off course. Don't be afraid to speak up and speak your mind—show how original you can be.

Monday, January 20 (Moon Taurus to Gemini 11:12 a.m.) This is a day you can make a personal appearance with great confidence. Not only should you look great, your intuition and timing should be absolutely on target. Take advantage of the situation by brightening up the atmosphere—possibly even in the clothes you wear. In a slightly more subdued scenario, family and/or personal differences will be settled and harmony will reign again.

Tuesday, January 21 (Moon in Gemini) Take a look at your financial picture and take heart; it should be a lot brighter than it has been in the recent past. If that is not the case, you will at least find something that you thought was lost and gone forever. Possibly even stolen. Be willing to change plans at the drop of a hat today, and show that you are willing to laugh at your own little faults. Don't take things too seriously. Have a great time with a Gemini, a Leo, or a Sagittarian—any of whom could be very good for you today. The lucky number is 3.

Wednesday, January 22 (Moon Gemini to Cancer 11:14 p.m.) Your past could loom up before you today—be ready for it. Memories of all kinds are activated and it could be a bit painful. For some, a separation may be relieved; realize that what's done is done and you must move forward. For some, the emphasis will be on matters of money and how to manage it. Take a tip from a Scorpio or another Taurus. The lucky number is 4.

Thursday, January 23 (Moon in Cancer) You should be able to engage in a heated debate today without getting heated up. Good for you! It's wonderful to realize that a class of ideas can be fun and not the occasion for ruffled feelings. Know who you are dealing with, however, and be ready to change tactics at the drop of a hat. For some, a short trip is possible.

Friday, January 24 (Moon in Cancer) Someone offers you a constructive suggestion today, and you should take it in the right spirit. There are things you think no one can do better than you; that is not necessarily the case. Some may have a delightful bit of communication with someone who has not been in touch of late. Try your luck with number 6 today.

Saturday, January 25 (Moon Cancer to Leo 8:47 a.m.) Your patience may be tried once again today. Try to be gracious and cooperate with someone who asks you to extend a hand. For some, it may be necessary to give some TLC to someone who needs it badly. Others may find that a former antagonist now swings over to their side. Rejoice!

Sunday, January 26 (Moon in Leo) Last year's full moon continues to shine for you—right in the sector of your chart that indicates "home," in every sense of the word. It may be necessary to practice restraint and to review some of your most cherished ideas. Possibly even change them. For some, a promise is fulfilled and some past memories are revived in a most emotional way. For the most part, Taureans should have a great sense of emotional security today. In fact, someone may count on your stability and your "Rock of Gibraltar" stance.

Monday, January 27 (Moon Leo to Virgo 3:51 p.m.) If there is a question in your mind, the answer is—let it go. Realize that it is best to get rid of a losing proposition when you are losing. Though you may feel momentarily unsteady, you will quickly feel more secure and back on familiar ground. Don't listen to anyone who has a get-rich-quick scheme—it is built on sand. Some should try their luck with number 9.

Tuesday, January 28 (Moon in Virgo) A pleasant relief from tension colors this day. In fact, you should feel positively renewed. And in the mood for pleasure. Be the one to take the initiative and show that you can make an independent, creative decision. If you accept the challenge, you will find you have some boon companions who are willing to help you. One could be a Leo, and you are lucky to have such a staunch individual in your corner.

Wednesday, January 29 (Moon Virgo to Libra 9:10 p.m.) Watch out for emotions that could dominate your logic today; do not act impulsively. You may get thrown off your pins when the status quo gets shaken up. Realize it is only temporary. More than that, realize that you can rebuild something in a much more satisfactory manner. For some, today's scenario should include tossing out of the old—and making way for the new. If in doubt, throw it out.

Thursday, January 30 (Moon in Libra) Some Taureans will find themselves focusing in on the state of their health—and their bodies. And deciding something must be done. Remember, where there's a will there's a way—and you will find it. Take time out to counsel someone who asks your good advice. On the other side, you may get some unexpected support when someone volunteers to help you. The lucky number today could be 3.

Friday, January 31 (Moon in Libra) Don't gloss over some small details; it is important to look at the fine print and check out everything you see there. It could be the original sources are not correct—or unreliable. Those who are excessively set in their ways may find themselves in a bind today; realize that change must take place, and that it is usually positive. You can't hang on to things, people, or ideas forever. A Scorpio could be a wise mentor. The lucky number today is 4.

FEBRUARY 1986

Saturday, February 1 (Moon Libra to Scorpio 1:19 a.m.) Today it should be a relief to get back on your usual conservative course. And you may take great pleasure in concentrating on basic issues and certainties rather than any kind of speculative venture. Relax and enjoy things familiar, but don't let anyone accuse you of being dull. Make an effort to be at least a little bit sparky.

Sunday, February 2 (Moon in Scorpio) Try to look at things in the large today and see the whole picture. That way little things will bother you less. Once again, home seems to be the best place for you. Don't make it a totally solo day however; those closest to you will want to talk about things that matter. Open up and divulge your feelings; you won't be sorry you did. Some should be thinking about travel.

Monday, February 3 (Moon Scorpio to Sagittarius 4:31 a.m.) You get a surprise today when you find out someone has been holding out on you. The surprise may be a pleasant one, however, when it concerns money someone has been stashing away. Whatever happens, you are able to start thinking about building, buying, or acquiring something new. Be sure to get advice from someone who has been there before. A rather unusual person charms you—give in to the feeling!

Tuesday, February 4 (Moon in Sagittarius) You start the day out on a fresh footing ready for change—and it comes your way. To some it comes in the form of an unusual message from someone unexpected. You could possibly find yourself involved where you didn't realize there was any involvement at all. Others may have to plow through a lot of useless information to get at the part that matters. It could be an important clue that can help you put your finances in order. All in all, it is a day that you will check off as not quite the usual. Don't let it pass unnoticed.

Wednesday, February 5 (Moon Sagittarius to Capricorn 7:02 a.m.) This is a day for bartering and bargaining. Some may find themselves in a tense but eventually productive discussion about money and budgets; the arena seems to be your personal rather than your professional life. It is an excellent time to create a new living arrangement that may be a bit unusual but more comfortable for all involved. Diet may be on your mind and you should be able to be strict with yourself. The lucky number today is 5.

Thursday, February 6 (Moon in Capricorn) You may find yourself doing some tough thinking about the current state of your income—both monetary and psychic. Some of you may decide the current job or profession does not yield a sufficient amount of either. You would do well to start looking around because opportunities should abound. Some may run into that "mysterious stranger"; don't let his/her surface glamour fool you—this is a quite everyday person with whom you could click. The lucky number today is 7.

Friday, February 7 (Moon Capricorn to Aquarius 7:35 a.m.) For some, good news comes in, and it may have to do with that subject of job or career that was on your mind yesterday. Whatever happens, most of you will have added responsibilities—but possibly increased return for them. Pressure is definitely on, and that goes for your relationships as well. Realize that one of your ties is getting much stronger; know where you stand and what you intend to do about it.

Saturday, February 8 (Moon in Aquarius) You may find yourself a star today; enjoy the recognition and the temporary fame. Also try to figure out how you can turn this to your advantage on a long-term basis. Some will feel proud of themselves when they figure out a way to cut costs and thereby afford something frivolous; go ahead and treat yourself! An Aries or a Libra could be an excellent boon companion.

Sunday, February 9 (Moon Aquarius to Pisces 11:32 a.m.) Yesterday pleasant developments give you a "fresh start" feeling today. Some should act upon it by getting rid of a losing proposition—you've spent all you need to on it. An important interaction takes place with someone in a position to give you all sorts of valuable information; realize it is not a casual encounter. The pleasure principle is quite strong today, but you can indulge yourself quite safely.

Monday, February 10 (Moon in Pisces) It is gratifying to find yourself taken seriously today; your opposite number could be a romantic interest you have had for some time. If that is not the case, you derive satisfaction from someone who listens to what you say when you define terms. All in all, you are in a stronger position by the end of this day. You may have to grant a request from someone close; now that person owes you one. The lucky number today is 2.

Tuesday, February 11 (Moon Pisces to Aries 6:21 p.m.) Most would simply like to go over the hill today and have a ball; unfortunately, not all of you will be able to have that kind of freedom. You can utilize this day right where you are by recognizing that the elements of luck and timing are with you. It is no accident that you find yourself smack in the center of all kinds of activity—possibly even a love scenario. Enjoy your popularity and whistle while you work if you must. The lucky number today is 3.

Wednesday, February 12 (Moon in Aries) Your instinct to remain quiet and lie low today is a good one. A certain amount of discretion is necessary if you are to find out what you want to find out. By day's end many of your doubts will have vanished. Many are rebuilding—slowly but surely. Realize that the small gains that you are making are permanent. Listen to a Scorpio who has some excellent hints.

Thursday, February 13 (Moon in Aries) Don't let this day go by without realizing what you have to offer. For some, that means accepting an invitation to join a new group or attend a special class. Understand that your presence is highly desirable. All should be ready for a change, and some should be ready for an overture from a member of the opposite sex. It is sincere. The lucky number today is 5.

Friday, February 14 (Moon Aries to Taurus 5:38 a.m.) Valentine's Day coincides with the moon in your sign—and it's a fabulous combination! Whatever form it takes, love is lavished on you and you should delight in it. That delight might take a very physical form; your sex drive is on high as well. Take advantage of your favored position today by getting someone to make a concession to you.

Saturday, February 15 (Moon in Taurus) This looks like an excellent day all the way, with you in the driver's seat. Nothing seems to happen halfway so you should be prepared for extremes of all sorts. Keep it all in perspective—even the fanfare and terrific reception you get. You may be the victor, but be sure to share the spoils.

Sunday, February 16 (Moon Taurus to Gemini 5:17 p.m.) Romance may definitely be on your mind today, but it could get you off course. Enjoy all your good feelings, but be sure to stay alert—especially when someone makes you a promise. You may have trouble collecting later on. If someone seems insincere, insist on evidence that he or she will come through for you. The lucky number today is 8.

Monday, February 17 (Moon in Gemini) Someone who attempts to trip you up today is due for a rude awakening when he/she realizes how really sharp you are. You may have a hint of your enormous potential and a sense that the sky is the limit; it is, but you must finish what you start. On the other hand, you will be able to dump a burden that was really not yours in the first place. Check in with an Aries or a Libra today—either could play a very significant role.

Tuesday, February 18 (Moon in Gemini) You may suddenly become aware that a jealous individual is doing his or her best to hinder your progress. The revelation should make you resolve to be more independent and more willing to go out on a limb occasionally. Whatever happens, don't get rattled—you are doing just fine, even if you are the only one who seems to notice. The lucky number today is 1.

Wednesday, February 19 (Moon Gemini to Cancer 7:39 a.m.) You may have a tendency to let your thoughts drift today. It's true that you have a lot on your mind, but if you calm down and think clearly, you will be able to clarify your sense of direction. You could be a bit moody and brooding today; try to overcome it. An older person who has your best interests at heart could boost your spirits. Spark to a suggestion for an unexpected excursion—it could do you worlds of good.

Thursday, February 20 (Moon in Cancer) You are able to shake off those down feelings of yesterday and get moving again today. Along with energy comes optimism, and you have a right to feel good because things are looking up. Give full play to your sense of curiosity today and get involved in something new that sparks your interest. In another interest, ask a lot of questions, and reject any superficial answers you get. The lucky number today is 3.

Friday, February 21 (Moon Cancer to Leo 3:25 p.m.) Home is where your mind is today; you may have some ideas you may want to put into practice but you should not be overbearing about them. Listen to the advice of someone who has been through it before and knows just what the limits are. Don't be afraid to confide in someone who seems to want to help you; you can count on his/her discretion. Try to hang loose today because there may be some sudden changes in plans.

Saturday, February 22 (Moon in Leo) Check, check, and double-check. You are on the right track but you must have all the evidence in hand before you act. A powerful person may seem to threaten your security, but actually you are on quite safe ground. Look for some relief toward evening when your excellent taste is in for a treat; just don't overindulge!

Sunday, February 23 (Moon Leo to Virgo 11:58 p.m.) There is a spirit of family today no matter whom you mingle with. It is a kind of reunion, and someone is trying to make amends for a recent mistake. Accept the gesture with grace, and do not brood over the past. Your diplomatic skills may be tried when someone acts rather childish; do not be condescending—you are occasionally guilty of this kind of performance yourself. The lucky number today is 6.

Monday, February 24 (Moon in Virgo) This full moon should be a particularly sweet one for you, full of love and romance and the feeling that you are cherished. In fact, you may have to protect yourself in the emotional clinches and realize that some sweet nothings are exactly that. For many, a wish comes true; however, you should realize that your own powers of persuasion were the ultimate factor. A Pisces could be very much in evidence today.

Tuesday, February 25 (Moon in Virgo) You may feel inclined to throw your weight around today because some restrictions are removed and you have a great deal more freedom. Go ahead and express yourself, because what you display today—including yourself—will sell very well. In fact, some may be invited to enter into a partnership, most likely in the business area. Realize this is serious business. For all, career opportunities should be picking up.

Wednesday, February 26 (Moon Virgo to Libra 4:07 a.m.) If you choose, you can sit back and hold court today; there are many who seek you out for advice, counsel, and just plain company. Someone who was rooting against you recently confesses that he/she did it out of envy. Accept the apology and realize that you have missed having the good will of this person. If your health has been a bit shaky, it should improve vastly now. For many it is because an emotional burden is removed.

Thursday, February 27 (Moon in Libra) You should be feeling revitalized and ready to take the new approach that is necessary. Stay alert, and you have nothing to fear. Someone wants desperately to get a sign of approval from you, and may do his/her best to do it. The bait could be something delicious—possibly even a gourmet meal. Whatever happens, most will taste true happiness today. The lucky number is 1.

Friday, February 28 (Moon Libra to Scorpio 7:05 a.m.) It is fortunate that you are in a rather broad-minded mood today, because you may have to deal with some sticky issues with your opposite number. When you give the other person the benefit of the doubt, you realize that in the long run you have made things better for everybody. Don't try to be a professional appraiser when it comes to something of value; get help. You may be brought up sharp when someone reminds you of a responsibility you tend to forget. A Cancer or a Capricorn could be prominent on the scene today.

MARCH 1986

Saturday, March 1 (Moon in Scorpio) There is a lovely rosy glow of cooperation over everything connected with your most important relationship today. In fact, the vibes are so good you will be in a mood to celebrate. It could be that you have recently made some accomplishment or gained some favorable notice. Whatever the scenario, there is sweet harmony and some rough spots of the recent past are totally forgotten by you and your opposite number. Enjoy! The lucky number is 3.

Sunday, March 2 (Moon Scorpio to Sagittarius 9:51 a.m.) However good yesterday was, today you will feel like a change of pace—and may even want to be alone. If necessary, insist on some privacy during which you should do some inventory taking—both real and personal. If you feel at a loss, do not hesitate to listen to someone who has been an important guide in the past. He/she will be there for you again. The lucky number today could be 4.

Monday, March 3 (Moon in Sagittarius) Even though things appear to be at an impasse, you should try to look ahead and reach beyond the here and now. Once again, one steps in to give you the benefit of experience, and possibly even some practical help. Some should be ready for a rather sudden change, and a new variety of sensations. Don't get carried away by same. A

Gemini, a Virgo, or a Sagittarian could be very prominent to today's little drama.

Tuesday, March 4 (Moon Sagittarius to Capricorn 12:56 p.m.) In the true Taurus fashion you may dig in your heels today and refuse to listen when someone gives you what is really quite good advice. Realize that you do not have to act upon it, merely incorporate it into everything else you already know about the situation. The point is that you are not always 100 percent right. Some will seize a pleasant communication—possibly even a gift. Be sure to give some reaction—but don't overreact. The lucky number today is 6.

Wednesday, March 5 (Moon in Capricorn) You should be at peace with yourself today, possibly even spiritually uplifted. It is good for you to occasionally contemplate higher values. You are not really mercenary, Taurus, but you do tend to live too much in the here and now. On a more mundane level, some instructions you have received will be clarified—and you will feel much more comfortable with the task at hand. A Pisces could clarify your thinking a lot.

Thursday, March 6 (Moon Capricorn to Aquarius 4:42 p.m.) Something you want very badly now comes within reach and you should go for it! That means putting out a little bit of extra effort, but it is truly worth the exertion. This is a day on which you can transform some mere ideas into tangible form. You are in luck because someone whose support you badly need is willing to give it, and will clear the path for you. If you do not make progress today, you cannot blame your fate.

Friday, March 7 (Moon in Aquarius) The work week winds up with you winding up a long-standing project. You should feel proud of yourself—and expect acknowledgment for what you've done. If it doesn't come, reward yourself by doing something pleasant—or buying something you have lusted after for a while. For some, the money situation will be much brighter. You should be feeling like a very solid citizen. You could try your luck with number 9 today.

***Saturday, March 8** (Moon Aquarius to Pisces 7:48 p.m.)* Try to apply some original thinking to an old problem; otherwise you will simply feel like you are going around in circles again. Test things out with some new contacts you have made and see if they can help you get to the heart of the problem. If nothing else happens, you will make some good new allies. Be willing to discuss differences in an intelligent manner today. Don't overdo with heavy work.

***Sunday, March 9** (Moon in Pisces)* Those of you who have felt unsure of their direction lately will have their confidence restored now. It could come through the intervention of another person—possibly a family member who understands your dilemma and steps in. Even those less troubled will feel more emotionally secure now—possibly even financially so. A strong hunch or intuition that seems to come out of the blue is most likely correct; act on your initial impression. It should make you realize that you don't always have to have things spelled out for you in order to make a decision.

***Monday, March 10** (Moon in Pisces)* Those who are in any kind of selling capacity will find they have to use very little pressure today; your powers of persuasion are extremely high now. Most anyone can get what they want by turning on the charm—and leaving it on. Some will receive an invitation they are inclined at first to say no to; you should accept instead. Something very unusual and gratifying could come out of it.

***Tuesday, March 11** (Moon Pisces to Aries 5:03 a.m.)* Even though you still feel quite in the dark, realize that a mystery is about to be solved—or a dilemma resolved. Even though you don't know it, someone is working for you behind the scenes and will eventually make things come out all right. Don't get so carried away with relief that you forget to show your gratitude, and indicate how much you are indebted to this person. In another scenario, you should relax and go with the tide, realizing that a delay is only temporary and will seem like a blessing later on.

***Wednesday, March 12** (Moon in Aries)* You may

have the opportunity to make an absolutely free choice today—something you do not ordinarily enjoy doing. If you are hesitant, realize that the more adventurous way is the more potentially productive one. As a matter of fact, you may run into someone who gives you an unexpected vote of confidence and sends your spirits soaring. It should teach you that safer is not always better. Some should get their thoughts down in writing, and attempt to communicate them to the appropriate person. There is a lot to be gained.

Thursday, March 13 (Moon Aries to Taurus 3:04 p.m.) The day starts out quietly but quickly picks up. One reason is that you are able to cast out some doubts, fears, and suspicions that have been plaguing you lately. Isn't it nice to know you were wrong? A very steady type—possibly another Taurus or Scorpio—is ready to go hand and hand with you. Accept! The lucky number today could be 6.

Friday, March 14 (Moon in Taurus) The time has come for direct action, and you should take it without hesitation. The moon in your sign corresponds with a great deal of physical and mental energy on your part. One cautionary note: Try to see things and people as they are and not as you would wish them to be. Your good spirits may make that a little difficult to accomplish but it is worth the effort. However, don't trust a hunch you have about where to place your interest—you are quite on the right track.

Saturday, March 15 (Moon in Taurus) This should be an absolutely splendid weekend with your lunar cycle at its monthly high. Most will be able to accomplish a great deal, but some should watch out for a tendency to overdo. Sure, you want to get involved, but it is wise to avoid overinvolvement at this time. Help and support come from someone who really surprises you by his/her actions; this is someone you never counted on! Try your luck with number 8.

Sunday, March 16 (Moon Taurus to Gemini 3:23 a.m.) You will have good reason to feel self-satisfied today—possibly even smug. When a reward or compliment comes in, resist the temptation to lord it over everyone else. There is no need to feel so insecure you have to prop up your self-esteem artificially. Instead, put the day to good use by planning your next move and envisioning end results. Spend some time catching up on necessary reading—there is much to be learned now.

Monday, March 17 (Moon in Gemini) You may feel uncharacteristically full of nervous energy today; be sure to direct it properly. Some feel like celebrating, even though there may be nothing in particular to celebrate. Don't use your verve as an excuse to self-indulge. You will regret it later on. Some may find that a member of the opposite sex is rather indiscreet in expressing his/her feelings; react accordingly. Do not get drawn into deeper waters than you can handle.

Tuesday, March 18 (Moon Gemini to Cancer 4:04 p.m.) No matter what your role in life, you may be called upon to play "teacher" today. Derive satisfaction from the fact that your advice and counsel are very much appreciated—even though the other person may not express it openly. Some of you may find yourselves digging through old memories to locate one which is the key to a present situation. Relax, and you will remember. Others may find themselves engrossed in all kinds of necessary activities relating to income and outgo. You may want to try your luck with number 2 today.

Wednesday, March 19 (Moon in Cancer) The pace definitely picks up today, and you may even find yourself moving around more than you would like to. Jump into the activity and enjoy it—you can rest up another day. Someone you have had a minor disagreement with recently gives in and acknowledges the fact that you were right. Don't gloat! Have fun with a Gemini or a Sagittarian.

Thursday, March 20 (Moon in Cancer) Today you are in the spirit of the swifter pace and ready to show your versatility. Some slight bad feelings that plague you in the morning are easily laughed off—don't waste time brooding. Some will have a surprise visit that seems like a dream come true. Could it be ESP? Even you should wonder. Once again, don' give in to laziness when someone suggests a break in routine. Try your luck with number 4 today.

Friday, March 21 (Moon Cancer to Leo 2:38 a.m.) Your sense of the dramatic is stimulated today and you should be able to state your case quite forcefully and with a sense of urgency. If you play your cards right, you will get the response you are looking for. If today you are successful where previously you failed, realize that your former attempts did not measure up to the situation. It is not an easy one. Many can find consolation from a deep philosophical thought with an intelligent person—possibly a Sagittarian.

Saturday, March 22 (Moon in Leo) Don't overreact and get your back up when somebody suggests a possible change—maybe even of residence. Nothing is wrong with talking as long as action does not follow. It could be a whim of the moment, but even then you should be willing to listen. There is no need to force another issue because what you want will come to you virtually effortlessly. Some will have to deal with a sticky problem mostly likely having to do with property.

Sunday, March 23 (Moon Leo to Virgo 9:39 a.m.) Today the subject of territorial rights and what belongs to whom may loom large and threaten to spoil the day's peace. Be willing to take a back seat this time and acknowledge that you may have taken more than your share. If you look at things in the long term, you will realize that pettiness is not necessary. Don't neglect someone who would be tremendously cheered by a call or visit by you. The lucky number today should be 7.

Monday, March 24 (Moon in Virgo) A rather moody spell is broken and today you can act with much more freedom of mind. In fact, you should feel confident enough to lay it on the line with someone you want to win over. It's okay to be forceful, but be a little creative. Bluntness is not always the way to someone's heart. For many, a relationship is growing much more intense. The lucky number today should be 8.

Tuesday, March 25 (Moon to Libra 1:22 p.m.) Be willing to toss off that old security blanket and let go of the past. You don't need it anymore. Not surprisingly, you get the green light to go ahead with a much-cherished project. You could be the one who allows you to do it. Don't overlook the offered help from a young, vigorous person; you can use it. Once again, love and romance are highly probable parts of the scenario.

Wednesday, March 26 (Moon in Libra) This particular full moon highlights your need to tend to the needs of others; that means some may be feeling rather overburdened now; however, for others, there should be a pleasant sense that one big job is over, and that a new one is beginning. All should be able to impress upon others their very special abilities, and to thereby feel a lot more independent. Remember, only you can do what you do. The lucky number today is 1.

Thursday, March 27 (Moon Libra to Scorpio 3:05 p.m.) Some excellent news—possibly concerning a test or competition—comes in and finds you very much ready for it. As your spirits lift, so does your general health. Some will have the additional boon of finding out that a wise person has put something aside for the proverbial rainy day. It's a nice money-in-the-bank feeling.

Friday, March 28 (Moon in Scorpio) Try to move slowly and rather cautiously today, but do not get lost in details. It is necessary to look at things in their entirety and see where you fit into the big picture. Your public relations ability should be on high now and it should enable you to get cooperation quite easily. Some energetic people you run into should energize you; decide to run with them. The lucky number is 3.

Saturday, March 29 (Moon Scorpio to Sagittarius 4:20 p.m.) You are coming out of the woods as far as relationships with those around you go. If you're smart, you'll still keep a low profile, however—especially in the earlier part of the day. Later on, things will lighten up—and your mood will, too. If you've got the time and the resources, taking in a good, knee-slapping funny film would be an excellent idea.

Sunday, March 30 (Moon in Sagittarius) You and someone else may "find" each other in a whole new way today. In your exploring mood, you may finally touch that right button, and someone will open up his/her heart all the way. In other cases, you will be feeling as if you need more tender loving care than usual; if you use a very subtle approach, you could sweet-talk someone right into giving it to you.

Monday, March 31 (Moon in Sagittarius) You may find yourself struggling with a desire to simply chuck it all and take off for a great walk in the wide open spaces. If you find you're "stuck" right where you are, take care not to let your mind wander too far off the main track; others are watching your performance. Make an effort to focus in on the here and now; you'll have plenty of time later to "take off" in a new direction.

APRIL 1986

Tuesday, April 1 (Moon in Capricorn) You're going to have to take a philosophical attitude toward things today and keep your sense of humor right at hand. You may not regard it funny at all when someone let's on he/she has been leading you down a primrose path of late. Focus on other things—like travel and other pleasurable pursuits. Some may have to go back to square one and start all over with an original approach to a problem. You'll get there! The lucky number today is 4.

Wednesday, April 2 (Moon Capricorn to Aquarius 10:11 p.m.) You will feel today quite over yesterday's annoyance. However, whatever happened has put you in a frame of mind where you are considering your own moral values and where you stand on certain important issues. Some will be much heartened when someone close to them—possibly a member of the opposite sex—comes through and says you're okay. Be sure to keep a light touch today, and ensure your chances of doing so by mingling with some lively types like a Gemini or a Sagittarian.

Thursday, April 3 (Moon in Aquarius) No matter how you try to avoid it, the subject of money will surface in some way today. It could be related to jobs or career, and your desire to have greater earning power. Make it more than a wish by resolving to do some self-improvement—possibly even taking an actual course. For others, this could be an expensive day—but what you spend it on is well worth the price. In fact, it could be something you have been lusting after for quite a while. Enjoy!

Friday, April 4 (Moon in Aquarius) Don't get rattled today when you find out what you thought you heard was not what someone was trying to say. It is simply a case of confusion and nothing to get bent out of shape over. However, make a note to ask more questions next time. It's an excellent time to clear out stuff that is no longer needed—that could include some old attitudes that are holding you back. Someone younger than you may set an example today by being particularly open to change. It's never too late for anyone! The lucky number is 7.

Saturday, April 5 (Moon Aquarius to Pisces 4:03 a.m.) Possibly because of extra effort on your part, something you've wanted now appears easy to get. Don't underplay your own role in making this come about. Someone may try to dump a responsibility on you that rightly belongs elsewhere; you could be "Mr. Nice Guy," but it won't get you anywhere. Keep your eye on your own long-range goals. If you are in the mood to speculate, the lucky number today should be 8.

Sunday, April 6 (Moon in Pisces) That old devil envy could plague you today; try to concentrate on what you have that others do not. As a matter of fact, it might help you to realize that there is someone who looks to you as an example of what is absolutely great.

And you could also be flattered by someone who confides an intimate problem and asks for your help. Try to be as objective as possible. An Aries or a Libra could be a key figure in a current dilemma—know who you are dealing with. The lucky number is 9.

Monday, April 7 (Moon Pisces to Aries 12:12 p.m.) Things are not what they appear to be today. Part of the scenario is that a wish of yours comes true, but in such an unusual manner that you almost don't recognize it. You may feel a bit cheated, but what you get is yours alone. Take a deep breath and make a definitive statement today; it is pointless to waffle about something you want so badly. If you display the courage of your convictions, others will believe you. A Leo could play a very important role.

Tuesday, April 8 (Moon in Aries) You could have a great feeling of relief today when a recently puzzling situation suddenly gets crystal clear. Now you can see where all the pieces fit. Perhaps because of this, your sense of direction is back and you like the feeling of being on familiar ground. For some, there could be a meeting of the minds with someone who has been a bit intractable of late. Enjoy the harmony, and try your luck with number 2.

Wednesday, April 9 (Moon Aries to Taurus 10:36 p.m.) You may start out the day feeling a bit "spooked," but try to realize that your fears are totally unfounded. The problem is you have begun to doubt yourself and that makes you suspicious of everyone else's stability. Some may find they are confined in some ways now; it is temporary. In fact, most are on the verge of an important change and should remain alert for signs of it. Optimism will get you everywhere! Try laughing it off with a Gemini or a Sagittarian.

Thursday, April 10 (Moon in Taurus) You should wake with a "new person" feeling, because the moon is in your sign and things will begin to go your way. Even your physical strength may seem renewed. Take advantage of the day by taking the initiative and realizing that your timing is excellent. Don't hesitate to speak up—even to someone who is a bit intimidating. Realize that someone who attempts to discourage you is merely envious.

Friday, April 11 (Moon in Taurus) The moon is still very much on your side and that means it's a day to make progress. One way is through the written word. Make your statement boldly and clearly. For some, romance is at a high point and physical attraction may be also. It is an excellent time to improve your relationships with the opposite sex—as long as you intend to keep them that way.

Saturday, April 12 (Moon Taurus to Gemini 10:51 a.m.) This should be an excellent weekend to feather your nest, in every sense of the word. Your immediate home environment could be undergoing a change, and that change should be very much for the better. In fact, for some there should be love and harmony where there has been discord recently. Others could experience a windfall, and it could actually be of the financial kind. At any rate, there is something very exciting possible in today's scenario. The lucky number is 6.

Sunday, April 13 (Moon in Gemini) Some of you may be feeling absolutely a live wire today. Put your restlessness to positive use—the best way would be through physical activity of some sort. Some verbal sparring is likely, and you are likely to enjoy it. Isn't it nice to have someone listen to your ideas? Take some time to catch up on necessary housekeeping and financial chores.

Monday, April 14 (Moon Gemini to Cancer 11:42 p.m.) Even if you start out the day feeling a touch of the blues, they will not last long. One reason is that you finally are able to see the results of some hard work you put in a while back. It should be gratifying—and possibly financially rewarding. There is the possibility of a face-off with a rather strong-willed person; do not dig in your Taurus heels. There is a way you can work out an accommodation with this other person. The lucky number today is 8.

Tuesday, April 15 (Moon in Cancer) There is a shake-up in the status quo today; but you needn't be shaken by it. In fact, if you keep an open mind, you will see that there are valuable new contacts to be made and interesting subjects to investigate. Something or someone comes along and gives your self esteem a boost, and it's a lovely feeling. Love is very much in the air today as is a contented feeling about finishing what you have started.

Wednesday, April 16 (Moon in Cancer) For many, this is a day when some excellent news comes in—most likely via the telephone. The general mood today is one of celebration, even if you have nothing in particular to celebrate. If you are into anything creative, you should put some time in on it today. Others should make it a point to zero in on a decision that needs to be made. You cannot keep putting it off indefinitely.

Thursday, April 17 (Moon Cancer to Leo 11:10 a.m.) This is a day to reach out and help others; if you don't, they will come to you anyway. Listen to a tale of woe that you hear and think "It could have been me." Count your blessings. Some will be called on to teach in some way, but will derive great pleasure from it. There may be a minor crisis during the day, but you'll know exactly what to do at the crucial moment.

Friday, April 18 (Moon in Leo) Today the pattern will be much more familiar, and you may breathe a sigh of relief at the fact that it's "business as usual." For most, that means a return to your usual conservative approach, and in this case it is the most effective. Social life should not be neglected, however, though you may want to keep it low key. The lucky number today is 3.

Saturday, April 19 (Moon Leo to Virgo 7:24 p.m.) You may have to be quite specific today in order to get things done or arranged as you want them to be. Don't overlook the fine print that could trip you up. If that is not part of your scenario today, there will be another one in which you realize that you must learn the rules before you break them. However, do not discourage yourself from taking independent action.

Just remember that blueprints are there for a purpose. You may get some surprising opposition from someone who is normally rather docile; it could be a Libra.

Sunday, April 20 (Moon in Virgo) Someone could make a surprise appearance today, and catch you off-guard. Don't get ruffled but think before you act or speak. There may be more to this event than is immediately apparent. Others may find that a change is beneficial and really long overdue. Children may figure big in the day's activities and should be a delight. A Gemini, a Virgo, or a Sagittarian could be very much on the scene.

Monday, April 21 (Moon Virgo to Libra 11:50 p.m.) It is not necessary to force an issue today, the commitment will come in due time. If the area is romance, you should know that the relationship is growing stronger—even if some of the surface elements are not there. Some may be forced to think about just how valuable something or someone is to them. Make your appraisal with great care. The lucky number today is 6.

Tuesday, April 22 (Moon in Libra) You get the distinct feeling that someone has been holding out on you, and you are right. Try not to be bitter about the situation; realize that he/she had your best interest at heart. It is definitely a day when you will have to focus on the work at hand—which could be considerable. You may feel as if simply *everybody* is counting on you. Just keep thinking how nice it is to be needed.

Wednesday, April 23 (Moon in Libra) Try not to take a ho-hum attitude when someone older—or at least more experienced—wants to give you more advice than you would like to have. Realize that there is something substantial here, and it could include money. Some will be feeling a bit out of shape and determined to do something about it; it is an excellent day to start any kind of diet or exercise regime. Try your luck with number 8 today.

Thursday, April 24 (Moon Libra to Scorpio 1:15 a.m.) This could be a particularly dramatic full moon for you, Taurus, because there is a total change in your game plan indicated. Don't fear it; flow with it. The important thing is to take it slow and maintain a low profile. Meanwhile, keep your eye on the ball and the technicalities that go along with it. You will come smiling through. Take heart and some comfort from an Aries or Libra.

Friday, April 25 (Moon in Scorpio) There is no question about it now; a new start is necessary. You should be reconciled to the fact that it's wise to let go of a losing proposition. The new one is far better. Some will find that a member of the opposite sex plays a key role and is enormously helpful in the situation. For others, there is the sweet feeling of vindication when you are proved right. Celebrate with a Leo, an Aquarian, or another Taurus.

Saturday, April 26 (Moon Scorpio to Sagittarius 1:16 a.m.) Recent events and changes are still making their mark—particularly in terms of a delay. Don't get impatient. Use the time to commune with your intuition and come up with a hunch that is so on target it could put you way ahead of the game. It is wise to cooperate as much as possible with family members and anyone around you now; it is important to avoid strained relationships. Don't get sucked in by a pie-in-the-sky scheme someone comes up with.

Sunday, April 27 (Moon in Sagittarius) Recent pressures are definitely relieved, and the day indicated could be a superb one. There should be all kinds of opportunities to expand your personal horizons—with new contacts, new ideas, and new pleasures. The lines of communication are wide open and a lot is coming through. It's an exciting scenario, and the lucky number is 3.

Monday, April 28 (Moon Sagittarius to Capricorn 1:41 a.m.) Don't accept any substitutes today—insist on the genuine article, no matter what form it takes. There is no reason for you to take anything less than top quality, because that is what you are worth. It may be a Scorpio from whom you gain additional knowledge that should help you enormously. It could be in connection with a legal matter. For all, there is a lot to be learned today and a lot to be gained from what you learn. The lucky number is 4.

Tuesday, April 29 (Moon in Capricorn) Some will know the wonderful feeling of meeting their ideal now. Even if the match is not perfect, you should no longer be feeling alone. If you are already involved, your main relationship will get a large boost today—a romantic one. Don't let love distract you from other important matters where you can make some dramatic forward moves now.

Wednesday, April 30 (Moon Capricorn to Aquarius 4:06 a.m.) The month winds up on an up note for you, and you should be feeling quite optimistic. The emphasis today is on ambition and how much of it you choose to exercise; don't be pushy, but don't be lazy either. Something good happens in your partnership or domestic sphere and the result is a nice warm feeling. Isn't it nice to feel secure? The lucky number is 6.

MAY 1986

Thursday, May 1 (Moon in Aquarius) Hooray, hooray, it's the first of May, sexy Taurus! And you know what that means. This should be a particularly lovely birthday month for Taureans, most of whom should be feeling rather comfortable right now. However, some could be sitting too pretty and not moving around enough. You do tend to get stuck in a rut occasionally, and it does tend to show. Think about doing some overhauling—both the personal kind and the kind that freshens up your surroundings. The lucky number today is 5.

Friday, May 2 (Moon Aquarius to Pisces 9:30 a.m.) A recent meeting is beginning to take on some significance; it was not a casual encounter. Don't brush off what this person could do for you in an important area of your life. Some settled Taurean could get a little nervous when someone with whom you share digs begins talking about a move. It may be temporary, but on the other hand you should be at least open to suggestions. Try your luck with number 6 today.

Saturday, May 3 (Moon in Pisces) It is generally not a good idea to mix business with pleasure; however, some may be sorely tempted to do that now. If you can maintain a serious relationship with a serious attitude toward your job at the same time, so be it. Some are experiencing the anticipation of a fond wish being fulfilled. It is good to be optimistic, but realize that nothing ever happens exactly as we wish it to happen. It's important to use imagination in putting yourself forward now; people are watching.

Sunday, May 4 (Moon Pisces to Aries 8:01 p.m.) Some may not be feeling on top of the world today; the reason may be a problem you are having difficulty coping with. Do not be too proud to reach out for help. You will be amazed at what a sympathetic ear you find and what a willing shoulder to cry on. Even if there is no apparent problem, the day may be tinged with blue feelings. Try to look within yourself and focus on some spiritual values. If your life seems empty, resolve to fill it with the right things. A Capricorn is a key person to keep in contact with.

Monday, May 5 (Moon in Aries) If you played your mental cards right yesterday, you should start off this day with determination—and a will to shake off your mood of yesterday. It is vital to finish what you start because that is the only way you can achieve a sense of accomplishment now. On the other hand, some will want to dump a responsibility into someone else's lap—where it belongs. Don't pass off a bit of information that drifts into your sphere of consciousness; it could be very important in the future.

Tuesday, May 6 (Moon in Aries) This should be a day you can wipe the slate clean and start to feel optimistic about the period coming up. Some may have reason to feel slightly suspicious about the activities of another, but if you examine things carefully, you will see there is nothing to fear. An exciting encounter is highly possible for some, while others may find it's a lie-low day. The lucky number is 1.

Wednesday, May 7 (Moon Aries to Taurus 5:59 a.m.) This new moon belongs to the sign of Taurus and should be one of the high spots of your year. You will have an excellent chance to see way down the road and get back your sense of direction. It is important to realize that what you feel today is genuine intuition; if you have doubts, check out what you sense with someone who really knows what is going on. For some, it will be an older person who could be extremely helpful in getting you where you want to go. A Cancer or an Aquarian could be prominent on the scene today.

Thursday, May 8 (Moon in Taurus) Once again the road is wide and clear, and the green light flashes for progress. If nothing that concrete occurs, you should enjoy a renewal of faith in yourself and a sense that you can make it—big! Whatever else happens, you will be in the right place at the right moment, and even have cause for celebration. A Gemini will play a key role and the lucky number should be 3.

Friday, May 9 (Moon Taurus to Gemini 5:26 p.m.) Stand tall, because someone will be looking up to you as an example. Don't be shy; be flattered. For some, special honor is due; for others, the rewards will be more subtle. All should be willing to take a look at something they have done or are doing, and be willing to revise it. No one's perfect! The lucky number today should be 4.

Saturday, May 10 (Moon in Gemini) If your cash flow has been a bit blocked as of late, expect it to start flowing more freely now. Some will have unexpected money coming in; others will finally get what they deserve. Even if you do not end the day literally richer, you will have something you did not have before. It could be something you thought you had lost. An element of excitement and romance colors the atmosphere; a Gemini, a Virgo, or a Sagittarian could be the focal point.

Sunday, May 11 (Moon in Gemini) You should be able to talk your way out of a tight situation today, or talk yourself into a quite interesting one. The key is to discuss the issues and to be as diplomatic as possible. You will be surprised to see how easily cooperation comes to you. Your living arrangement may be the subject of the discussion you get into; realize that someone has to give in, and it may have to be you. A Libra, a Scorpio, or an Aquarian could make your life a lot easier.

Monday, May 12 (Moon Gemini to Cancer 6:18 a.m.) Something may come out of the blue and threaten to throw you off-balance today; stand firm. It is important not to give in to the aura of confusion that exists. Keep your wits about you and be ready to laugh off some small annoyances. The key to success today is to remain flexible and try to bend with circumstances. It is an excellent day to play private eye and find some missing pieces to the puzzle. A Pisces could be extremely helpful in this or another endeavor.

Tuesday, May 13 (Moon in Cancer) You could amaze everyone by coming up with a prediction today that is uncannily accurate. The reason is that your antennae are operating particularly well and you are able to perceive a pattern where others see nothing at all. Many will find themselves in a position to make a power play—go for it! Others will simply feel on much steadier ground than they have of late. The lucky number today is 8.

Wednesday, May 14 (Moon Cancer to Leo 6:15 p.m.) This is one of those days when warmhearted Taurus could meet his/her match—and even fall madly in love! All signs point to excitement, fulfillment, and getting right at the heart of things. If nothing that spectacular happens to a particular Taurus today, he/she will feel in the mood to celebrate anyway. The reason is a sense of accomplishment and the fact that a big hurdle has been hurdled. Join hands with an Aries, a Virgo, or a Libra to form a perfect circle.

Thursday, May 15 (Moon in Leo) Someone extends a hand today, and you should take it. The offer of help is sincere and in no way will compromise your desire for independence. In a rather embarrassing or delicate situation, it is important to be as direct as possible. You cannot afford to waffle now. For some, patience will seem like a heavy burden, but it is necessary. However, do not hesitate to take the first step in what could be a very creative project. The lucky number is 1.

Friday, May 16 (Moon in Leo) Don't grumble about that big obstacle standing right in your path, and don't try to shove it out of the way. There is nothing you can do now but wait it out. A long-standing arrangement surfaces and in some ways makes you feel more secure. Realize that you have both emotional and moral support—and that the monetary kind would be there if you needed it.

Saturday, May 17 (Moon Leo to Virgo 3:45 a.m.) You should be able to focus and direct your energies today in any direction you like; most of you will opt for the pleasure route. You will be pleasantly surprised when something that strikes your fancy comes within easy reach. For some, that could be romance—and a new quickening of the heart. Others will find it a day in which they are particularly popular, and have the opportunity to match wits and share a few laughs with some particularly lively people. The subject of education may arise, and you should consider continuing yours. The lucky number today is 3.

Sunday, May 18 (Moon in Virgo) Someone may try to get on your nerves today; refuse to let him/her intimidate her. Realize he/she is trying to manipulate you—out of envy. Divert any excess energy into some fix-up projects that badly need doing. Some may find themselves involved with a rather heavy type who threatens to cast a pall over the day. Stay out of range.

Monday, May 19 (Moon Virgo to Libra 9:41 a.m.) Someone could walk right up to you today and say, "You're the greatest." Don't be embarrassed; be flattered that your recent performance merits that kind of rating. Your mellow Taurus voice could be heard quite clearly today—don't hesitate to use it. Some will have a rather unusual exchange of ideas; others will experience something quite new. Don't hang back—be adventurous. You might even try your luck with number 5 today.

Tuesday, May 20 (Moon in Libra) Make it a point to start out the day with a sense of self-esteem—you may need it. It may seem as if people want you for all the wrong reasons today; it may also seem as if no one can do anything without you. It is not necessary to play the martyr. Some will have their day brightened by a sentimental gesture from someone important. Others will try to lift their spirits by starting on a new health and diet regime. Good for you.

Wednesday, May 21 (Moon Libra to Scorpio 12:02 p.m.) Today could be a touch better than yesterday, but still far from perfect. However, realize that what appears to be a loss will end up being a blessing in disguise. A delay that seems merely frustrating will in the long run benefit you. You may want to retire into your own private world today and review events of the recent past. If you're feeling stalled, understand that some of the problems lie within yourself. Get rid of anything you don't need—including old and superfluous negative attitudes. Get in touch with a Pisces for solace.

Thursday, May 22 (Moon in Scorpio) Some may find themselves getting deeper into a situation or a relationship than they had planned. Proceed with caution, and do not trust your mood of the moment. For all, it is a day to move slowly and deliberately—that is, in your usual mode. Permanent and sure alliances prove comforting now, as they should. Be aware of your contractual obligations. A Capricorn could walk on the scene and immediately make you feel more secure. The lucky number is 8.

Friday, May 23 (Moon Scorpio to Sagittarius 11:57 a.m.) This full moon should find you strengthening your ties with the most important person in your life.

In fact, there may be a kind of reunion or pleasant calm after the storm. However, it is also a day in which you may find yourself at odds with someone whose ideas clash with your own. It is possible that the subject is a legal matter. Realize you will eventually emerge the victor.

Saturday, May 24 (Moon in Sagittarius) A seemingly important incident during this day has serious long-range implications; stay alert and don't let anything escape you. Some of you could be calmed by a big-talking individual who really cannot deliver. Be skeptical and ask a lot of questions, insisting on straight answers rather than clever evasions. A clear-thinking Aquarian could be extremely helpful in this or another tricky situation you may encounter today. The lucky number today is 1.

Sunday, May 25 (Moon Sagittarius to Capricorn 11:15 a.m.) A rather unusual dream—or uncommon conscious thought—should be analyzed very carefully. Realize that you are on to something and that you should not take things at face value. Allow yourself to dig deep and to tread areas that you normally would avoid. There is nothing to fear; in fact, you have a great deal to gain. A sensitive Cancer or a practical Capricorn could help you sort things out. The lucky number is 2.

Monday, May 26 (Moon in Capricorn) A new degree of self-insight should help you make an important break now; that break could be with a person, or simply with a way of thinking. Some may realize that it's time to move on to more productive areas—possibly in a job or career. Others may be feeling a bit unnerved, but should realize things are not as haphazard as they seem. You are heading in the right direction. The most important thing is to reach beyond your current expectations.

Tuesday, May 27 (Moon Capricorn to Aquarius 12:00 noon) You should begin to see that it is possible to achieve your goal much faster than you originally thought. The reason may be that there is an extremely important person in your corner. Don't feel shy about accepting the help that is offered. It may be necessary to take the long view now and try to rise above a petty quarrel. You may not be directly involved, but it could hit pretty close to home. Regard as simply an annoyance, and let it go.

Wednesday, May 28 (Moon in Aquarius) No matter at what level you operate, your status should be elevated and notched today. It is important to keep alert and to welcome change and variety. Some may have a promise fulfilled that they had almost forgotten. Others may find they can successfully deal with a person or group that has been difficult in the past. The lucky number today is 5.

Thursday, May 29 (Moon Aquarius to Pisces 3:54 p.m.) Take any opportunity that comes along to display your creative talents. It could be as simple as cooking a meal. Whatever the case, you will have the chance to impress someone very favorably now. Don't blow it! Some may simply find the drive toward pleasure and comfort particularly strong today; give in to it, but don't go overboard. Another Taurus could be a great deal of fun to team up with.

Friday, May 30 (Moon in Pisces) Intense emotional involvement colors this day. Beware of a tendency to dramatize a situation or to overreact to an advance someone makes. For some, it is an excellent day to put forward a case and swing opinion in their direction. Let someone less emotional than you today help you analyze some special data or information. You are not up to it.

Saturday, May 31 (Moon Pisces to Aries 11:43 p.m.) You are swinging into a high cycle and should realize it. What seems like luck may simply be your ability to make clear-cut decisions, and know exactly what end is up. Some obstacles seem to vanish and someone you thought was quite indifferent will extend a hand for you to take. Take it! The lucky number today is 8.

JUNE 1986

Sunday, June 1 (Moon in Aries) You should have a nice warm feeling throughout this "comfy" day. Events contribute to your excellent mood—especially one which involves your financial situation. Some will get the facts they need to wrap something important—others will reap the benefits of a major consensus someone makes. You may be asked to meet someone in secret—there is no danger.

Monday, June 2 (Moon in Aries) It should be clear now what your ability to make a decision has accomplished. Now you need hold back no longer. In an interpersonal matter, define your terms and insist that the other party does, too. The person is too important to your current and future situation to allow things to remain fuzzy. Brush up a new technique you learn because it will be very useful later on. The lucky number is 7.

Tuesday, June 3 (Moon Aries to Taurus 10:45 a.m.) Your high cycle begins to peak and you should have a winner of a day! The only problem today may be the number of choices that are presented to you; you cannot take them all. But isn't it nice to have some options? Some will reestablish a relationship that has faltered a bit; others will get back something that was taken away from them. Share the wealth of this day with a Cancer or a Capricorn who is close to you.

Wednesday, June 4 (Moon in Taurus) Don't be smug when you find you have the last laugh; realize what an enviable position you are in versus another. Today is pay-off time for efforts you put in in the past. Enjoy the money-in-the-bank feeling and realize what freedom you now have. Also resolve not to be intimidated in the future or hesitant about expressing yourself surely. The lucky number on this lovely day is 9.

Thursday, June 5 (Moon Taurus to Gemini 11:26 p.m.) Take a chance on yourself today—you've got what it takes! A positive attitude is key to positive developments, in love, money, or whatever it is you want.

Test yourself to be in the right place at the right time and let your intuition take you where it will. However, if you get too carried away you run the risk of a face-off with another person as hardheaded as you. Be willing to bend.

Friday, June 6 (Moon in Gemini) Many Taureans will have reason to cheer today, as their lucky streak continues. In some cases, it could mean an actual gain or promotion. All of you should be feeling optimistic and full of vim and vigor. If you cannot seem to find yours, you may not be going with the flow. Try something new and see if that does the trick. A key player in the day's events could be a Cancer or a Capricorn; don't count him/her out before you get the whole story.

Saturday, June 7 (Moon in Gemini) Now you are in danger of having too much of a good thing. Slow down a bit and watch the signs on the road. It's possible you may want to stop and rest a bit. However, for most there will be ample opportunities to keep on the go and mix and mingle with sundry inspiring individuals. Stick to your guns about diet and health resolutions, no matter what the day brings.

Sunday, June 8 (Moon Gemini to Cancer 12:16 p.m.) The time of year may make you take a good look at your body and decide that some major repairs are needed. Don't get discouraged if you can't accomplish everything immediately; today, simply put on a happy face and a bright image. Some of you will be experiencing a change in plans that is momentarily unsettling. You should be able to make a quick comeback. Others may get a hot tip on a sure winner. Act on it only if you can afford to.

Monday, June 9 (Moon in Cancer) If you are feeling uneasy today, put it down to moodiness and not to anything really threatening. A frank talk with someone important in your life could clear the atmosphere, and make you feel a lot more secure. Don't hesitate to initiate it. Some may be embarking on a holiday trip, and should realize there are better days ahead. The lucky number today is 5.

Tuesday, June 10 (Moon in Cancer) Most should be feeling much more in harmony with themselves today. Isn't that adjustment easier to make than you thought? You shouldn't fight change the way you do at times. There should be some good news coming in, and it should make you happy on behalf of someone else. Be magnanimous, even though the gain is not your own.

Wednesday, June 11 (Moon Cancer to Leo 12:11 a.m.) Your imagination can run away with you today if you let it. The cause could be a "mysterious stranger" who drifts onto the scene. Don't make more of it than is really there. You may be feeling quite romantic, but you are better off directing that feeling toward someone who is a more known quantity. If you feel a bit down on yourself today, realize that you have plenty to offer—even if you don't recognize it all the time. Pisces could be very helpful in letting you see your good points.

Thursday, June 12 (Moon in Leo) Don't fight it when someone wants to change the status quo today; you could use a bit of shaking up. It is possible to change your habit patterns even if you cannot see that now. In the end, you will feel a lot more free and able to move about. Whatever your work, you should be quite productive today and able to see tangible results.

Friday, June 13 (Moon Leo to Virgo 10:18 a.m.) Someone tells you he/she has your best interests at heart. Test it out by making a couple of demands and see what happens. If it causes a shake-up, so be it. When it comes to your living environment, it may be time to get someone else's viewpoint on how it could be made more comfortable/ship secure. The lucky number today is 9.

Saturday, June 14 (Moon in Virgo) You should be in for some fun and variety—and your energy level should be high. However, it is important not to overdo, especially in the area of sports and other forms of physical exertion. Put your mental energy to work in a pioneering project, and show how original you can be.

You may be very inspired by a Leo. The lucky number today is 1.

Sunday, June 15 (Moon Virgo to Libra 5:38 p.m.) Someone may disappoint you today, but realize that you may be overreacting. You could have a tendency to brood now. Accept a temporary separation philosophically and realize it is in everyone's best interest. Make it a point to mingle with the young—even if they are merely young in heart. You may get the opportunity to learn by teaching.

Monday, June 16 (Moon in Libra) Remain flexible no matter what happens. You may have more to do than is comfortable, but you will have some room for maneuvering. Some may receive an invitation that involves travel; grab it! It could add luster to a day that is otherwise rather basic, in every sense of the word. You may have to pay some attention to your health—or the health of a dependent. The lucky number is 3.

Tuesday, June 17 (Moon Libra to Scorpio 9:36 p.m.) Someone may try to get something out of you on the strength of a very flimsy promise; insist on more tangible proof. It would be returned. There may be a rather important decision that must be made now; do not do so without some excellent advice. You need a real heavy—possibly a Scorpio—to lead you through this one. Your personal magnetism may be quite high now, and the physical side of a relationship could become pronounced. But that's the way Taurus generally likes it.

Wednesday, June 18 (Moon in Scorpio) You've got to exchange ideas with someone before you can put something into perspective. The matter is possibly a legal one, and you should not trust yourself to be objective. All kinds of contracts—including marriage—are up for grabs now. Be sure you know your own mind. A very lively type may skip across your scene today; have fun matching wits. The lucky number today is 5.

Thursday, June 19 (Moon Scorpio to Sagittarius 10:36 p.m.) You could receive a special gift from a special person—although it may not be the kind you unwrap. Whatever the case, show your gratitude and respond in kind. Some of you will have a clear-cut opportunity to improve their financial status; this is one time he who hesitates is lost. Others may learn the true facts about a situation and be grateful that they can now drop their suspicions and doubts. They were an uncomfortable burden.

Friday, June 20 (Moon in Sagittarius) Someone may tell you more than you want to know today; it could be the kind of confidential information that could have serious consequences if revealed. Maintain your silence. A relationship is growing in intensity and you should be aware of it. If you want to make things permanent, now is the time to strike! Don't let anyone else speak for you.

Saturday, June 21 (Moon Sagittarius to Capricorn 10:00 p.m.) For some this may be a day to get all your facts and figures into one neat pile so that you can deal with them. It is not the pleasantest task in the world, but you will feel much more comfortable when it is done. In fact, you may get a few surprises—pleasant ones. Things are not as bad as you thought. The flip side of the day involves closeness—most likely of the romantic kind. Permit yourself to get to know someone a lot better, no matter how long you have known him/her. The lucky number today is 8.

Sunday, June 22 (Moon in Capricorn) Whatever else this full moon brings to you, it should make you take a broad, philosophical look at your situation. You may feel the need to recuperate from a recent draining experience, and the way to accomplish that is on your own and by yourself. You will not feel lonely. Keep your spirits up with the knowledge that you are on the brink of an important new development.

Monday, June 23 (Moon Capricorn to Aquarius 9:50 p.m.) You should start out the week feeling refreshed and ready for contest. Your rather playful mood will make you hit upon an original approach that surprises and pleases those you work with. Use originality in dealing with an interpersonal situation as well, because it too needs a "face-lift." Open up the lines of communication, and you will be heartened to see the result. Have some fun with a Leo or an Aquarian. The lucky number today is 1.

Tuesday, June 24 (Moon in Aquarius) Someone close—most likely a family member—will prevail on your goodness today and make a special request. Do everything you can to grant it—even if you do not feel it is totally deserved. Your time will come. Realize that this person's sense of direction is a bit off right now, and that you are the more secure one. Pay some attention to your own ambitions and keep your eye on the main chance—because there may be one now.

Wednesday, June 25 (Moon in Aquarius) A potential mix-up can be avoided by stating things clearly and getting others to repeat what they say. However, no matter how hard you try, someone is going to change his/her mind today and you may get thrown off-balance. Don't worry, because you will regain your equilibrium almost immediately. Put the finishing touches on a creative project, or start some work on yourself. That could mean an improvement project like a diet or exercise regime. You may take a look in the mirror and not be happy about it.

Thursday, June 26 (Moon Aquarius to Pisces 12:12 a.m.) You could easily get away with some fancy maneuvering today and end up in a much better spot. You don't even have to knock anyone else down in the process. However, you may have to change your way of doing things in a certain area; a little revision never hurt anyone. Most Taureans should be feeling very popular and loved. If you're not, a downer attitude may be the problem.

Friday, June 27 (Moon in Pisces) This is a day you could make a killing, or at least put some new reserves in your emotional or financial bank. Fulfillment is indicated as is the pleasure principle. Splurging will be easy now, but you should be able to prevent yourself from going too far. A Gemini or a Sagittarian will add a light touch to an already lighthearted day. The lucky number is 5.

Saturday, June 28 (Moon Pisces to Aries 6:35 a.m.) You will have an acute awareness of your surroundings today and a lively interest in everything going on around you. Some may be inclined to join a new group or break into a whole new sphere of interest. Let yourself go! In the process, do not forget to remember a person who badly wants to hear from you. Avoid someone who would waste your time with pointless discussion.

Sunday, June 29 (Moon in Aries) Something that happened yesterday makes you resolve to be more selective today. That could mean you choose to be with fewer people. Even with your circle smaller, you must take care to protect your own interests. Someone could tempt you to go way out on a limb where there is little security and no safety net. Make sure you know what you are getting into. The lucky number today is 7.

Monday, June 30 (Moon Aries to Taurus 4:54 p.m.) If you sense an undercurrent today, you are quite correct. There is something going on behind the scenes that directly involves you. Don't jump to any conclusions and exercise discretion no matter what you hear. This is one time you could open your big mouth and blow the whole deal. Some will get a chance to show how clever they are and impress even themselves in the process. The lucky number today is 8.

JULY 1986

Tuesday, July 1 (Moon in Taurus) No matter what you do today, it will be difficult to go wrong. A personal dilemma is resolved almost without your having to lift a finger, and it is a tremendous relief to have that off your mind. Your charisma quotient is quite high now and you would find yourself sought after by all kinds of interesting people. Among them may be a Pisces or a Virgo who strikes your fancy. For all, romance should be flourishing.

Wednesday, July 2 (Moon in Taurus) Today you appear to be the instant expert who comes up with a winning solution. You should be handsomely rewarded; if it does not come from others, do something nice for yourself. Some are due for greater recognition in job or career, and should feel satisfied with a job well done. Accept a new responsibility with a smile and regard it as a challenge. Speaking of challenges, you may get one from a tough customer—possibly a Cancer or a Capricorn. The lucky number is 8.

Thursday, July 3 (Moon Taurus to Gemini 5:32 a.m.) You may celebrate Independence Day early by relieving yourself of an annoying burden that you never felt was yours anyway. As your load lightens, the atmosphere brightens and puts you in a mood to celebrate. A splurge purchase is possible. Don't overlook something you already own, however, because it could serve you quite well, too. The lucky number today is 9.

Friday, July 4 (Moon in Gemini) Don't let an undercurrent of worry spoil your holiday; you will find that your concern is excessive, and that the difficulty that you are anticipating will be easily resolved. Focus your energies on your special feeling for someone else, and do something to move the relationship forward today. The time is ripe for it. In fact, some can make a new start in a long-standing partnership.

Saturday, July 5 (Moon Gemini to Cancer 6:19 p.m.) Don't be afraid to follow your feelings today; your initial impressions are likely to be quite correct. However, someone could surprise you by making a quick turnaround; you will like the results. Some may find themselves trying to locate a person or an object that is temporarily lost. No matter what your quest, it will be successful. The lucky number today is 2.

Sunday, July 6 (Moon in Cancer) Most will wind up this holiday weekend on a high note, and they may find themselves the center of attention. Show how quick your wit can be and how snappy your sense of humor can be. Some may be feeling the effects of overindulgence; you could try cooling your appetite for the good things in life. There are lots of high times to come. A Gemini or a Sagittarian could spark your interest—or even give you a new interest in life.

Monday, July 7 (Moon in Cancer)   For many, it will be a jolt to come back down to earth and face reality. One way to deal with it is by reviewing what you've done and making some constructive changes. Some may have to stay very alert in order to avoid getting tripped up by a minor mistake someone makes. Some kind of good news comes in and makes an ordinary day rather special. The lucky number today is 4.

Tuesday, July 8 (Moon Cancer to Leo 5:52 a.m.) Someone or something makes you feel important today and that makes it easier for you to deal with a rather intimidating person. Refuse to be put down by his/her overbearing attitude. Some will find themselves enchanted by a recent or new acquaintance—possibly a Gemini or a Sagittarian. Realize that you could fall under his/her spell. Nothing wrong with that if you are ready for it.

Wednesday, July 9 (Moon in Leo)   Some Taureans will be considering a change of residence now and should keep in mind that others' needs are involved as well. It is important to come to an agreement about what kind of lifestyle will satisfy everyone. Someone you respect bolsters your ego by asking you what you think about a sticky problem; give the answer your best shot because this person deserves it. The lucky number today is 6.

Thursday, July 10 (Moon Leo to Virgo 3:50 p.m.) Once again the spotlight is on matters of home and property—and the necessity to satisfy everyone's needs and wants. Realize that the entire burden is not on you. All should take great care to define their terms now, because there is the possibility of misunderstanding. More important, all should attempt to be as realistic as possible and not to look at the world from proverbial rose-colored glasses. It's time for reality. Do something nice for someone older, and try your luck with number 7.

Friday, July 11 (Moon in Virgo) You should have little trouble showing off your special style today; in fact, you should be feeling strong, vital—and even romantic! Long-term commitments are emphasized, and if you are contemplating one this is the excellent time to make a move. Some will feel particularly ready for new sensations and possibly even "cheap thrills." Don't let it get too expensive! Those involved in creative work will shine.

Saturday, July 12 (Moon Virgo to Libra 11:40 p.m.) You should have the opportunity to help someone today—possibly someone who came to your rescue in the past. Indulge your desire to make a humanitarian gesture, but do not go overboard. It's possible to be a good friend without going broke. Many of you will come to the end of a cycle and say, "That's that," while finishing off a big project or assignment. It should be a good feeling. The lucky number today is 9.

Sunday, July 13 (Moon in Libra) You are acutely aware of the necessity for a change of pace; the pressure has definitely been building up. As you relax, you should feel your powers return and your vitality make a comeback. It is an excellent time to put a relationship back on more solid emotional ground. Some may receive tender loving care today, and should express their gratitude for it.

Monday, July 14 (Moon in Libra) You will still feel a need to slow down, and should do so. No matter how heavy your work load, take on only those things you know you can finish. People around you should be supportive, however, so you can count on a team effort. Some will get involved in a family conference; realize it is necessary in order to decide on future direction. Let someone else take the lead.

Tuesday July 15 (Moon Libra to Scorpio 4:58 a.m.) With the pressure off, you are able to bounce back and deal with things as they come. Most will find they have more room to move around in and that certain restrictions have been lifted. Make it a point to accept an invitation that puts you in contact with stimulating people; you could use a shot of adrenalin. A Gemini or Sagittarian could give you a whole new outlook on things. The lucky number is 3.

Wednesday, July 16 (Moon in Scorpio) If you overstep your bounds today you will find yourself smack in the middle of a sticky situation. In fact, you could have a rather serious confrontation and should do everything to avoid it. That means be willing to compromise and agree to a reshuffling of the status quo. Some may find their most important partnership (possibly marriage) undergoing a review. Don't fight it, join it.

Thursday, July 17 (Moon Scorpio to Sagittarius 7:34 a.m.) Try to apply your powers of analysis to a current situation that baffles you. If you are sharp, you will discern what someone's real motives are, and consequently be able to deal with things better. A frank discussion may be necessary—have it, even if you feel it endangers a special relationship. A key to success now is selectivity and the choice of quality over quantity. Let a discriminating Virgo lead the way for you.

Friday, July 18 (Moon in Sagittarius) Some will be in the mood to change things today. You should be able to accomplish your goals—if they are realistic. It is possible you may have to settle for less than what you would ideally like. For all, the focus is on the resources of others—both personal and material. It is possible you have sized someone up incorrectly; take the proper measure of him/her now. The lucky number today is 6.

Saturday, July 19 (Moon Sagittarius to Capricorn 8:10 a.m.) If you are persistent, you will get to the bottom of a situation that has been annoying because of its inconclusiveness. When you find out what really is involved, you may realize that nothing can be accomplished without a joint effort. That means you may have to make allowances for someone else's weak points. Some should be careful not to take anything for granted when money is concerned. Someone may be simply spinning moonbeams. The lucky number today is 7.

Sunday, July 20 (Moon in Capricorn) A more optimistic mood prevails today as circumstances swing in your favor. Some may actually be able to get their hands on something that's been unavailable or out of reach. Others may see an opening to improve their financial situation. Whatever happens, you will be less inclined to brood and more able to look on the bright side. A Capricorn or a Cancer could considerably lighten the atmosphere.

Monday, July 21 (Moon Capricorn to Aquarius 8:17 a.m.) The full moon in a higher part of your natal chart should make you look forward rather than backward. You should also be able to rise above the pettiness of everyday annoyances and be able to take a broad view of your current situation. A careful analysis will convince you that one of your obligations can easily be dropped. Let someone else carry the load for a while. Someone special—possibly an Aries or a Libra—would be the ideal companion for your mental journey today.

Tuesday, July 22 (Moon in Aquarius) This is one of those rare times when you get a chance to undo something you were not happy with the first time. Make the most of it! Some will find they have new authority and more responsibility; an actual promotion or job move is possible. No matter what your sphere of influence, you will find yourself mingling with the movers and shakers today. Take the opportunity to make points for yourself.

Wednesday, July 23 (Moon Aquarius to Pisces 9:59 a.m.) You have an excellent opportunity to take someone by surprise today and thereby improve your position immensely. It is important to take the opportunity while it is there. Some should experiment with new ways of doing things; prove that you are not as unimaginative as some say the sign of Taurus is. Bowl them all over by following through on a hunch. A Cancer or an Aquarian could be extremely helpful.

Thursday, July 24 (Moon in Pisces) If you have set your sights on someone special, now is the time to zero in on the target. Don't hang back or waste time; you've been putting it off long enough. If it's rejection you're afraid of, cast off your fears and take the proverbial bull by the horns. Those in sales should have an excellent day. All should find themselves meeting people and making valuable contacts. The lucky number is 3.

Friday, July 25 (Moon Pisces to Aries 3:02 p.m.)
Make a pledge to yourself that you will follow through on a very positive offer that is presented today. A lot of people may try to discourage you, but in your heart of hearts you know it's what you've been preparing for. Some may feel a bit boxed in now, but the confinement is only temporary. Console yourself with a Scorpio, a Leo, or an Aquarian.

Saturday, July 26 (Moon in Aries) Someone will try to tell you something—something you might rather not know. Face up to it! It is possible to be open to suggestions without being gullible; listen with a clear mind and a willingness to learn. You are highly subject to flattery now, so keep on the alert for hidden motives.

Sunday, July 27 (Moon in Aries) Conflicting forces may tempt you to practice sidestepping tactics; once again, it is necessary to meet the situation head on. By being diplomatic with a group that is not in agreement, you will be able to restore harmony—and come out looking like a hero! Some money may be burning a hole in your pocket and you may be looking for ways to spend it. Invest in something valuable.

Monday, July 28 (Moon Aries to Taurus 12:11 a.m.)
The moon shines on you with a lovely light all day long. Now is the time for all good Taureans to come to the aid of their cause. Your judgment should be sharp and your timing honed to the split second. If you're not feeling the full effects of these positive vibes, bolster yourself by wearing something bright and by thinking up thoughts. The more optimistic you appear, the more reason you will have to be so. The lucky number is 7.

Tuesday, July 29 (Moon in Taurus) Just making your presence known is enough to get things started today. Follow up with a dynamic presentation of your wants; you may be amazed at how easily things come to you. The key is not to hold back but to take the lead. A love relationship is intensifying and you may be blinded by the light; step back and observe.

Wednesday, July 30 (Moon Taurus to Gemini 12:19 p.m.) Finally recognition comes to you for a good deed or excellent job you did but none seemed to notice. It should be an excellent feeling. Most should find that they can spread themselves around now and reap a lot of personal benefits. There is even the possibility of getting a second crack at something you just missed a while back.

Thursday, July 31 (Moon in Gemini) You should have a money-in-the-bank feeling; for some, it will be a reality. No matter what else happens, you should discover that your financial picture is better than your recent pessimism has led you to believe. Be prepared and willing to stand on your own now because it is the way to a brand new start in a new direction. A romantic reunion is possible for many.

AUGUST 1986

Friday, August 1 (Moon in Gemini) Those around you may be envious of what they see as your luck. Don't let their ribbing make you forget how hard you worked for this boon. Even without a specific incident, you should have a resurgence of confidence in your own techniques and your own talents. Hang on to the feeling. The lucky number today is 8.

Saturday, August 2 (Moon Gemini to Cancer 1:04 a.m.) Critics care little about helping you overcome what they see as shortcomings. Remember that it's up to you to assess your own performance and to make adjustments accordingly. Peace is restored around you, and you should feel relieved. Some will be annoyed by a hindrance that appears to be a limitation. You are able to reach beyond it. An Aries or a Libra could play a key role today.

Sunday, August 3 (Moon in Cancer) You should

start the day with a new attitude and a determination to be more positive. You may have to ward off feelings of paranoia about the actions of someone who made a promise, then seemed to break it. You are not a target! For many, love is part of the scenario and it will be possible to lay some cards on the table.

Monday, August 4 (Moon Cancer to Leo 12:26 p.m.) Someone may try to use nostalgia as a tool to divert you from your purpose. Resist falling back on the past when you know you should be moving toward the future. Let the practical side of your nature help you keep going in the right direction. Trust your first impressions—especially in matters of the heart. The lucky number today is 2.

Tuesday, August 5 (Moon in Leo) Unexpected changes may threaten to upset your plans, but you should be resourceful enough to know how to come up with a new set of plans quite quickly. Your competition may be mind-blown by how quickly you can recover from a crisis. By day's end, you have greater freedom of thought and action. The lucky number today is 3.

Wednesday, August 6 (Moon Leo to Virgo 9:44 p.m.) This is a day to check up on some work in progress and to check out possible pitfalls. Slow down enough to catch up with yourself and you will avoid some unnecessary hassles. Some may find it a bore to renegotiate an agreement, but someone just wasn't listening the first time. An Aquarian or Scorpio or another Taurus could be a great help.

Thursday, August 7 (Moon in Virgo) Get up, get out, and get going. You should be aware by now that you do have the wherewithal to make a success of a project once you apply yourself to it. For many, an emphasis today will be on pleasure and change. You'll feel stimulated by new experiences, and more alive in every sense of the word. Go out and play with a Leo. The lucky number today is 5.

Friday, August 8 (Moon Virgo to Libra 5:05 a.m.) Your patience really comes to the fore now, and it is a good thing. The longer you are prepared to wait, the better the news will be. The message today is: Don't push it. The pleasure principle is still very much in effect, and you may want to pamper yourself with a good meal or a shopping spree.

Saturday, August 9 (Moon in Libra) It is best to be careful not to ruffle anyone's feelings, because you may blow your own chances of getting what you want. Tread lightly and opposition will fall away. Spend some time looking into your own resolutions—about work habits and health habits. You may find you need to do some reevaluating.

Sunday, August 10 (Moon in Libra) Someone will insist that you reconsider some of your plans; listen and don't object. It is a time to realize the ball is in someone else's court. The more receptive you are and the less you say, the more easily you will be able to get over this rough spot. In another matter, you may find it necessary to be discreet. Pretend you never heard what you heard.

Monday, August 11 (Moon Libra to Scorpio 10:36 a.m.) Finish something today rather than start something new. It's a time to tie up loose ends and keep a low profile. You may soon be thrust right into the middle of a mix-up, and you should start practicing keeping cool right now. Be careful not to say anything that could be misinterpreted. Deliberate rather than participate.

Tuesday, August 12 (Moon in Scorpio) You are coming out of the woods and should be ready for action. Try to shake off your conservative attitudes and be open to a break with the past; it is possible to dance to your own tune now. Partnership matters are emphasized—and that includes marriage and other live-in arrangements. Is yours all it should be? Talk it over with a rational advisor and you may see the situation more clearly. The lucky number is 1.

Wednesday, August 13 (Moon Scorpio to Sagittarius 2:17 p.m.) Insist on your right to see your own job to the finish. You don't need to accept someone else's lazy attitude if you feel it's impeding the progress you've been working so hard for. Stick to your goals and you can accomplish great things. Speak softly but carry the proverbial big stick—and follow through on a hunch. Keep it low key all through the day.

Thursday, August 14 (Moon in Sagittarius) It may look like a battle of the sexes, but it's strictly a misunderstanding that you two can quickly settle if you each explain fully. A big problem is communication. State your case fully and openly, and understanding will quickly follow. Some may find themselves making some exciting long-range plans; it might be wise to check out the financial resources of the person who makes them with you.

Friday, August 15 (Moon Sagittarius to Capricorn 4:22 p.m.) Recent events may have proven to you that you've got to get more into long-range planning. It is not likely to live from day to day, but you have been avoiding some problems right under your nose. Don't be afraid to end an arrangement that is no longer productive. For many of you, money is involved, and it would be wise to seek the advice of an expert. The lucky number is 4.

Saturday, August 16 (Moon in Capricorn) This is the time to let the love life glow and to let your romantic feelings flow. You can make a relationship work for you if you resolve to hold up your end of the bargain. One requirement is that you express all of your feelings—not just the positive ones. Something you read may provide inspiration about how to make the tide flow in your direction. The lucky number today is 5.

Sunday, August 17 (Moon Capricorn to Aquarius 5:44 p.m.) Some may find themselves on a sentimental journey today. As old memories are revived, you may find yourself feeling very mellow. Don't let that affect a hard decision you have to make—possibly concerning a family member. Tension should lessen with regard to a financial matter. In fact, a revamping of your whole financial structure may now be paying off.

Monday, August 18 (Moon in Aquarius) Now that you've decided to take your share of the credit for the work you did, go a bit further. Take your well produced project to someone who can help catapult you into a better future. Some may be invited to join a club or organization; consider it seriously. Others may find they may have to define their terms much more clearly in order to get people to understand. Realize that it may be frustrating, but it is necessary.

Tuesday, August 19 (Moon Aquarius to Pisces 7:52 p.m.) Attention all Taureans; this month's full moon lights up your house of career and achievement. Use the influence to your best advantage, but don't overplay your hand. Exercise power in a quiet determined manner for best results. For many, the pressure will be on and there is the possibility of jangled nerves. Keep cool! On the personal side, all your emotional responses will be heightened and you should watch out for going overboard—possibly romantically.

Wednesday, August 20 (Moon in Pisces) Some may find themselves experiencing full moon "hangover." Emotional excesses of yesterday may come back to haunt you today, but you shouldn't torment yourself. It's a day to recognize that you are no longer bound by restrictions and that an open road lies before you. Some will be flattered when their opinion is sought by a person whose status is impressive. Don't let that color your response. The lucky number today is 9.

Thursday, August 21 (Moon in Pisces) If you allow yourself a feeling of adventurousness, you will be pleasantly surprised. A challenge you've been hoping would come your way now presents itself in all its complexity; don't be intimidated. Grit your teeth and plunge in feet first. Some may be amazed at how much they are able to influence a person or a situation. It should make you understand how much weight your words really do carry.

Friday, August 22 (Moon Pisces to Aries 12:27 a.m.) Don't be surprised if someone very close to you tells you how much you've changed and how pleased he/she is at what is happening. Obviously you should continue on your current path. Some may be told something in confidence, and should resolve to keep it that way. Don't neglect someone who's not as free to move around as you are. A Cancer, a Capricorn, or an Aquarian could play a key role today.

Saturday, August 23 (Moon in Aries) Stay loose today for best results. Show that you do have a sense of humor and can be flexible when plans change. You know that Taurus can sometimes be considered a rather earthbound creature. Enjoy the spotlight and the interesting people you interact with today. The lucky number today is 3.

Sunday, August 24 (Moon Aries to Taurus 8:36 a.m.) Wrap up a situation that requires close attention to details, and get ready for an exciting busy couple of days. Things may start slow, however, and you may have to work behind the scenes today. In fact, you may even have to deal with some sticky details you would rather avoid. Be sure to read behind the lines, and to listen to a canny Scorpio.

Monday, August 25 (Moon in Taurus) This is a good day to take charge—and to charge into a new situation you can handle with ease. Don't let shyness hold you back; realize that you have been handed something on the proverbial silver platter. Whoever says your plans are impractical will soon learn otherwise; stick to your convictions and you'll be showered with compliments before long. Today you are the leader others will follow.

Tuesday, August 26 (Moon Taurus to Gemini 8:00 p.m.) Today you can prove to those who doubt that you are able to handle a hot situation with icy aplomb. You see! You can hold your Taurus temper in check. When you display your cool, others quickly warm up to your suggestions. The accent is on originality and initiative—be the first to broach a rather delicate subject, possibly about a change of residence.

Wednesday, August 27 (Moon in Gemini) It's a day

to ride with the tide and not force any issues. Someone may attempt to take all the credit for him-/herself for something you really have done. Don't give in to the temptation to make a scene about it. Instead, take inventory of your personal talents and attributes, and you will see that you are by far the better person. In a matter of property, it might be wise to get a professional appraisal. A Pisces or a Virgo could be key in today's events.

Thursday, August 28 (Moon in Gemini) If you find yourself in a bout with people who simply don't seem to understand, maybe it's because you sent all the wrong signals. Correct wrong impressions immediately. It is not a time to hide your light under a bushel; no one will notice you if you don't step right out in front. Try to enjoy the thrill of open competition.

Friday, August 29 (Moon Gemini to Cancer 8:40 a.m.) Are you aware that you are flirting with fame? Keep on reaching toward that goal and you have every possibility of reaching it. In this cycle, your money situation should improve and you should begin to feel more optimistic about the future. Even if there is no tangible growth in your bank account, you should be feeling the beneficial effect of your own talents and capabilities. If this is not the case, do some soul searching with a close friend—possibly a Cancer or a Scorpio. The lucky number is 9.

Saturday, August 30 (Moon in Cancer) You are in a position to dictate terms; be reasonable, even though the trend is with you. The secret of your solid position is that you are very much needed. Enjoy the emotionally secure feeling that you get from this set of circumstances, but do not lord it over others. An Aries, a Leo, or an Aquarian might offer another perspective. The lucky number today is 1.

Sunday, August 31 (Moon Cancer to Leo 8:08 p.m.) Your emotions could easily dominate your logic today if you allow them to run away with you. Express your feelings, but maintain balance and humor at all costs. Realize that you are definitely going places and that others value your companionship very highly. There is no need to impose yourself on them. A short trip may come up. The lucky number is 2.

SEPTEMBER 1986

Monday, September 1 (Moon in Leo) Be willing to put the past aside and look forward. You may experience a temporary sadness but in the long run you will feel much more lighthearted. The key is realizing that your destiny is in your own hands. Some may get into a discussion of basics—like home and residence. Don't panic, but be willing to consider change. Others may find that love is very exciting now. The lucky number is 9.

Tuesday, September 2 (Moon in Leo) Isn't it nice to know someone cares? Since he/she has decided to be open about it, you should respond in kind. If it isn't love that comes your way, it will be an outlet for your great creative talent. Even if things have not panned out in the past, realize that a fresh start is possible. The lucky number today is 1.

Wednesday, September 3 (Moon Leo to Virgo 5:06 a.m.) It's a day with a lot of options built in and you should be prepared to make some choices. Just realize you can't have it all. You may be amazed to find out how right you were about someone you sized up; it should make you value yourself as a judge of character. For many, the element of luck is built into the day.

Thursday, September 4 (Moon in Virgo) Many will be extremely aware of body image today—possibly even uncomfortably aware. Circumstances push you into the spotlight and you may wish you had paid more attention to matters of diet and exercise. Nobody's really noticing except you, but the experience should determine your calorie intake in the coming weeks. Some will have more demands on their time than they like; realize you can't please everybody.

Friday, September 5 (Moon Virgo to Libra 11:33 a.m.) What appears to be an obstacle could actually be a healthy challenge. There really is no great impediment to your progress now. However, not everything you have done so far may be usable, and you may have to go over some old ground again. Stick with it! A Scorpio could give you a lesson in determination.

Saturday, September 6 (Moon in Libra) This could be a very workaday day—even though it's theoretically a day off. There's an awful lot to be accomplished in the way of service to others. Don't play the martyr! A telephone call or message could considerably lighten an otherwise humdrum twenty-four hours. Be willing to lend a sympathetic ear to someone who needs consoling. The lucky number is 5.

Sunday, September 7 (Moon Libra to Scorpio 4:12 p.m.) Events today take a more positive turn, though they still center around homebase. You may reach agreement with one who shares the same roof about improvement projects that are sorely needed. No matter how off-the-wall someone's suggestion appears, be receptive. It may contain hidden gold. Accept a peace offering or token of affection.

Monday, September 8 (Moon in Scorpio) Your legendary Taurus patience should come in very handy today. In fact, if you play a waiting game, you will totally upset your opponent's game plan. Just be sure to check your sources and be sure they are reliable. Some may find themselves in an interpersonal relationship that has reached a Mexican standoff; something's got to give. A Pisces could show you how to be more subtle.

Tuesday, September 9 (Moon Scorpio to Sagittarius 7:40 p.m.) A relationship is definitely growing stronger, and also requires more responsibility on your part. It should not be difficult for you to manage. Others may discover that it's time to decide about an important commitment; make up your mind about how much involvement you would be comfortable with. Love and support from someone older or more experienced will come as a welcome soft spot in the day. The lucky number is 8.

Wednesday, September 10 (Moon in Sagittarius) Don't give up just as the end is in sight; now you can finish what you sometimes wish you had never started. It should give you a great feeling of accomplishment. Some of you may have to keep alert in an emotional entanglement; someone may be trying to milk you dry. Relax with a Leo or an Aquarian whose upbeat attitude is good counterpoint to your own serious mood.

Thursday, September 11 (Moon Sagittarius to Capricorn 10:28 p.m.) You should now know that your fears about someone's seriousness were unfounded; he/she is here to stay. Some may be avoiding the situation because they are uncertain of its outcome; this is one case where the truth should make you happy. Get to the heart of it. Someone may question your authority today, and you should be willing to listen.

Friday, September 12 (Moon in Capricorn) The mystery of some puzzling messages should be solved and you may find that you are being tested. You proved your loyalty, now let someone else do the same. You may have a sneaky feeling about something and should let it serve you as a guide. You are definitely on the right track. Open up a discussion someone else is avoiding.

Saturday, September 13 (Moon in Capricorn) Kicking up your heels is far better than kicking because someone upsets some of your plans. It should only be a minor annoyance in this pleasurable day. An interesting invitation is possible—and for some could involve travel. Enjoy, but don't overdo. Remember that you have resolved to be in control of your body image. The lucky number today is 3.

Sunday, September 14 (Moon Capricorn to Aquarius 1:07 a.m.) Your ego should get a large boost when someone you respect comes and asks for your help and support. You are lucky to have him/her on your side and in your corner. Consider getting more active in the affairs of your immediate environment. And don't be afraid of a clash of ideas. Conflict can often be creative.

Monday, September 15 (Moon in Aquarius) Although signs seem to indicate you're on a blind alley course, the fact is you will soon take a surprise turn that leads you right to your goals. That is why you should be open-minded in a discussion today—though not goal. Listen selectively. Many will be able to get their points across dynamically and graphically; it's not necessary to charge forward as the bull sometimes does in a manner that irritates others. Variety is definitely on the menu. The lucky number today is 5.

Tuesday, September 16 (Moon Aquarius to Pisces 4:27 a.m.) It should be a tremendous relief when someone has a change of heart that brings back harmony to your domestic sphere. There is nothing you desire more than peace in your place of refuge. A compliment for a gift may come your way today and signal to you that you are more appreciated than you thought. The lucky number today is 6.

Wednesday, September 17 (Moon in Pisces) You could all too easily be conned by a sob story or sales talk today; ask for evidence before you "buy it." You should be feeling better about yourself now and realize that occasionally you must give yourself a pat on the back. You can't always expect it from others. Apply your renewed confidence to a difficult task and you will be way ahead of the game. Return a phone call you are inclined to ignore; it could be important.

Thursday, September 18 (Moon Pisces to Aries 9:33 a.m.) This could be a quite pleasant and fulfilling full moon for you. That is, if you use its energy properly. Don't hang back in a situation where you must speak out. You do have the power to control things but you must speak with the voice of authority. A Cancer or a Capricorn could be key to the day's events. The lucky number is 8.

Friday, September 19 (Moon in Aries) This could be a crucial point in your current self-advancement program. You must be prepared if you are to move ahead, but you must also be willing to roll with the punches. That means some things may not go exactly as you had planned. Don't get rattled! Some may find themselves the center of attention—when they would rather not be. Play it cool! The lucky number today is 9.

Saturday, September 20 (Moon Aries to Taurus 5:25 p.m.) Advance three spaces today, as your cycle begins to move up. Those who wish to can wipe the slate clean and start off on a whole new footing. Sense your power, and realize you are in control of what happens to you now. Keep an eye on your emotional responses today, and you may find out you are feeling more strongly about someone all the time. A Leo or an Aquarian could offer you some interesting insights now.

Sunday, September 21 (Moon in Taurus) Today may be too much of a good thing. One possibility is that you may be forced to choose between two excellent alternatives—or so they seem. Follow your instincts, but hopefully they will take you down the conservative path. The unfamiliar will not bring you happiness now. Trust a Cancer or a Capricorn who knows how much you love peace—sometimes at any price.

Monday, September 22 (Moon in Taurus) With the moon still in your sign, you should make the most of your creative efforts. It should be easy as circumstances should favor you over others. You can afford to be a little smug when you receive applause from a group of your peers. Take a bow, and decide you like being on the receiving end. The lucky number is 3.

Tuesday, September 23 (Moon Taurus to Gemini 4:13 a.m.) The emphasis shifts to that area of your chart that signifies money in all its manifestations. That means you should be super careful about details, especially where any kind of figures are involved. Some might be wise to schedule a session with a financial advisor who knows all the angles. You are generally pretty good at such things, but this is one time when you may need help. The lucky number is 4.

Wednesday, September 24 (Moon in Gemini) This

could be good news day where money or income are concerned. That goes double for those who heeded yesterday's message. Some may simply relocate something they thought was lost, missing or stolen. It's nice to have it back in your possession again. If you're burning with curiosity about something, you could do some personal detective work. Only keep it subtle. The lucky number is 5.

Thursday, September 25 (Moon Gemini to Cancer 4:44 p.m.) You may be tempted to stamp "fragile" on your emotions today. Instead of feeling sorry for yourself, plunge into a big job that's possibly the cause of your minor depression. You can do it much better than you think you can. Some of you may receive a gift—or at least a sign of approval from someone who counts. In spite of yourself, you could turn this into an excellent day.

Friday, September 26 (Moon in Cancer) Take an opportunity that comes along to clear the decks of what you no longer need. You'll be surprised to discover how much it's been cluttering up your life when it is gone. Be sure to keep your options open and utilize your powers of perception; someone may not be what he/she appears. This is one time first impressions are likely to be deceptive. Take time out to plan a trip.

Saturday, September 27 (Moon in Cancer) This is an all or nothing day and you should be aware of it. Don't think you can put in one foot without getting wet all over. A fairly major decision may be involved and you should be prepared to make it. If you decide it's "no deal," don't be tough on yourself for being chicken. It would be a major responsibility. On the lighter note, try your luck with number 8 today.

Sunday, September 28 (Moon Cancer to Leo 5:39 a.m.) Today should be somewhat of a relief, especially when you are relieved of a burden—or the necessity to make a choice. Your generous nature could take a lot of testing now as many people make demands on you. Be prepared to separate the phony sentimentality from the messages of real affection. You should know who your real friends are. Check up on some safety measures you may have neglected of late.

Monday, September 29 (Moon in Leo) You may feel like backing off from the world today and going into temporary solitary confinement. Do so if it is at all possible. You need a second emotional wind and privacy is one way to get it. Some will find that a new policy allows them greater independence of thought and action; use it wisely! Isn't it nice to be alone but not lonely?

Tuesday, September 30 (Moon Leo to Virgo 1:57 p.m.) You may have to utilize your talent as a character analyst today. Someone is a puzzlement and it's up to you to figure out what he/she is really up to. Your space is expanding and you definitely should take advantage of it by making new contacts and exploring new opportunities. Someone you meet will turn out to be a steady, cooperative, and loyal ally. The lucky number today is 2.

OCTOBER 1986

Wednesday, October 1 (Moon in Virgo) You may be tempted to speak ill of someone who hurt you badly. It is understandable, but not recommended. You will simply sound like a bad sport and make others weary of your temper. The best way to handle this situation is to smile broadly and dazzle the enemy. You'll be the winner. In fact, you might have a stroke of luck today that others will envy. The lucky number today is 1.

Thursday, October 2 (Moon Virgo to Libra 8:03 p.m.) Your desire to see justice done may be a bit more radical than it should be. Give the object of your apparent anger the benefit of a defense and be willing to listen to both sides of an issue. You should focus on finding a new direction for yourself rather than trying to direct others. An experienced individual—possibly a woman—could play a major role today and benefit you more than you can imagine. Pay some attention to a minor health problem.

Friday, October 3 (Moon in Libra) Don't dig in your heels and play "typical Taurus" today. Things may be moving rather fast and you will have to move with them. The sphere of activity appears to be your job and your dependents. If you find yourself down a blind alley, back up and try another direction. There is no real threat to you.

Saturday, October 4 (Moon Libra to Scorpio 11:35 p.m.) You've got right on your side, and you can prove it. If you are feeling a little shaky, focus on how many friends and supporters you really do have. A job that needs doing requires a lot of determination and you may have to call on some hidden resources. The day may be more strenuous than you like.

Sunday, October 5 (Moon in Scorpio) This day is themed with a much lighter note. Make it a point and get around, and find some outlets for your nervous energy. Some may find it an excellent time to catch up on phone calls and other forms of personal contact. Others may find themselves smack in the middle of a new romantic liaison. Whatever happens, enjoy!

Monday, October 6 (Moon in Scorpio) Listen carefully when someone you love makes a request; there is more to it than meets the ear. In fact, someone could actually be testing your love and loyalty. Respond accordingly. The spotlight is on domestic relations and the status quo. Perhaps you should examine yours. A Libra could play a very important role today. The lucky number today is 6.

Tuesday, October 7 (Moon Scorpio to Sagittarius 1:48 a.m.) Remain wary in what could be a secret meeting. Don't divulge anything you shouldn't and do not put yourself in a compromising position. For some, it is an excellent time to do something constructive for those less fortunate. Even if you think your participation is that important, you will really be making a contribution.

Wednesday, October 8 (Moon in Sagittarius) Many will have the chance to prove just how important they are in someone else's life. A relationship has come to a critical point and has passed the mere flirtation stage. Others should refuse to give up something for nothing; be aware of the value of what you have. Something happens today that you may be inclined to ignore— don't! Talk it over with a Cancer, a Capricorn, or another Taurus and find out how important it is. The lucky number is 8.

Thursday, October 9 (Moon Sagittarius to Capricorn 3:52 a.m.) Don't be misled by glowing statements someone makes. You may just be blinded by the light. In everything, stay alert, and look only to your own judgment for guidance. Take heroic measures if necessary to keep things from getting more complicated. Don't get mired in the mud, but look beyond the immediate and draw up some objectives.

Friday, October 10 (Moon in Capricorn) Some have been making quite a splash lately and may be asked what their secret is. Avoid taking any bait that will hook you into telling more than you should. Some will find out exactly where they stand with a very special person and should be prepared to do likewise. Assert your own needs and refuse to be a scapegoat. A Leo could be very prominent today.

Saturday, October 11 (Moon Capricorn to Aquarius 7:45 a.m.) Progress is the name of the game for the ambitious Taurus who has been practicing his/her best shots. A new venture is proving successful and the state of your finances should show it. Someone close—possibly a family member—offers help in the form of contacts; don't turn it down. And don't get rattled when a short trip means a change in plans.

Sunday, October 12 (Moon in Aquarius) Your gift for making a romantic event truly memorable becomes evident again. Someone special is your inspiration and lets you know just how perpetually fascinating you are. In any encounter today, use your sense of humor and show that you are capable of laughing at your own little foibles. A Gemini or a Sagittarian could help you do it.

Monday, October 13 (Moon Aquarius to Pisces 11:03 a.m.) Someone you respect indicates that he/she respects you by asking your opinion in a rather important matter. Give your answer serious consideration and do not show off. It's a day to get a lot done or start an ambitious new project. Don't sign anything at the moment. A delay will be to your advantage. The lucky number is 4.

Tuesday, October 14 (Moon in Pisces) Someone could pull strings on your behalf and give you a nice boost up the ladder. Some may be feeling very expansive and inclined to make big plans. Make sure they include everyone you love—including children or young people. You should be particularly sensitive to nuances today, and should apply this condition to a close relationship. Have you been missing something?

Wednesday, October 15 (Moon Pisces to Aries 5:13 p.m.) Don't get bull-like and attempt to force an issue today; a smile and a handshake will get you a lot farther. Someone may demand an explanation of recent expenditures; the arena could be job or home. Be prepared to give complete answers, but don't be ashamed of your penchant for the perfect. Let people know that quality is your style. Another Taurus or Libra will understand.

Thursday, October 16 (Moon in Aries) Wishful thinking could be disastrous today; be your realistic Taurus self in all areas. A tendency to deceive yourself is understandable, but unadvisable. For many, light will be shed on an area previously shrouded in mystery. It's good to know where things are at. Others will receive a clean bill of health and feel a lot easier about things.

Friday, October 17 (Moon in Aries) This full moon could find you a bit unsettled and unnerved by something you cannot unravel. For some, the problem may be a romance that is going through a rocky period. For others, it may simply be that the sense of direction is temporarily missing. Your best course is to talk things out with sympathetic friends. Or you might consider a brand-new activity that will get your mind off things. Try your luck with number 8 today.

Saturday, October 18 (Moon Aries to Taurus 1:35 a.m.) There is a dramatic shift in your mood as the moon moves into your sign. The clouds pass away and you have a sense of your own power. Perhaps that's why you are able to turn events in your favor—and make a critical decision that is 100 percent on target. Burn off some energy by mingling with exciting people or participating in a ground-breaking project.

Sunday, October 19 (Moon in Taurus) The status quo gets shaken today and it may be you who does the shaking. Your optimism and self-confidence should make you willing to branch out—and take a chance on your own abilities. If you think someone finds you rather attractive, you are right; and this could be an important new relationship. Many will have a right to celebrate today.

Monday, October 20 (Moon Taurus to Gemini 12:15 p.m.) Realize that you can't have it all today; if you try to, you could wind up with a case of psychic indigestion. For some, there may be overindulgence in sense pleasures, and it is wise to keep moderation as a goal. Don't turn down an opportunity to make a personal appearance, even if you feel shy about it. You undoubtedly will be a smashing success today. The lucky number is 2.

Tuesday, October 21 (Moon in Gemini) You are beginning to sound as if you know exactly what you want, and the truth is—you do! Before you let anyone talk you out of your goals, prepare your arguments and be ready to present them. On the other hand, be willing to be flexible and to make some revisions. Some may receive a surprise when repayment of an old debt comes in—it could take monetary form or simply be a long-delayed thank you.

Wednesday, October 22 (Moon in Gemini) Be sure you are not spending on things you don't really want. Use your good instincts to sniff out the real bargains and curb your urge to buy junk. All should make an assessment of what they already own and become aware of the value of their possessions. You may be in for some surprises. Be willing to try doing things a new way when someone asks you to.

Thursday, October 23 (Moon Gemini to Cancer 12:37 a.m.) You may find it difficult to believe that someone could deliberately be lying, but it is possible that you are not getting the whole truth. It is not enough to know what happened; you must find out why it did. In this or another matter a frank discussion with a member of the opposite sex is highly likely. If you are open, your opposite number will be too. Clear communication is the key to resolving things. The lucky number is 5.

Friday, October 24 (Moon in Cancer) Give of yourself very carefully now. Your high principles make you an easy target for those who would capitalize on your good nature. On the other hand, believe someone who previously was indifferent to you and now expresses enthusiasm. It is real! Use diplomacy with someone difficult—possibly a relative. A Libra could give you a clue.

Saturday, October 25 (Moon Cancer to Leo 1:02 p.m.) What seems to be the best course (and the best always appeals to you) may be deceptive. Check out every claim before you make any kind of commitment. Sometimes what appears to be solid gold is just cheap glitter. You generally know the difference, but even you are fallible. Dump some unnecessary objects and expenses. If you streamline your life, it will be a lot more manageable. Let a pleasant message boost your morale as it should.

Sunday, October 26 (Moon in Leo) Stick to familiar ground today, and that goes for people too. Someone from out of nowhere may presume to know more about you than he/she should. Be wary, and aware that someone may be setting you up. Go out of your way to visit or call someone who is confined to home or hospital. Others may have to remember a special anniversary.

Monday, October 27 (Moon Leo to Virgo 11:20 p.m.) Expect to hear words you've waited to hear for a long time. Venus is shining a lovely light and love is much favored during this period. If you don't receive a visit from cupid, you'll at least be able to get your message across and to swing people over to your side. Have fun with a rather flamboyant person who tickles your sense of humor. Watch out for some hidden signals.

Tuesday, October 28 (Moon in Virgo) You may be getting some rather puzzling vibes from those around you. You may even feel you're being left out of too much. Realize that you could be hypersensitive—or that you need to make some moves in a relationship yourself. It is an excellent time for changes of all sorts. Hold your tongue when you are tempted to bad-mouth someone. The lucky number today is 1.

Wednesday, October 29 (Moon in Virgo) You are generally a pretty good judge of character; use that ability now in assessing someone new who crosses your path. He/she may have a lot to say but really say nothing. Don't panic when some challenges to your authority come along from unexpected quarters. You are obviously going to have problems for a while in what is relatively a new situation.

Thursday, October 30 (Moon Virgo to Libra 6:04 a.m.) Though it's a bore, stick to your resolutions about diet and health, even when someone tries to talk you into goofing off. You know you've got to do the necessaries and clean up your life before you can relax with a clear mind. Those you help and care for today will show their appreciation. The lucky number today is 3.

Friday, October 31 (Moon in Libra) Although Halloween is hardly a major holiday, you may find this year's "spook day" an excellent excuse to brighten up your surroundings and do some entertaining. You will need some fun to alleviate what could be an otherwise rather tedious day. In any work that you do today keep the caution lights in your mind; you could easily trip yourself up and make a silly mistake—one that will not have dire consequences, but which could prove rather annoying. A rather basic family issue could come up for review and require your attention.

NOVEMBER 1986

Saturday, November 1 (Moon Libra to Scorpio 9:19 a.m.) Take advantage of this low-key day by stepping back and viewing your situation in the large. You may discover that some small anxiety you feel is the result of worrying about the trees rather than the forest. Some people you deal with today make it clear that they are interested in results, not rhetoric. You too should take a pragmatic view of things and deliver action—not talk. Be sure to add some kind of light touch to your day; you might try your luck with number 2.

Sunday, November 2 (Moon in Scorpio) The moon phase could easily cause some turbulence in your "house of partnership." In simple terms, that means tread lightly today where others are concerned—particularly those with whom you share a roof. On the other hand, it could be the ideal time to bring a sticky situation out into the open and confront it. Don't let pride or stubbornness prevent you from taking this opportunity. Some will get a delightful message by mail or phone—and it could renew a sense of optimism. Others may simply decide to put a trip on the agenda; now is definitely the time to plan. You might include a lively Gemini or Sagittarian in the scenario.

Monday, November 3 (Moon Scorpio to Sagittarius 10:19 a.m.) You may have a touch of the Monday morning blues today; it is just as well that you do not feel like plunging into things immediately. Go back and check over some things you've done already, because you may find a couple of rather gaping holes in your work. Some more thought is necessary before you can turn what is really a good idea into a workable procedure. Don't sweat it, but don't be afraid to tear up what you've done and start all over again. No matter what your environment, today will be rather quiet in the sense that more is going on inside your head than around you. Another Taurus or a Scorpio could be an excellent boon companion now. The lucky number today is 4.

Tuesday, November 4 (Moon in Sagittarius) You run the risk of getting overly emotional about something today. It's possible someone may hit a nerve and throw you off balance, but you do not need to overreact. It's not worth ruining your day for. Some will find it profitable to do some personal detective work now; go ahead and satisfy your curiosity. You may find to your surprise that someone who has made a great show of things really has little to back it up. You will be tempted to gloat, but that would not be very productive. The lucky number today is 5.

Wednesday, November 5 (Moon Sagittarius to Capricorn 10:49 a.m.) Get back in the mainstream today, but ease in rather than plunge. Steady as she goes should be your watchword today. Spend your time putting things in order; it will make you feel a lot less disorganized. In another arena, do not force issues; this is a time to smile sweetly and get what you want without bowling others over. You may be forced to be more honest in a relationship than you would like to be at this time.

Thursday, November 6 (Moon in Capricorn) You are very much back on the track now—so much so an idea you had buried surfaces again and you can see new possibilities. This is one time you are operating on pure intuition; make a mental note of how productive that can be. A subtle individual can help untangle some rather confusing details; relax and enjoy the help. A Virgo may also be prominent today. The lucky number is 7.

Friday, November 7 (Moon Capricorn to Aquarius 12:29 p.m.) Along with a friend—a rather inventive one— you could easily get involved in something off the beaten track. You will love the diversion, and the novelty of being a bit unorthodox. For many, serious involvement is the order of the day—even of this whole period. This applies to both the personal and professional areas of your life. Don't skate through things; consider how ready you are for the additional responsibility. Talk it over with a Capricorn.

Saturday, November 8 (Moon in Aquarius) You are *número uno* today, and don't forget it. You may even get credit for something you did in the past, and it is long overdue. Or you might even find promotion a distinct possibility. If neither of these is the case for you, at least realize you can reach beyond your current expectation. You are seriously undervaluing your potential. Take it as a compliment when someone comes to you for advice and counsel; it just proves how important you are to others.

Sunday, November 9 (Moon Aquarius to Pisces 4:30 p.m.) You should be feeling pretty mellow today—in fact, emotionally fulfilled. Your pleasant mood moves you to see where you can be particularly helpful to others. The help you give may involve a purchase of something that makes life easy for everyone involved and you should feel the expenditure is worth it. Someone may compliment you on your very original style— keep it up! Try your luck with number 1.

Monday, November 10 (Moon in Pisces) You can afford to relax a bit and rest on your laurels today. The pressure is off, even if only temporarily. You're quite popular now and might even have the tendency to be a little smug with people you would like to impress. Don't push it—you should know by now that you know the secret of winning friends and influencing people. Someone—possibly a family member—has a request to make. He/she is sincere, and your response should be a favorable one. A Cancer or a Capricorn could cross your path in a significant way.

Tuesday, November 11 (Moon Pisces to Aries 11:14 p.m.) If you don't watch it, you could be all over the place today, scattering your forces and not getting anything significant accomplished. Focus in on one thing— the most important one of course. For some, that may be a hobby or part-time activity that has been particularly fulfilling lately. Stick with it; you never know what can happen. Some may get a lovely but last-minute invitation. Grab it!

Wednesday, November 12 (Moon in Aries) The

tempo is not as good today and you may be feeling a bit down. In fact, some could be experiencing annoying delay or restriction. Realize that it is necessary and in the nature of things. A frank talk may be in order in order to get a relationship back on the track. Don't turn green with envy when a dynamic individual steals the show; you will have your day.

Thursday, November 13 (Moon in Aries) Even though you feel it may help, curb a tendency to spill everything you know and reveal the secrets of your heart. This is no time for confessions. If you must do something about your emotions, jot them down on paper and you may feel more clearheaded. There are no easy answers now; you will have to do some digging. But it will be worth the effort. Talk things over with a philosophical friend—possibly a Sagittarian.

Friday, November 14 (Moon Aries to Taurus 8:24 a.m.) As you move into your high cycle, you may be feeling very expansive and inclined to say yes when someone asks you for money—don't get carried away. It is possible to accommodate others without putting a strain on yourself. Some of you may find that a "wayfaring stranger" turns up on the doorstep and asks for temporary refuge. It could be a very interesting experience. Try your luck with number 6 today.

Saturday, November 15 (Moon in Taurus) For some Taureans, there will be a very dramatic turn of events today; you will end the day much better off than you began it. Even if there is no bolt from the blue, it will be as if you were shot with a cannon today. The very power of your will and personality will bring about changes even you are surprised at. Don't be afraid to let go of the status quo and jump into the driver's seat. Some important people will find you important today; don't let them down. Show them your ambition. The lucky number today is 7.

Sunday, November 16 (Moon Taurus to Gemini 7:26 p.m.) This is the most important full moon of the year for Taurus. You should be full of power, determination, and passion. All your emotional responses will be intensified and you will come out the winner if you direct your energies properly. There is the danger of being carried away, but remember that you are in control. Some of you will be dealing with older individuals or people of authority. You can handle anything that comes along.

Monday, November 17 (Moon in Gemini) Today may be a bit of a letdown after the highly charged atmosphere of the last few days. However, some will find it a relief. Make sure to finish what you start today and don't let small distractions deflect you. It is an excellent time to put your financial house in order and see where you stand. Your glimpse of great things should hearten you about the future; realize what could happen if you removed some obstacles from your path.

Tuesday, November 18 (Moon in Gemini) It's a hustle-and-bustle day with the emphasis on doing a lot of different things simultaneously. Some will be making a purchase and should make absolutely sure they're getting the most for their money. You need an infusion of new ideas, and a lively type—possibly a Gemini—could prove to be the one to provide it. Some will have to face truth as it exists, especially with a member of the opposite sex.

Wednesday, November 19 (Moon Gemini to Cancer 7:46 p.m.) Stick to a straight-and-narrow course today, and you will sail right through. Check, check, and double-check some plans you have made and be sure they are airtight. It's a good day to examine some new possible sources of income. Some will turn up an article they thought was lost and gone forever. The lucky number today is 2.

Thursday, November 20 (Moon in Cancer) This day could find you in "fat city"—in every sense of the word. You will be tempted to overindulge in everything, from fun to food. Your mood is excellent, however, and you should be able to face problems squarely—and emerge victorious. Someone may ask you to join a new group; do it!

Friday, November 21 (Moon Cancer to Leo 8:25 p.m.) You could be faced with a heavy number today—in the form of a person or a situation. Don't be intimidated, no matter what odds you seem to be working against. Resolve to be self-reliant and open about the situation. Some may receive information that is incorrect; check everything out before you react. You can make progress now, even though some may feel they are pushing a proverbial rock uphill.

Saturday, November 22 (Moon in Leo) Today you feel very inclined to reach out to people, and the first place you do it is home. The reaction is warm, and you are pleased that you are able to make someone feel comfortable. On the other hand, some may find themselves dealing with a person whose ego just won't quit; don't let him/her ruin the day. And don't get competitive. Laugh it off with a lighthearted Gemini or Sagittarian.

Sunday, November 23 (Moon in Leo) It's a good thing you know how to keep your mouth shut, because if you tip your hand too early, you run the risk of messing up a long-range scheme. People will know soon enough. Someone you like may give you something you like—and you will be touched by the gesture. Like most people, you love being surprised, and you should let the giver know it. Try your luck with number 6 today.

Monday, November 24 (Moon Leo to Virgo 7:46 a.m.) Be prepared to dump old ideas and old attitudes today. You should be able to see they are nothing but excess baggage. Your mood is realistic and that is a good thing, because you may have to reassess your opinion of someone. He/she has feet of clay, and you should know that now. Some will be thinking about a solid purchase, possibly land or real estate. Get all the facts.

Tuesday, November 25 (Moon in Virgo) You feel a lot better with yesterday's problem out of the way, and are more than ready for a change—and some fun. Fun runs right into you in the form of a rather fascinating person. He/she likes a lot of the same things you do so there's plenty to talk about. Some may want to keep on talking forever. A Gemini may give you competition, but you are up to it. The lucky number today is 8.

Wednesday, November 26 (Moon Virgo to Libra 3:59 p.m.) You may decide it's the fair part of valor to take on a task that is assigned to you today with grace and a willing smile. You can handle it, and you can win yourself a lot of points by doing so. Your salesmanship quotient is quite high today and you should take advantage of it. The holiday mood is coming in, and you should be starting to focus on those people you love and those things you are grateful for. There is a lot of genuine affection around you.

Thursday, November 27 (Moon in Libra) Some Taureans may experience a rather offbeat holiday this year. Something will be different, even if it's only the food. Most will find themselves learning something today—something rather unexpected, especially in a holiday atmosphere. Others should take back seats when it becomes obvious that someone is taking over the scenario. It could be a Leo, and you should take him/her with a grain of salt.

Friday, November 28 (Moon Libra to Scorpio 8:13 p.m.) Stick to the basics today. You may feel as if you are being pulled in two different directions and you know you can't serve two masters. Make your choice on the basis of the path that is most familiar. This is not a good time to start down a whole new road, especially when you do not know what is at the end of it. What's most familiar is what's most safe.

Saturday, November 29 (Moon in Scorpio) Don't jump the gun today, or you will regret it. The time to start has not yet arrived. Hold back and let the other side do the talking; you'll get your chance later on, and it will be a much better one. Be as discreet as possible and do not let others know your game. Someone may make you a rather unique proposal; consider it, but do not immediately give a response. The lucky number today is 5.

Sunday, November 30 (Moon Scorpio to Sagittarius)
You get an excellent opportunity to dump an old way of doing things and thereby give yourself a lot more breathing space. Don't be afraid to say "I was wrong" because one does not often get the chance to correct a past mistake. Somebody wants you to make suggestions about how to build on your secure financial base; even if you do not feel you are an expert in this, you know more than this person does. Be helpful.

DECEMBER 1986

Monday, December 1 (Moon in Sagittarius) Love could be on your mind today, and it may not be making you feel altogether happy. Perhaps you are holding back where you should speak out; it is possible you are letting your Taurus stubbornness get in the way of progress? Some may find their checkbooks suddenly fatter with money from an unexpected source. Others may emerge from a social gathering with a whole new travel plan. That's right, think ahead! The lucky number is 3 today.

Tuesday, December 2 (Moon Sagittarius to Capricorn 8:26 p.m.) You have every reason to be confident in a rather tricky situation; if you check your hand, you will discover you are holding the trump card. Let others forge on ahead while you clean up your act. The more fact checking you do, the better off you will be. Just remember you are on solid ground. Check in with an Aquarius or Leo who has been down this road before.

Wednesday, December 3 (Moon in Capricorn) Many will have to face a kind of showdown with the most important person in their life today. Try dancing around the central issue, be as tactful as possible, and don't push your luck. In fact, why not get something nice in the way of a gift to help smooth things over. In another area, a rather murky situation becomes crystal clear and you should feel less threatened.

Thursday, December 4 (Moon Capricorn to Aquarius 8:23 p.m.) This is a good day to take stock of all your resources and see where you can make a good thing even better. As you put it all together you are helped by someone close to you who has your interest at heart. Home is definitely where your heart is and your attention is centered on making it a happier and more harmonious place. You will be successful. Some may find a real bargain; grab it off right away. The lucky number today is 6.

Friday, December 5 (Moon in Aquarius) You've got a sneaking suspicion something is going on you ought to know about. It isn't paranoia you will discover, when you talk to someone who is willing to clue you in. By being realistic you will steer clear of a situation that smells like trouble. This is one time you should look a gift horse in the mouth. You may find something you don't like.

Saturday, December 6 (Moon Aquarius to Pisces 10:48 p.m.) It pays to be the boss when someone wants to make you decide and you are not ready to. You can simply pull rank. Those who can should do that—and thereby give themselves the time to clear their minds and look at things in a new perspective. You can use the moon energy to give your career a boost today; give free rein to all your aspirations and ambitions. The lucky number is 8.

Sunday, December 7 (Moon in Pisces) Sometimes you are too free with a dollar—or simply with your goodwill. Now you should see that one burden you carry is unnecessary, and that it can be shifted to someone else. All should be in harmony with those around them now, and for some a dispute can be resolved to everyone's satisfaction. Unless you are causing yourself a lot of trouble, you should have inner peace at this time. With just a little effort, some could make a wish come true.

Monday, December 8 (Moon in Pisces) You've never been more ready for new things to happen—and it's good that you are. Today the ground work is laid and you should do your own part in finishing off a project and getting it out of the way. Your persuasive powers are great now and you should put them to work—possibly in a relationship that seems stalled at the moment. Those who try can get a commitment where they want it. Friends and good feelings should be the order of the day. And the lucky number should be 1.

Tuesday, December 9 (Moon Pisces to Aries 4:49 a.m.) Take time out to play "teacher" today. In that way, you will make a good friend out of someone who has been holding back on you. In fact, you will be surprised to find out how much he/she softens up. People are talking behind your back, and it is extremely favorable. Trust your hunches today and test out your first impressions. A Cancer or Aquarian could figure importantly in the day's events.

Wednesday, December 10 (Moon in Aries) A private meeting could be the start of something big. If secrets are confided to you, make sure you uphold your promise to keep them under your hat. Discretion is the way to gain status now. Keep flexible in every way, and try not to get stuck in old ways of thinking. You can be a lot more versatile than that. The lucky number is 3.

Thursday, December 11 (Moon Aries to Taurus 2:10 p.m.) Now things are beginning to fall into place and you can much more easily see where you are going. The prize is in sight. However, don't get overconfident; continue to plan ahead. You may have to make a snap decision when something falls into your hands. Many of you will be doing some soul-searching and perhaps should start keeping a journal. It's surprising how beneficial it can be to see your own thoughts in writing.

Friday, December 12 (Moon in Taurus) Here you go, off on your "moon high" for the month. You can take the world by storm if you choose. Most will probably chose to do things in a more quiet way. However, don't hide your excellent creative sense—and do play up your excellent sense of proportion. Remember, even the moon can't make others notice you unless you open up. Pay a special visit that you've been putting off for a while. It could pay excellent dividends. Some should be careful to protect their ideas by making sure they get only to the right people.

Saturday, December 13 (Moon in Taurus) You should be king—or queen—of the roost this weekend. It would be highly unusual if you did not find everyone around you highly cooperative. They may also be looking to you for guidance and inspiration. In a certain situation, use your talents as a character analyst to steer someone in the right direction. This is one time you really know more than he/she does. Another Taurus or a Libra could add a special glow to the day.

Sunday, December 14 (Moon Taurus to Gemini 1:41 a.m.) You are still in a very strong bargaining position; however, don't spoil the harmony by going all out to get your way. Your smartest course now is to play a waiting game in a financial matter. People will come to your terms soon enough. A pleasant but rather gabby person brings some surprises; now you know what's been going on.

Monday, December 15 (Moon in Gemini) Some will get back money owed them—just in time for holiday shopping! For others, the additional finances are potential rather than actual. Don't miss out on a chance to say yes when you are offered some extra responsibility. You have nothing to fear from a challenge now. An authority figure could be prominent; stand your ground. The lucky number today is 8.

Tuesday, December 16 (Moon Gemini to Cancer 2:09 p.m.) This month's full moon offers you an opportunity to put yourself in a much better financial situation; be sure you recognize that opportunity. It may mean giving up something now but the end results could be spectacular. For many Taureans love is very much in bloom and could provide a very heady experience today. Go ahead and enjoy.

Wednesday, December 17 (Moon in Cancer) You may sense that the moment has come to move on to other things—or people. Your independent streak is very strong today, and it could make new horizons open up to you. Respond when someone expresses interest—you never know where this could lead. Don't beat around the bush when you must make your opinion known; being frank and direct is the only thing you can do. Your lucky number is 1.

Thursday, December 18 (Moon in Cancer) Don't despair. What looks like a lost cause may have a second life. You'll find that your position is stronger than you thought. If you stick to familiar ground, your position will be a lot stronger than you think. Later on, feed both your body and your soul with some excellent food and good companionship. A career hint may be dropped; be right there to pick it up.

Friday, December 19 (Moon Cancer to Leo 2:44 a.m.) A big break is indicated; keep your wits about you so you will recognize it when it presents itself. Wisdom and courage may be required, but you will find it well worth the effort. Keep your cool, however, and your sense of humor. Some should pay attention to their health and diet.

Saturday, December 20 (Moon in Leo) Matters of home and property are high on your list of imperatives today. You may have to make some extra efforts to ensure getting the proper amount of goods and services for your money. In reminiscing with a friend or relative, you may notice some striking parallels between what is happening now and what has happened in the past. Learn the lesson. Someone may challenge your territorial rights; be ready to stand your ground.

Sunday, December 21 (Moon Leo to Virgo 2:30 p.m.) You are beginning to get in the holiday mood and the events of the day should contribute to your good spirits. In fact, some may receive a very exotic and unexpected gifts. Others will find themselves in a mentally stimulating discussion with a new and exciting individual. It's an anything-can-happen day, and you should make the most of it. Something comes along and shakes up the status quo, but it leaves you in much less restricted position. Do you like the feeling of being a free spirit? Even if nothing so dramatic happens, your personal magnetism should be on high, and you should keep yourself open to new people and new experiences. Your timing should be great and you could easily take a flier on something.

Monday, December 22 (Moon in Virgo) You should be very much in tune with the holiday mood, and your mind should be very much on things that bring pleasure to others. You may be tempted to go overboard and really splurge on one particular individual; check yourself to see if you are simply trying to buy love! The work ethic will probably be strong in you today; use it to get a lot of small things cleared up so you can really enjoy the coming holiday.

Tuesday, December 23 (Moon in Virgo) Now enough is enough, and you must give your logic equal time with your instincts. Realize that somebody may want something for nothing, and you could be the main target. However, your good judgment should help you protect yourself in the clinches. Don't shrug off an invitation to a group of "in" people. You could get many of the answers you are looking for if you attend.

Wednesday, December 24 (Moon Virgo to Libra 12:05 a.m.) Your money has been flowing rather freely this holiday season—all in the opposite direction from your wallet. If you are tempted to go overboard with last-minute shopping, it is wise to take stock of where you are financially. Did you ever think of giving others the gift of your services? By taking some tasks off someone else's shoulders, you could give the best gift of all. Have fun with a Sagittarian who arrives bearing gifts. The lucky number today is 8.

Thursday, December 25 (Moon in Libra) This holiday arrives finding you feeling extra secure, with people around you you love and trust. You may find yourself in the middle of a discussion about some practical matters of planning. Even the gifts you receive will be on the more useful than the frivolous side. It suits your mood today, and your mind is on matters of self improvement. Like a good Taurus you know that if you hold back today, you can splurge later on.

Friday, December 26 (Moon Libra to Scorpio 7:06 a.m.) Most should be feeling refreshed and ready for a new start. You should feel in control and realize that you have every reason to be optimistic. Both love and a sense of the rightness of things make you willing to be patient and to compromise where others are concerned. Some may be coming to the realization that a new relationship is worth pursuing. Go for it!

Saturday, December 27 (Moon in Scorpio) Some may be feeling rather edgy today, and your energy may not be very high. All should realize this is not the time to play games with anyone—particularly a member of the opposite sex. Someone may be ready to commit to you, and could be easily hurt by your lack of response. Honesty will work best—but waiting until tomorrow will work even better.

Sunday, December 28 (Moon Scorpio to Sagittarius 8:20 a.m.) Don't feel you have to call all the shots today; step back and let other people express their views—particularly in partnership arrangements. Follow your own heart in a matter that can't be solved by logic. You could have an amazing experience as a result. Luck could come to you today with the number 3. A more relaxed mood prevails and someone who's been out of touch suddenly appears on the scene. Even though he/she is a bit late, be gracious. This is no time to burn any bridges. As you act your charming self, you are able to firm up plans for a New Year's celebration. Admit that you were getting a bit nervous about it. Don't worry; lots of people love you.

Monday, December 29 (Moon in Sagittarius) Don't get concerned if you feel you are straying a bit off course today. Your intuition is leading you in a new direction, and it is the right one. Sometimes you are too hung up on doing things the same old way; now it's time for a change. In your romantic life, you may find that someone is leaning on you in a way you are not particularly comfortable with; talk about it.

Tuesday, December 30 (Moon Sagittarius to Capricorn 7:54 a.m.) A strange kind of excitement takes over today and you find you are looking forward to the new year in a new way. You've learned something this year; that is, change can be very stimulating. Don't waste time with someone who is only talking to hear him-/herself talk. You've got a lot better things to do.

Wednesday, December 31 (Moon in Capricorn) The moon's position on this day bodes very well for the coming year. Your thoughts should be idealistic ones and your resolutions on a fairly high plane. Yes, the coming year you should be able to drop grudging attitudes and be more gracious with other people. Don't forget to build a marvelous and long trip into your plans for the year. Enjoy!

About This Series

This is one of a series of
Twelve Day-by-Day Astrological Guides
for the signs in 1986
by Sydney Omarr

About the Author

Born on August 5, 1926, in Philadelphia, Omarr was the only astrologer ever given full-time duty in the U.S. Army as an astrologer. He also is regarded as the most erudite astrologer of our time and the best-known, through his syndicated column (300 newspapers), and his radio and television programs (he is Merv Griffin's "resident astrologer"). Omarr has been called the most "knowledgeable astrologer since Evangeline Adams." His forecasts of Nixon's downfall, the end of World War II in mid-August of 1945, the assassination of John F. Kennedy, Roosevelt's election to a fourth term and his death in office ... these and many others ... are on record and quoted enough to be considered "legendary."

SIGNET Books of Special Interest

(0451)

- [ ] **WRITE YOUR OWN HOROSCOPE by Joseph F. Goodavage.** A leading astrologer tells how you can chart your individual horoscope with the accuracy of a trained professional. This ancient science is explained with explicit details and rare clarity that will unlock the secrets of your character—and your future—as no other book can. (130936—$3.50)*

- [ ] **YOU CAN ANALYZE HANDWRITING by Robert Holder.** Here is the fascinating book that explains, stroke by stroke, the significance of every type of handwriting including that of famous public figures like Richard Nixon, Helen Gurley Brown and Walter Cronkite. A practical tool for self-knowledge and personal power. (115422—$2.95)

- [ ] **FORTUNE IN YOUR HAND by Elizabeth Daniels Squire.** Let this world-famous authority guide you into the realm of fascinating perceptions about the past and future, about yourself and others through the science of palmistry. (080610—$1.75)

- [ ] **1001 WAYS TO REVEAL YOUR PERSONALITY by Elyane J. Kahn, Ph.D. and David Rudnitsky.** This authoritative book by a prominent psychologist lets you use all your actions, preferences, and habits to tell you more than a mirror about yourself and those around you. (120124—$3.50)

- [ ] **YOUR MYSTERIOUS POWERS OF ESP by Harold Sherman.** Explore the whole new world of your mind—and unlock the secrets of your own amazing psychic sensitivity! One of the world's great sensitives, writers, and lecturers on psychic phenomena explains why and how mind-to-mind communication is possible, exploring: telepathy, extrasensory healing, communicating with the dead, and out-of-body travel. With documented testimonies and case histories. (093151—$1.95)*

*Prices slightly higher in Canada

Buy them at your local bookstore or use this convenient coupon for ordering.

NEW AMERICAN LIBRARY,
P.O. Box 999, Bergenfield, New Jersey 07621

Please send me the books I have checked above. I am enclosing $_____ (please add $1.00 to this order to cover postage and handling). Send check or money order—no cash or C.O.D.'s. Prices and numbers are subject to change without notice.

Name _____

Address _____

City _____ State _____ Zip Code _____

Allow 4-6 weeks for delivery.
This offer is subject to withdrawal without notice.

COUPON

PROF. LALLEMEND
Dept SO-8 • POB 252
BROOKLYN, N.Y. 11204

516 Fifth Ave., NY., NY. 10036

Dear Reader,

You do not have to 'merely believe' Professor Lallemend, the renowned astrologer, because he will **PROVE** to you how he can help you make your life better!

Just fill out this form and mail it. Professor Lallemend will prepare **YOUR HOROSCOPE** and predict—without charge **TWO ESSENTIAL EVENTS IN YOUR LIFE.** You will be thoroughly convinced by the precision of the forecast and will also learn how you can gain success and inner contentment, as well as avoiding everything which can be an obstacle in the path of your happiness. You will receive his advice absolutely free of charge. All you have to do is, answer the questions below, and mail the coupon TODAY

Please send me free of charge and without any obligation on my part my horoscope and two predictions in an unmarked envelope.

My Birthdate ....
Time .... Place ....

Please let me know as well, my lucky numbers. I enclose here a number between 0 and 9 which suddenly comes to my mind:

_____

NAME.......................
ADD. ....
....
CITY........................
STATE :......... ZIP ....

How well do you know yourself?

This horoscope gives you answers to these questions based on your exact time and place of birth...

How do others see you?
What is your greatest strength?
What are your life purposes?
What drives motivate you?
How do you think?
Are you a loving person?
How competitive are you?
What are your ideals?
How religious are you?
Can you take responsibility?
How creative are you?
How do you handle money?
How do you express yourself?
What career is best for you?
How will you be remembered?
Who are your real friends?
What are you hiding?

Many people are out of touch with their real selves. Some can't get ahead professionally because they are doing the wrong kind of work. Others lack self-confidence because they're trying to be someone they're not. Others are unsuccessful in love because they use the wrong approach with the wrong people. Astrology has helped hundreds of people with problems like these by showing them their real selves.

You are a unique individual. Since the world began, there has never been anyone exactly like you. Sun-sign astrology, the kind you see in newspapers and magazines, is all right as far as it goes. But it treats you as if you were just the same as millions of others who have the same Sun sign because their birthdays are close to yours. A true astrological reading of your character and personality has to be one of a kind, unlike any other. It has to be based on exact date, time, longitude and latitude of your birth. Only a big IBM computer like the one that Para Research uses can handle the trillions of possibilities.

A Unique Document Your Astral Portrait includes your complete chart with planetary positions and house cusps calculated to the nearest minute of arc, all planetary aspects with orbs and intensities, plus text explaining the meaning of:

★ Your particular combination of Sun and Moon signs.
★ Your Ascendant sign and the house position of its ruling planet. (Many computer horoscopes omit this because it requires exact birth data.)
★ The planets influencing all twelve houses in your chart.
★ Your planetary aspects.

Others Tell Us "I found the Astral Portrait to be the best horoscope I've ever read." —E.D., Los Angeles, CA
"I could not put it down until I'd read every word. It is like you've been looking over my shoulder since I arrived in this world!" —B.N.L., Redding, CA
"I recommend the Astral Portrait. It even surpasses many of the readings done by professional astrologers."
—J.B.,
Bristol,
CT

Low Price There is no substitute for a personal conference with an astrologer, but a good astrologer charges $50 and up for a complete chart reading. Some who have rich clients get $200 and more. Your Astral Portrait is an analysis of your character written by some of the world's foremost astrologers, and you can have it not for $200 or $50 but for only $22. This is possible because the text of your Astral Portrait is already written. You pay only for the cost of putting your birth information into the computer, compiling one copy, checking it and sending it to you within two weeks.

Permanence Ordinarily, you leave as astrologer's office with only a memory. Your Astral Portrait is a thirty-five page, fifteen-thousand-word, permanently bound book that you can read again and again for years.

Money-Back Guarantee Our guarantee is unconditional. That means you can return your Astral Portrait at any time for any reason and get a full refund of the purchase price. That means we take all the risk, not you!

You Hold the Key The secrets of your inner character and personality, your real self, are locked in the memory of the computer. You alone hold the key: your time and place of birth. Fill in the coupon below and send it to the address shown with $22. Don't put it off. Do it now while you're thinking of it. Your Astral Portrait is waiting for you.

© 1977 Para Research, Inc.

Para Research, Dept. BT, P.O. Box 61, Gloucester, Massachusetts 01930 I want to read about my real self. Please send me my Astral Portrait. I understand that if I am not completely satisfied, I can return it for a full refund. ☐ I enclose $22 plus 1.50 for shipping and handling. ☐ Charge $23.50 to my Master Card account. ☐ Charge $23.50 to my VISA account.

Card number		Good through Mo.	Day	Yr.
Mr/Ms		Birthdate Mo.	Day	Yr.
Address		Birthtime (within an hour)		AM/PM
City		Birthplace City		
State	Zip	State	County	

Know in advance the changes in your life

Wouldn't it be useful to know when important events in your life are going to happen? How would you respond? What will you experience emotionally, intellectually and psychologically? And how will these experiences affect your life.

Your transits can provide valuable clues to various trends or stages of personal growth. This is especially true for the slower moving outer planets—Jupiter through Pluto. The transits for these planets are long lasting and profound in their psychological consequences. Many occur only once in a lifetime. The Astral Forecast is all about the outer planets.

This horoscope provides a reliable tool for astrological forecasting. The Astral Forecast will show you how the outer transits affect your sense of timing, that is, the times that are appropriate for you to take certain kinds of actions and inappropriate for others. This horoscope includes every significant transit to your outer planets that occurs in a twelve-month period. You can use your Astral Forecast to better understand how the outer planets affect such important life issues as career, child rearing, love, marriage and more.

For example, when Jupiter is in the first house, this transit represents a major growth cycle in your life. This is the best time for you to explore who you really are as an individual. Under this transit, you will feel more secure about yourself and the impression you make on others. Therefore, understanding yourself and your influence on others can make this transit an especially powerful and

important time in your life. This is also a time for learning and gaining new experience. All this is part of your present need for personal growth, which affects not only yourself, but also the way you deal with the world as a whole. This is one time when persons and resources are likely to be drawn to you, and you should take constructive advantage of them.

You can find out in advance what your transits are going to be. But if you do it on your own, you will have to consult several astronomical tables to find the positions of each of the transiting planets every day and then compare them mathematically to the positions of the planets at the time of your birth.

There's an easier way to learn of your transits. Our IBM System/36 computer will handle all the calculations and provide you with information on all your outer transits based on your exact time and place of birth. With the Astral Forecast you not only receive the most accurate calculation of your personal transits for the next twelve months, you will also receive an extensive printout interpreting the character and significance of your individual transits.

Your Astral Forecast is the most accurate and authoritative guide to the outer transits that you can receive. It is based on the work of Robert Hand, one of America's most famous astrologers, and the author of several astrology books.

Like all Para Research horoscopes, the Astral Forecast is inexpensive. For just $16.00 you can have the same kind of advice that would otherwise cost you hundreds of dollars. This low price is possible because the astrological data is stored in our computer, and can be easily formatted and printed. Also, the mathematical calculations can be done in a matter of minutes. Your only cost is the cost of putting your personal information into the computer, producing one copy and then mailing it.

When you order your Astral Forecast, you receive an unconditional money-back guarantee. This means you can return your Astral Forecast at any time and get a full refund of the purchase price. We take all the risk.

Order your Astral Forecast today. Discover how the transits can bring energy to each part of your personality, fulfill your potential and help you gain more control over your own life.
© 1983 Para Research, Inc.

Para Research, Dept. BT, P.O. Box 61, Gloucester, Massachusetts 01930 Please send me my Astral Forecast. I understand that if I am not completely satisfied, I can return it for a full refund. ☐ I enclose $16 plus $1.50 for shipping and handling. ☐ Charge $17.50 to my MasterCard account. ☐ Charge $17.50 to my VISA account.

Card number		Good through Mo.	Day	Yr.
Mr/Ms		Birthdate Mo.	Day	Yr.
Address		Birthtime (within an hour)		AM/PM
City		Birthplace City	State	
State	Zip	Start calendar with Mo.		Yr.

Don't Let A TERRIBLE THING HAPPEN TO YOU!

SECRET KNOWLEDGE REVEALED THAT HAS BEEN HANDED DOWN THROUGH HISTORY· TO HELP GIVE YOU A RICHER, LOVE FILLED, HAPPIER LIFE.

Will The POWER Of The OCCULT DOLL Work For YOU?

● **OCCULT SUPPLIES** — For centruies it was and still is a tradition that in Secret Ancient Rituals and Magic of Haiti, Africa, and Latin America, dolls and spells were used to carry out every purpose desired. Used for Love, Luck, Riches to gain power. These ancient rituals were rare a constant source of comfort and hope to those who practice.

We have been making these OCCULT DOLLS and RITUALS for certain customers with Special Problems to see if they were able to help. We are happy to tell you that we feel they have been a great success. Each Doll is made of a certain color with Amulets, Charms, and Herbs sewn in. Believed to attract WHAT YOU WANT. Each Doll is handmade with Great Care by one who knows and believes. Comes with full instructions.

● **LOVE DOLL**
We feel the Most Powerful Love Occult Ritual is done with Red, and special items sewn in. Used to bring a love back to you or get your relationship back to the love and excitement you once had we believe. Comes with special Red tipped pin, powerful instructions.
D300 .... 5.98

● **MONEY DRAWING DOLL**
Green Doll handmade with coins and herbs sewn inside. We believe that Green has the power of attracting money to you in need. Strong money directions included.
D500 .... 5.98

● **OCCULT RITUAL HANDBOOK**
Everything you always wanted to know about Occult Rituals and Magic—songs, chants, spells for every purpose. Use of Roots, Herbs, Oils plus ceremonial rites and more. The secrets are here.
Bk120 .... 4.98

Triple Win BINGO BAG

Did you ever wonder why some people always win at BINGO? Do they have a secret? Now you can have your own secret! Your own BINGO BAG to carry with you.

NOW YOU CAN WIN TOO!
When your numbers are called, you be the one to shout BINGO! You get Bingo Oil, Gemstone, Charm, Seal plus Green Bag and full instructions.
KK795 All 7 items 7.95

LOVE RUB

Rub on your hands or body — or on the body of the one you love. Get what you want and use it wisely.

K371-Red-Passionate Love
K372-Pink-Win love and conquer Evil
K373-Green-Money Drawing
K374-Light Blue-Power to Find a Job
3.98 Any 3 for 11.50

FOLLOW ME COLOGNE

Comes with "LUCKY FORTUNE" A Few Drops Does the Trick. To attract your love, wear this whenever you go out. Sprinkle in your draws also.
K297 Large 4 oz. size
4.98

SPIRITUAL OILS

Used by many thousands of satisfied people because the fragrance charms the senses. Try them today!
2.25 Save 77¢
Order any 3
Only 5.98

K-4 — Attraction	K-14 — Lady Luck
K-100 — Commanding	K-11 — Lodestone
K-2 — Compelling	K-112 — Lovers
K-101 — Concentration	K-113 — Lucky Money
K-102 — Crossing	K-114 — Lucky Hand
K-103 — Dragon Blood	K-9 — Money Drawing
K-16 — Fast Luck	K-7 — Power
K-104 — Finance	K-117 — Protection
K-105 — French Love	K-121 — Spirit
K-106 — Good Luck	K-8 — Success
K-107 — High Conquering	K-122 — Uncrossing
K-109 — Holy Spiritual	K-123 — Van Van
K-110 — Jinx Removing	
K-111 — King Solomon	

SPECIAL INCENSE   2.25
Save 77¢ Order any 3 Only 5.98

Burn incense to attract, to dispel wicked odors. Best incense available, attracting fragrances, satisfying results.

NUMBER IN EVERY BOX
People are used to buying incense with a number. And considering it lucky. We don't claim these numbers as such.

K-77 — Commanding	K-48 — Success
K-42 — Compelling	K-34 — Jinx Removing
K-78 — Concentration	K-84 — Lady Luck
K-97 — Crossing	K-86 — Lovers
K-80 — Dragon Blood	K-87 — Lucky Hand
K-41 — Fast Luck	K-88 — Lucky Money
K-33 — Finance	K-91 — Masters
K-81 — French Love	K-47 — Money Drawing
K-82 — Good Luck	K-39 — Power
K-83 — High Conquering	K-43 — Van Van
	K-35 — Uncrossing

Write to: **ANN HOWARD DEPT.SY1 200 West Sunrise Highway, Freeport, N.Y. 11520**

$5 Dollar Deposit on all C.O.D. Orders! Prepaid Orders Please Add $1.95 for Postage. FREE- Latest Catalog-Candles, Oils, Incense, Spells, More. Just Write. No claims are made. These alleged powers are gathered from writings, books, folklore & occult sources. Sold as curios.

"Next to my mother, you have been the greatest inspiration of my life."

You'll be amazed!

When you read what Marguerite Carter has to say about your life in the year ahead you'll be amazed. She delves into the most important areas of your life: romance, money, goals, and significant changes. You'll find out all the wonderful ways you can live a better life when you have your Unitology Forecast prepared for you by Marguerite Carter.

She'll help you.

Marguerite Carter has counseled thousands of enthusiastic followers around the world for decades. She has been the guiding light and helping hand for people from all walks of life: business leaders, hollywood stars and just everyday folks. There is a good reason why they seek her services year after year. They get the help they need in the most important areas of their lives!

'. . . it was amazing.'

People write all the time telling about how Marguerite Carter has helped them.

MARGUERITE CARTER

". . . it was amazing. I just can't believe it." W.C., Canada

". . . could not put it down until I read it cover to cover." M.L., Illinois.

"Without a doubt, next to my mother, you have been the greatest inspiration of my life. Many others could probably say the same thing." M.A., PA

In letter after letter people comment on the realistic guidance they've received for getting what they want from life. They've found the help they need in times of decision or resolving personal problems. These are judgments by a caring counselor, not some impersonal computer.

Hidden Opportunities

The things you want most may not be out of reach. Marguerite Carter says, "Many people are completely unaware that the opportunities for money, love or advancement are passing them by almost daily . . ." Without knowledge of when the conditions are favorable or unfavorable, the chances for success and happiness are greatly diminished.

Get your Unitology Forecast with special notations by Marguerite Carter. It will be prepared to your specific birthdate information. Remember that you will receive a full year of guidance, regardless of when your request is received, and you'll know that your forecast has come from one of the world's most highly respected astrologer-counselors.

O-6

Marguerite Carter • P.O. Box 807 • Indianapolis, Indiana 46206

☐ Yes Miss Carter, Please send me my Unitology Forecast for the year ahead. Enclosed is my remittance of $9.95 plus $1.00 for postage and handling. (First Class $1.30) Make all checks payable in U.S. funds. Allow 4 weeks for delivery.

Name _____
Address _____
City _____ State _____ Zip Code _____
Birthplace _____
Month _____ Day _____ Year _____
Place _____ Hour _____

ASTROLOGY QUESTIONNAIRE

Help us bring you even better astrology guides by filling out this survey and mailing it today.

A. Book Title (Sign): _____

B. Using the scale below how would you rate this astrological guide? (Place one rating from 0–10 in the space provided.)

Poor	Not So Good	O.K.	Good	Excellent
0 1	2 3	4 5 6	7 8	9 10

Rating

Overall Opinion of book

Essay On:
1. Defining Terms _____
2. Your House of The Sun _____
3. The Geometry of Relationships _____
4. Twelve Places at the Table _____
5. Moods of the Moon _____
6. Venus and Mars _____
7. Venus Sign Position Chart _____
8. Mars Sign Position Chart _____
9. The Planets as "Stars" _____
10. Astrotrivia _____
11. Sun Sign Changes _____
12. Your Sign: The Big Picture _____
13. Your Sign: Objectives and Obstacles _____
14. Pairing Off With Your Sign _____
15. Your Sign's Sex Role Dilemma _____
16. Your Sign: Female _____
17. Your Sign: Male _____
18. Your Sign: Help Wanted _____
19. How "Pure" a _____ are you? _____
20. Find Your Rising Sign _____
21. Your Sign: Astro-Outlook for '86 _____
22. 15 Months of Day-By-Day Predictions _____

C. In total about how many astrology guides have you purchased for yourself in the past 12 months?
# of books _____

D. What topics would you be interested in having Sydney Omarr write about in the 1987 Astrology Guide?

_____

_____

E. What is your education?

1( ) High School   3( ) 4 yrs college
2( ) 2 yrs college   4( ) Postgraduate

F. What is your occupation? _____

G. What is your marital status?

1( ) Single   3( ) Divorced   5( ) Widowed
2( ) Married   4( ) Separated

H. Age: _____   **I.** Sex: 1( ) Male
                                          2( ) Female

Please Print Name:_____

Address_____

City_____ State_____ Zip_____

Phone # ( )_____

Thank you. Please send to New American Library, Research Dept., 1633 Broadway, New York, NY 10019